BLOOD PLAGUES AND ENDLESS RAIDS

BLOOD PLAGUES AND ENDLESS RAIDS

A HUNDRED MILLION LIVES
—~ IN THE ~—
WORLD OF WARCRAFT

ANTHONY R. PALUMBI

CHICAGO
REVIEW
PRESS

Copyright © 2017 by Anthony R. Palumbi
All rights reserved
Published by Chicago Review Press Incorporated
814 North Franklin Street
Chicago, Illinois 60610
ISBN 978-1-61373-684-5

Library of Congress Cataloging-in-Publication Data
Is available from the Library of Congress.

Cover design: Marc Whitaker / MTWdesign.net
Typesetting: Nord Compo

Printed in the United States of America
5 4 3 2 1

"As we wash our body so should we wash destiny, change life as we change clothes."

—Fernando Pessoa, *The Book of Disquiet*

To the many millions who made their way to Azeroth, whatsoever they accomplished, whomsoever they played with, however long they stayed. And to our parents, partners, and friends, whose birthdays and baby showers we missed.

CONTENTS

ACKNOWLEDGMENTS

First, thanks to my wife and best friend, Liz, with whom I hold a mutual sanity pact: nobody gets to go all the way crazy. Thanks also to my parents, Steve and Mary; my in-laws, Judy and Beto; and all the family who never gave me too hard a time about this video game fixation. This work would not exist without the tireless advocacy of my agent, Dawn Frederick of Red Sofa Literary, nor the foresight of my editor at Chicago Review Press, Yuval Taylor. It was vastly improved by all the *World of Warcraft* players who shared their stories and voices with me, particularly Rumay "Hafu" Wang, Chris, Noah, Chelsea, Gabriel, Jessica and Aaron, Everett, Laura, Max, Dan, and Steven. Tremendous love to T K T and Elitist Jerks, two families who adopted me. Thanks to everyone I ever played with, especially Paches, Meaning, Tyrawick, Gurgthock, Mem, Zkar, Loderunner, Hornsbuck, Savena, Yueng, Kalick, Salem, Slipo, Modu, Anwyn, Karma, Kaetau, and Malicia.

PLEASED TO MEET YOU! PLEASE DON'T USE MY NAME

◆

I fell from sleep when the car stopped, cringing at the fluorescent glare of gas station floodlights. Acrid tobacco smoke curled like cream through a dark brew of muttered conversation. The windows were down, and even at four in the morning the South Texas air weighed warm and damp on our shoulders. The car emptied, three grown men unfolding themselves from the bench seat in the back. I'd had the foresight to call shotgun back in Houston. A battered passenger van sat alongside us at the pump; a dozen migrant laborers milled about, crunching on bags of Doritos, their Spanish soft like they feared waking the sun.

Ten hours and a hundred dollars in bribes later, across the Rio Grande and past the seething, desperate border town of Reynosa, Eric's dusty red station wagon soldiered along in the 115 degree Fahrenheit air. Shrubs, grasses, and stunted trees hugged the ground around us—all shockingly green for a murderous Mexican August. The air conditioner roared against the heat with all the success of men cursing God. Heat had long since pacified the conversation when the car swerved dramatically to the right. We flailed about and were pulled left again, correcting back to the center of the road as Eric cut loose with a stream of incredulous profanity. "The dogs," he bellowed when at last his brain made sense of things. "Dogs in the road!" And suddenly we were turning around, pulling a U-turn on the two-lane highway.

"Horns?" asked Tim from the front, too distressed to recall Eric's real name, instead abridging his gaming handle, "Hornsbuck."

"Look at this!" Eric insisted as we roared back to the spot. The hazard came into view: three dogs in the center of the highway. The one with the white-blond coat was the biggest. She lay dead in the road, the victim of an earlier passing motorist. The others had discovered the body and were attempting to mate with it. The little black one had climbed her corpse and now worked furiously at its summit. The ragged brown mutt sat patiently in the median, waiting his turn. The asphalt's heat rose around them in shimmering waves. The regal iron-gray ladies of the Sierra Madre Oriental mountains sat in quiet judgment. In the car, the odor of weed resin mingled with hours-old sweat. We turned around once more on a dusty service road, and as we continued on our original course we got a third and final look. Brett insisted the little black dog was "lined up wrong"; the humping was just a display. I've chosen to believe him.

Our house outside Cadereyta was a pastoral dream of white stucco and cerulean tile inlay. A fountain loomed by the front door, dry and spattered with road dust. Storm clouds had begun to churn in the distance. Our hosts came out, and we exchanged greetings in the withering heat. They introduced themselves with the names we knew, names attached to a virtual world. This man was Modu; that one Plastico. We responded in kind, discarding the given names we'd used in the car. It was instantly comfortable; they said there would be a mariachi band at dinner. When your *World of Warcraft* guild holds a retreat in Mexico, video games will not be the first priority.

Inside the ranch house waited a dozen young men. Many appeared to be Mexican and spoke Spanish, while others had the lighter pigmentation and uprooted bearing of foreigners. Some assembled a battery of computers against the wall while others napped on a flotilla of mattresses arrayed across the white tile floor. We'd never met, but we knew each other well. Plastico sidled up, put his arm around my shoulders, and pressed a cold glass bottle into my hand: Tecate, a Monterrey-brewed beer I'd only ever seen in cans. He clapped me on the back and wandered off—the only acknowledgment I'd see that week of the burden we shared. Leadership was a mantle he wore unconsciously, almost obliviously, and one I'd taken up only recently and only in desperation.

I sucked down my beer and luxuriated in the air-conditioning. A very thin man from Singapore ("by way of Malaysia," he explained, in a prim accent, "before it went to the fucking dogs") introduced himself as Malicia. A warlock: one of our best, meticulous in his preparation, unforgiving of sloppy play. We shook hands, and his was clammy with sweat—he'd overdressed for the heat in a long-sleeved white linen shirt and black slacks, and flowing strands of black hair clung to his cheeks. A shock of dyed magenta hair ran tastefully over his scalp. Not wanting to refer to this man by his female in-game handle for the next week, I asked his real name. He wouldn't tell me. Once, months before in the heat of battle, I had said some intemperate things to Malicia. He seemed disinclined to forget them.

Stepping out the back door, I took in the expansive coral-painted deck. There was a pool, its bottom striated with dark blue tiles matching the house's facade. Leaning against a tree in the backyard, admiring the wide landscape swollen green by recent rains, I felt a hard wind pull. A pair of threadbare ranch dogs sprinted past, one nipping at the other's flanks. The clouds had descended; tall trees thrashed in the gale. I didn't know the time of day. A peal of thunder set the dogs to yelping. The smell of rain weighted the air and I stumbled inside, where my fellow gringos had busied themselves with what seemed like miles of Ethernet cable. Wire cutters in hand, they snipped and stripped and threaded the copper entrails into square plastic heads. Tim did his best to converse in Spanish with Plastico, who would occasionally break the conversation to bellow good-natured abuse at us.

"'Ey, Ghando!"—he addressed me as my avatar. "I hear you so long, and I imagine your ugly face, and now I am in love," the last word pronounced *lub*. He was a small man, short and sporting a nascent gut, but his voice boomed nonetheless, the way I'd grown accustomed to hearing through my computer's headset. I had always assumed he kept the microphone too near his mouth. Clearly I was wrong.

"Plas, I can't believe how short you are," I replied. The cheapest shot, the quickest, the lowest-hanging fruit.

Plastico threw back his head for a belly laugh. "Ghando, I punch you in the head." Our juvenile exchange was utterly in character. The man was a constant joker and hated nothing more than discord, ill feeling, or unpleasantness—feelings he derisively lumped together with the catchall term "drama." It was therefore crucially important to him that everyone had as much fun as possible at all times. He was the life of the party, his magnetic online charisma translating perfectly to this tile-floored, air-conditioned room in the mountains of Nuevo Leon. He pushed more Tecates into our hands. Sleep-deprived and dehydrated as I was, the room quickly grew fuzzy. The floor mattresses beckoned me. I felt like they might honestly save my life.

Memo woke me up: a snaggletoothed young man with a long, thin face and wide white eyes. "Time to eat, *pendejo*." Memo was a priest, a fellow healer and one of the guild's junior officers. I stumbled after him toward the patio, peeling my eyelids back with fingertips, letting them snap back to moisten my sandpaper contacts. The rain had come and gone, though giants stirred above us. Tables were set, with all the deck illuminated and coals smoldering in an enormous grill. The iron was raised with a hand crank; Plastico held half an onion in each hand, waxing designs on the surface that quickly hissed to fragrant steam. My guild scattered themselves between tables adorned with bottles of tequila and more Tecate.

"Drinking Tecate is a must," Plastico explained, quoting the guild's official theme song. While some guilds might play their favorites over private voice chat servers (where we could don headsets and banter out loud like friends in a bar) we had our own original track, written by a hip-hop producer in Los Angeles who in a past life had pulled duty as a backup dancer for Vanilla Ice. Watch music videos from the old days and you'll see him. *Teenage Mutant Ninja Turtles II*, the "Go Ninja Go" sequence: he's there, lean and young in parachute pants with a killer faded flattop. Kojak, as we called him, had a wife and kids keeping him rooted at home and away from Mexico. Into my brain popped a question about the week's raiding schedule*—if we had computers set up, after all, might we be able to clear some dungeons? This was how I'd started thinking in the months since taking charge. The game always ran in the background, persistent in my brain the way it was on countless server farms, seeking the sharpest edge or the freshest goal. But Plastico's happy glow kept me silent. He wouldn't countenance shoptalk, not with tortillas to layer like fish scales over the raging grill.

The guild's founder—a wealthy electronics retailer with a round belly, scruffy beard, and easy smile who'd fronted the cash for this adventure despite rarely having time to play the game anymore—stood up at the start of dinner. Slipo was more than our patron for the week; he was the *patron*, the guild's spiritual father, held in a kind of reverence that extended beyond the game. His ex-wife, still a close friend and the guild's honorary mother, sat nearby with their beautiful children. Though Slipo spoke some English, he insisted on Memo translating for him. A man in his position does not stand before guests in his own homeland to struggle with a foreign tongue. He thanked us for being there, for traveling so far as many had. He bade us eat and drink, he introduced the band, and then he sat. With the first round of quesadillas in my stomach, I felt sturdy enough to sip Tecate with lime. It suddenly seemed very natural, being in this place with these people. Shared time and sacrifices had brought us here, and I decided I wanted to stay. Not just at the ranch house—everything already booked and planned—but in this guild, with these people, with their warmth and what we'd built together. I'd given so much already, holding things together when any sensible person would have walked away and done something easier. Did I not own this thing, whatever it was, as much as anyone?

---

* "Raiding" is among *World of Warcraft*'s most common player pastimes. While the game contains many "dungeon" areas with monsters and treasure for parties of five players, it also includes steeper challenges for larger groups called "raid dungeons." Any group of players larger than five is also called a "raid," whether it's adventuring in a dungeon or in the open game world. Chapter 5 explores raiding in great detail.

The music kicked up. It played soothing and busy, the singer's ululations and the sharp slaps of his palm on his guitar binding up time like leaves of paper. For the first time in my life I understood why people enjoy mariachi music. Eric threw Plastico in the pool about an hour later; Brett, short and round and red as a tomato with liquor's flush, declared he would fight anyone who tried the same on him. Gnats cavorted overhead through the beams of buzzing electrical lamps. The band played with barely a breath between songs, but never for a moment did they rush.

NOVEMBER 2004

One doesn't find oneself attending a weeklong *World of Warcraft* party on a lark. It takes a long time to plumb that particular depth; one makes a great many choices on the way. Personally, I never planned to play *WoW*. It wasn't my type of game, I declared, having never played *EverQuest* or *Dark Age of Camelot* or any of *WoW*'s other competitors in the massively multiplayer online role-playing game (MMORPG) genre.

"But Tony," Chris pressed his case across the table at a Friendly's diner in Waltham, Massachusetts, eighteen months prior to my Mexican excursion. "It's going to be really great. Noah and I are playing with some guys I met playing *StarCraft*. The game world is *huge*, like the size of a real continent. There's all these classes, with dungeons and other people to fight against. You won't have to play alone. We'll own noobs together! I know how you feel about noobs." I don't wish to belabor this common Internet jargon; suffice it to say that anyone less skilled than the speaker at a given video game is a noob, and to beat a noob is to own him.

It was Thanksgiving, and I'd come back east for the long weekend. The nation had just seen fit to reelect George W. Bush and I was visiting my New England hometown, seeing friends before returning to college in California. In the end, those friends convinced me to play *WoW*. We went to a local mall together to pick up our copies, forging between us a Musketeerish brotherhood. We approached the game, even then, as something inherently dangerous. Like if we didn't cling together we'd be washed away by the vastness we knew awaited us in *WoW*'s virtual world, or possibly addicted to software as mind-warpingly powerful as any drug. These seemed like real possibilities.

By the time I booked my trip to Mexico I was the last one standing—the last still playing. That night at Friendly's was long gone by then, buried under a new history I'd made for myself, so distant it may as well have happened to someone else. I had new friends. I lived a different life, into which the Cadereyta convention became an initiation. This trip was my personal portal—a threshold crossed from one world into another.

The metaphor ran deeper still; just days before setting out for Mexico, I'd walked in my graduation from Stanford University. Tom Brokaw spoke, for some reason. His trademark nasal thrum fused with the suffocating Palo Alto heat, and it became remarkably difficult to stay awake. A bruising hangover didn't help, and all I really remember was an admonition not to become overly consumed with technology. You can imagine how well this message went over with my cohort, an overwhelming number of them bound for jobs at Google and Facebook and Apple. This was 2006—just at the cusp of the mobile revolution—and more than a few of them are now millionaires. I knew I'd never join them.

School always came easy to me, and I'd chosen to direct that talent toward a degree in English with an emphasis on creative writing and a minor in astrophysics. I was then, and remain now, functionally unemployable. Still, I beat the odds and secured a position at the bottom rung of a small Bay Area film company, earning $1,000 per month before taxes. For $400 of those dollars I secured a basement room in colorful conditions of hippie squalor. I returned from Mexico and jumped right into "real life," cutting video by day and slaying digital monsters by night. I would build a creative career alongside my online reputation as coleader of T K T, the world's top Spanish-speaking guild. That was the life I wanted.

For years this second life ran in parallel to the first, buttressed it, stole from it, informed it, and on occasion threatened to swallow it entirely. I stood as one of millions and stood apart from those millions as one of their highest elite. I plunged down the deepest of rabbit holes, laughed and cried and triumphed and despaired, paying a fifteen-dollar subscription fee each month for the privilege. I'm ashamed of how much it mattered. I would do it all over again, and I still enjoy *WoW* today. I wouldn't trade those times for the world.

And I'm not alone.

WASHED UPON A SHOAL

Everyone who ever entered the World of Warcraft did so on equal footing. There may have been a box or a digital download; perhaps one read, as I did, the ponderously, tantalizingly thick manual printed on glossy paper designed to resemble parchment. Once the software installed itself and your credit card information had been verified, you selected a "realm server" on which to play. The World of Warcraft is actually more than a hundred identical worlds, each separate from the others. This breaks up the titanic player population into techno-logically manageable chunks, keeping communities small enough to feel intimate. A player's *WoW* identity is strongly linked to her realm of origin.* Three types exist, corresponding to the game's three major avenues of achievement: player-versus-player (PvP), player-versus-environment (PvE), and role-playing (RP). The first allows players to battle each other with few restrictions, while the lat-ter two allow PvP combat only under special conditions. Role-playing servers observe unique rules for player interactions and are covered in detail in chapter 9. At launch, North American players could pick between forty-three PvP realms, forty-one PvE realms, and five RP realms. In practice, you played on whatever server your friends used. For me that meant Sargeras, a PvP server where Chris's friends had already started a little social group named T K T.

---

* Players use the terms "realm" and "server" interchangeably.

Logging into a realm server for the very first time, everyone meets the same screen: a dizzying palette of choices to help you fashion yourself a character, an avatar, what some colloquially dub a "toon." For those familiar with traditional role-playing games, the process was second nature: cycling through hair colors and goatee styles, skin tones and tattoos. But the game's highly effective marketing campaign drew in countless new gamers—people suddenly forced to make intimidating choices of identity with very little information.

Which of the game's two warring factions to choose, the traditional high-fantasy heroes of the Alliance or the darker, more outwardly barbaric Horde? From there, which of eight distinct classes to pick, determining the character's abilities and basic play style? Which race of fantasy creatures to pick, knowing each race conferred certain bonuses, not knowing which was best? Some people spent hours customizing their characters, from eye color to hairstyle, and this made sense at a time when every cosmetic choice was permanent. That would change, years later, but at the time each decision felt like it had to say something about my identity. When anyone looked at my character, they'd see neither my personality nor the contents of my heart—only an anthropomorphized bull standing on two hoofed feet, great muscular neck dipping like it bore the world's weight, yellow eyes glaring under a charcoal shock of mane. They would see the tauren shaman Ghando of the Horde—named for a friend's Great Dane, itself named after a Norse giant. Satisfied, I clicked the fat red button marked ENTER WORLD.

Ghando appeared, as have five hundred million other *WoW* characters to date, in a strange and open land wearing nothing but rags. As a tauren, he arrived in the Horde territory of Mulgore, with just a crude mallet in his hand and some meager provisions in his backpack—his only wards against the world's cruelty. Turning my new character in a circle, I spotted a fellow tauren, albeit one controlled by the game (a non-player character, or NPC). She offered me a quest: exterminate a bit of the local wildlife in exchange for a few copper coins. I accepted and surveyed my surroundings, flushed with purpose. Flat grassy plains stretched in all directions, budding groves of tall conifers in the spots where they edged up to meet the encircling mountains. Brightly painted canvas tents and mighty totem poles had been arranged around a dusty playa to form the settlement of Camp Narache. A few other tauren players ran about, bounding about with determined gaits, marked with names meaning nothing to me. Eager to connect with my friends Chris and Noah, I opened the game's Social menu and tried to message them. Both were offline; I was struck by a sudden and very surprising sensation of loneliness, facing a world both strange and vast with no friends and barely any tools. Then again, I reasoned to myself, you've got this mallet, and those animals aren't going to bludgeon themselves.

After successfully slaying several large, flightless birds, I began to grasp the game's most basic combat mechanics. Though defeating the feeble things wasn't much challenge, I quickly ran into a conundrum: there weren't enough of them. Oh, at some point in the past there might have been, but at present the plains of Mulgore were dotted with avian corpses and my fellow players hunting them down as quickly as fresh prey could materialize into the game world. New "spawns" were snatched up before I could close in to malleting range, and only rarely could I score one for myself.*

What to do? I considered teaming up with one of my fellow players, allowing us to share credit for each dead bird, but decided against it for fear of rejection. This is a recurring issue in my life. The next-best option seemed to be running in circles, seeking out new birds as the game materialized them into being, using a magic spell to zap the birds from long range and claim them for myself—but the first time I did this, another player responded with a breathtaking stream of textual profanity. Though he wasn't allowed to attack me, he clearly wanted to. In the end I wandered off to find my own section of plains on which to hunt, and completed the quest. But in just a few minutes I'd managed a serious violation of the game's unwritten social code!

---

* For many years a constant staple of *WoW* was its "tapping" mechanic, which awarded credit for a monster kill only to the first player or group that damaged it. This was changed in 2016's *Legion* expansion, which made kills nonexclusive. Up to five separate players of either faction who "tap" a monster by dealing damage to it (also known as "tagging") share in the credit and any loot.

I felt like a feeble waif. In video gaming culture, the adage goes, anyone who's played the game five minutes less than you is a noob. Anyone who's played five minutes more is a nerd loser with no life.

No single feature sucked me in during those first hours and days, but neither could I deny the game's infectious quality. *WoW* has always offered players a very pleasurable loop of gameplay: you engage a monster, use various damaging spells and abilities to reduce its hit points to zero, and loot its corpse. The red health bar dwindles to empty, loot box opens and closes, and you pick the next monster. All the while colorful visual effects pop to emphasize the damaging strikes back and forth between opponents; they fit in nicely with the bright, welcoming, slightly cartoonish environment. I always appreciated that *WoW* never really punished me for making mistakes—even death only meant a ghostly jog from the nearest graveyard back to my body, which cast the world in soothing shades of spectral gray and offered a few moments' reflection on what I'd done wrong. And in the cities where players gathered to chat and trade and shout the latest online meme, a social order slowly assembled itself.

The moment anyone entered the World of Warcraft, she began a performance. Until the moment she logged out, every word she uttered and every action she took reflected, in some small way, her identity. At any moment, she might be subjected to withering criticism from a crowd of total strangers. Yet the game offered few hints on navigating this constant emotional minefield—certainly not in the manual, which was long on the history of the game's locale, the war-scarred planet of Azeroth, but short on useful social tips. Players found themselves awash in possibility but lacked the tools to successfully deal with each other. They had to carve out their own spaces, to define social norms, to communicate and enforce them.

More than a decade later, online communities and social networks are old hat. We have all become cyborgs. Facebook started as a convenient way for college students to check whether their crushes were single, but its early adopters have long since watched in mounting horror as their parents and grandparents made accounts to post old photos. We have watched countless careers implode because of tasteless Tweets. The organic process of building self-regulated and self-sustaining online communities has been reduced to flowcharts in Silicon Valley boardrooms, though anyone who can actually pull it off is still worth millions. But back in 2004, before Twitter's founding or the very first iPhone, this process was far from established. It wasn't understood even by those actively participating, and so the task of defining personhood in *WoW* fell to the players themselves.

This is no easy task, laying down a society's rules. Typically, societies come together from groups of people sharing some commonality: geography or ancestry, faith or ideology. *WoW*'s disparate and varied player base had none of these advantages, and further complicating the matter was the game's very unreality. Virtual interactions don't carry the same weight as those in real life, so getting players to agree on social norms became all but impossible—they couldn't even agree where reality stopped or started! Nowhere near consensus, players did what human beings often do in such situations: they balkanized, establishing their own separate organizations ("guilds") with independent rules and agendas. With dozens if not hundreds of organized guilds on every game server, necessity birthed a new generation of leaders practicing a different style of leadership. Teenagers led guilds of grown men through sheer force of personality; paraplegics charged into battle freed from pitying gazes. Most guilds, even casual guilds, boil down to a lively assortment of individuals who gather for light, semianonymous socializing after work. Think of the classic sitcom *Cheers*, without that whole boring mess between Sam and Diane. The Guild chat channel was the place where everyone knew your name—or at least your character's.

WoW is an emotional escape vehicle for the vast majority of players, and the more hardcore the player the more he tends to value the separation—though it's possible he develops those attitudes to validate the huge amount of time invested in the game. Decoupled from the worries of real life and an economy that's shunted young people into unsatisfying part-time work, Azeroth becomes a magical, welcoming place filled with eminently achievable goals. Its systems are logical, comprehensible, and reward players for diligent work. Losses are temporary, gains are permanent, and an essentially limitless stream of entertainment is available at your fingertips for less than fifty cents a day. Players love the portal because everything on the far side is so appealing. This is, by the way, why most people consume any kind of immersive entertainment. Casual smartphone games are portals. Books are portals. MMORPGs are just another variant on the form.

WoW's publisher, Blizzard Entertainment, produced a fine piece of entertainment software, but its true function was that of a community-building platform. Ultimately these communities would become the most valuable part of the game, fueled by players chasing their own ideas of fun. Millions of people sunk huge amounts of time and energy into this game; many don't regret a moment. Ask them why and you'd get no single answer. Every one of them has a story, an explanation of why and how this video game came to mean so much.

So what happens when the portal's breached? Intense feelings not deeply felt are the essence of *WoW*'s appeal. Once the game starts to hurt, it's no longer healthy. But conflict cannot be excised from the human condition. If hundreds of guilds and thousands of people occupy the same virtual space, they will eventually collide. The terms of those conflicts derive from the established values of the guilds themselves—wildly variable, never more so than during *WoW*'s early years. Given the massive emotional investment by many players in the game, tragic misunderstandings were inevitable. Some even rose to the level of atrocities.

The outside observer's biggest hurdle to appreciating the *World of Warcraft* has always been the simplistic objection: *But it's not real!* If one were to concoct a one-sentence argument against this book, one would start there. A philosopher might reply with penetrating questions about what constitutes reality and what separates it from the alternatives. I point instead to a very famous, highly polarizing event from *WoW*'s history that made news headlines, offended the moral sensibilities of millions, and brilliantly bridged the gap between real and virtual events. Half political speech and half act of terror, it was immortalized by its perpetrators on the Wittenberg church door of their age: YouTube.

IN DEFENSE OF FUNERAL BOMBINGS:
SERENITY NOW AND THE MORAL MULTIVERSE

We begin with lilting guitar strings in a minor chord. Paul McCartney soon joins in dulcet tones, picking his way through a wistful melody, pining for a day not too long departed when all his troubles seemed so far away. The screen displays text, a series of posts from *World of Warcraft*'s cavernous online message boards: rage and castigation, denouncing unnamed individuals in the harshest possible terms. They call for the agonizing deaths of close relatives followed by funereal desecrations. The juxtaposition of soothing music and inchoate rage is vaguely artistic, like a bedroom decorated by an angsty teen.

Finally we get a scrap of context. It's an earnest message of mourning from a player on the US-based realm server Illidan:

On Tuesday of February 28th Illidan lost not only a good mage, but a good person. For those who knew her, Fayejin was one of the nicest people you could ever meet. On Tuesday she suffered from a stroke and passed away later that night.

I'm making this post basically to inform everyone that might have knew her. Also tomorrow, at 5:30 server time March 4th, we will have an in game memorial for her so that her friends can pay their respects. We will be having it at the Frostfire Hot Springs in Winterspring, because she loved to fish in the game (she liked the sound of water, it was calming for her) and she loved snow.

If you would like to come show your respects please do. ☺ Thanks everyone.

And then—timed by the video's anonymous editor to coincide with the end of McCartney's classic tune—a follow-up posting on the same thread by the same warm-hearted person, with a concluding sentence that should make the heart of any experienced online gamer drop like a stone down a well:

We're planning some cool stuff and we're going to make a video of it to show her family. ☺ So I would appreciate it if nobody comes to mess things up.

Smash cut to a wide earthen tunnel carved through a mountainside. A driving bass line tumbles from a fuzzy vac-tube amplifier.

The singer is now Glenn Danzig, boisterously belting the first verse of the Misfits' "Where Eagles Dare." We see at least a dozen *WoW* avatars riding an assortment of colorful beasts: tigers purple and white, armored white horses, even a tiny gnome astride a mechanical birdlike contraption evidently powered by steam. They are heavily armed and armored; a ruddy-bearded dwarf spurs his big-horned ram, his brow adorned by a crown of pure fire. They ride with swift and terrible purpose. This is a war party.

Smash cut once again to a serene snowscape: the Frostfire Hot Springs in the far frozen north of Azeroth's westernmost continent of Kalimdor. Steam rises from water bordered by thin ice crunching under heavy boots like spun confectioner's sugar. Mozart's serene if trite Requiem has replaced Danzig's aggressive tenor. At the lake's edge stands a slender female figure clad in a dress of snowflake white. This is the avatar Fayejin, of late owned by a late woman whose name has remained mercifully unyoked to the events described. Mourners have assembled themselves into an orderly line, paying their respects one by one to the dead woman. Most are Horde members, like Fayejin herself; most eschew armor and weapons for black-tie dress. The avatar filming this shot, a human rogue of the Alliance, takes her place at the end of the line.

"Nice day for a memorial," she remarks casually.

"Guess you could say that," her neighbor in line replies, seemingly put off by her wording but unwilling to make a scene. It is a somber occasion indeed.

We see the war party once again, now clear of the underground tunnel and riding amidst comically engorged conifers towards the Frostfire Hot Springs. They are less than a minute out. Danzig declares he "ain't no goddamned son of a bitch!" Nobody at the funeral has any idea what is about to happen.

Cut back to the funeral, where our rogue heroine has slipped away from the crowd under cover of Stealth mode. She creeps invisible up to Fayejin at the water's edge, avatar for a woman recently deceased and obviously beloved even by people who never met her face-to-face. Strings, brass, and chorals crescendo . . . into the sudden psychic arrest of a vinyl record scratch. The rogue's knives come out; Scatman John's '90s novelty nonsense hit "Scatman" erupts through the speakers. Instantly and with a savage coup de grace, the rogue drops Fayejin's hit points to zero. She dies; the game accords the murdering rogue an appropriate number of "contribution points." For a moment nobody seems quite sure what to do. A tauren warrior—one of the very few attendees equipped for battle—approaches with his weapon drawn. The rogue slips past him and lays into the nearest mourner as the video's frame rate slams to single digits. Arcane energy flares in lashing purple novae. A dance beat undergirds Scatman John's infernal gibbering. The war party has arrived.

What follows is not a battle but a massacre. Most mourners are butchered in the first fifteen seconds, and the rest soon follow. That first warrior, having actually worn his armor, is among the last to die. A warlock's demonic minion, a giant, flaming infernal, runs about directionless, a headless chicken without its dead summoner, until at last the murderers spare themselves a moment to crush it. Dark crumpled bodies dot the snowscape. The rogue, still filming, approaches Fayejin's fallen form.

"She loved fishing," she says to the dead and also to the living, those she knows will be watching. "And snow. And PvP," slamming one scornful nail after another into the bloodlogged wood of this coffin.

"Sorry for your loss," a white title snarks against a black background. Another follows: "Yes, we know we are assholes :D" The murderers announce themselves: the guild Serenity Now of Illidan. This video, headlined "Serenity Now bombs a World of Warcraft funeral," accumulated several million views on the now-defunct Google Video service before its migration to YouTube, where to date it has over six million views. These figures do not include the video's many popular online mirrors, adding millions more.

The events described took place on March 5, 2006. They would not become widespread public knowledge for some time, as the tidal wave of outrage spread from the Illidan server's provincial forums to the larger *WoW* community and online society at large. And by far the most common reaction was indeed outrage. The term "funeral bombing" has a way of taking on moral weight.

What really happened here? Examined in a vacuum, the deed seems so obviously wicked it barely warrants discussion. Civilized people do not, as a general rule, assault funeral parties. Even bitter enemies grant each other quarter to retrieve and honor the fallen. A woman of the Horde was dead; surely the Alliance owed them the favor of peace in which to mourn.

That judgment rests on a crucial assumption: that the death in question is real and equally acknowledged by both sides. As noted, the early World of Warcraft was short on consensus and long on combat. Fayejin's friends placed little space between the woman and her avatar; Serenity Now saw little connection between the two. With such fundamental disagreements over life and death, some players were bound to cross social lines. But who was really right and who wrong? Brutal though Serenity Now's tactics were, the massacring party arguably deployed a more accurate moral compass than the massacred.

The bombers operated under a code of conduct solely defined by the virtual world of Azeroth, in which the game's hard rules are the only guide. Under this code, opposing players are fair game at all times. To condemn Serenity Now is to hold two moralities: acknowledging the virtual world's unreality while also asserting real-life morality as a guiding principle. Game philosophy theorist Stacey Goguen coined the term "dual-wielding morality" in a 2009 paper to describe this idea. As *WoW* characters may wield weapons in each hand, so too must human beings engaged in virtual worlds always wield two distinct types of moral agency. They may slaughter their foes but must ultimately check themselves before virtual slaughter becomes genuine abuse.

After some discussion of the Serenity Now incident, Goguen decides this dual-wielding morality is the best approach; "the humorous, light-hearted aspect of the ganking* is apparent. However, the fact

---

* Popular gaming shorthand for "gang killing." Ganking often involves an outnumbered victim, but not always; a one-on-one encounter can be a gank if the victim is attacked while fighting monsters, has low starting hit points, or is otherwise disadvantaged. A fair, straight-up fight is almost never called a gank.

that actual people had a request to respect their grieving disregarded outweighs in significance the humorous aspect of this issue . . . yes, this story is funny, but the members of [Serenity Now] are still jerks for what they did, and what they did is not an acceptable ethical interaction between people, even if it is within a computer game."

Goguen makes a good argument, insofar as she attempts to define a universal standard of virtual conduct. One ought not, as a general rule, hurt the feelings of others. But never did *WoW* attempt to lay down such a standard, and never did the community evidence any collective desire for one. Numerous provisions governing interplayer conduct appear in the official terms of service, but overwhelmingly they refer to verbal harassment of other players via in-game text message—particularly harassment of a sexual, racial, homophobic, or otherwise hateful nature. Thus Blizzard Entertainment signals to its customers even before they enter the game world that speech is to be regulated, actions not. Perhaps this smacks of a corporate lawyer's cold calculation, but solid game-design reasoning lies behind: verbal abuse is no fun, not even for those stunted, angry people inflicting it (about whose opinion few care anyway). What's more, the harms of offensive speech aren't much mitigated by a virtual portal. Text is virtual by its very nature—at this moment you hear the voice of a virtual author in your head—and so it hurts equally whether on- or offline.

In a video game, however, physical adversity isn't suffering. Instead it's a challenge, one the player generally has the means to overcome. In gaming, you don't get mad; you get even! A player ganked repeatedly by other players could flee the area—or she could have fun with the situation, hunting down her attackers. Outnumbered, she might call in support from her guildmates or cleverly employ local monsters as a distraction. The game's wide-open "anything goes" nature was precisely what made it fun. Many of my fondest *WoW* memories were enormous brawls sparked from isolated, unremarkable gankings somewhere in the literal Hinterlands of Azeroth's Eastern Kingdoms. However twisted Serenity Now's motivation in attacking Fayejin's funeral, her friends had the opportunity to fight back. They could have hosted the gathering in friendly Horde territory, rather than the contested zone of Winterspring. Nobody made them remove their weapons and armor, and no one coerced them into prioritizing the snowy setting over safety. They were merely operating with different intentions and values—values Serenity Now had no obligation to respect.

One group of people tried to use a video game for mourning while another used it for fun. Ask yourself, whose values are more aligned with "real" society? From the massacre itself to the YouTube video's perfectly silly music selection, Serenity Now certainly knew how to have fun. Outrage didn't fuel those millions of views; amusement did. A certain kind of gamer—and here I admit I am this kind of gamer—sees it and breaks up belly laughing. Personally, the request "I would appreciate it if nobody comes to mess things up" strikes me as so jaw-droppingly naive it practically begs for transgression. To issue this plea and expect it might be honored is to assert one's particular values as universal, but in the World of Warcraft that was never going to happen. Existence in Azeroth was a constant negotiation between many poles, many agendas, many ways of thinking. It was, in other words, a premonition of the ever-connected and multidetermined world we now experience every day.

HIDDEN IN PLAIN SIGHT

To this point we've considered the experiences of millions as they entered the World of Warcraft and examined the consequences when their competing moral universes inevitably collided. From a great height, large populations may seem homogenous—great herds driving up mesas of dust over a wide plain—and even as a conscientious author it's easy to wrap messy reality in gauzy conclusions. Every one of the millions of WoW players built and lived an avatar as unique as though etched in nucleic acid. Though we live in an age of breathless confessionals ("I Spent My Twenties in the World's Biggest Game and You Won't Believe What Happened Next"), this approach shrinks the world and trades its most fascinating features for a self-aggrandizing promise of brutal honesty. Not everyone who passed through the virtual world felt the same way about it.

Max is a soft-spoken young man with a conspiratorial smile, hair shorn to a buzz, and a thickness of limb suggesting he enjoys the gym. The letters PUNX sit tattooed across the knuckles of his left hand in homage to Rancid frontman Tim Armstrong. Max got his MMORPG start as a high school sophomore, dabbling in several games before joining *World of Warcraft* at its North American launch in fall 2004. He made his home on the Illidan server, joining the successful raiding guild Saga—ultimately a sister guild of sorts to Serenity Now. Players from both guilds often collaborated, particularly on "world PvP," the unstructured open-air battles with other players of which Serenity Now was so fond.

Max describes the relationship: "We were friends with them because they were all funny bros, but they were kinda shitty." Elitism runs bone deep in gaming, and even Max can't help noting Serenity Now's players were neither particularly skilled nor dedicated. Their material accomplishments were few—but then, as I've theorized, that was kind of the point. Far from the "power guilds" Max played in and I'd come to lead, Serenity Now was a collection of puckish figures committed to their own amusement.

Though he wasn't at the bombing and doesn't appear in the infamous video, Max was aware of the events in real time as Serenity Now mustered over the voice chat server the guilds shared. Voice-over-Internet programs, VOIPs, ran on private servers with monthly fees, so guilds often shared voice chat venues. Many competitors exist, from TeamSpeak to Ventrilo (often shortened to Vent) to more recent inventions like Curse Voice and Blizzard's own in-game voice chat. Saga's well-equipped fighters, busy in a raid dungeon, could not make an appearance. They were aware of Fayejin's funeral in advance and considered the plea for comity absurd. "I saw the forum post . . . talking about the funeral and asking politely to keep things respectful . . . and I knew the guys at Serenity Now. It was very much something that they would do."

He wholeheartedly approved of the funeral bombing and its accompanying video. "I think it's a game and you can do whatever you want. If you want to host an in-game funeral for a friend, that's fine. But if you host it in a contested zone and then essentially announce on the forums where and when a bunch of unsuspecting Horde [players] are going to be, then don't get mad if someone is playing the game in a different way. . . . Blizzard designed the game to be open so that different groups of people could have fun in different ways. Some people thought it would be fun, or honorable or whatever, to host a funeral, and some people thought it would be fun to sneak attack it."

For Max, the game's appeal lay in its wide-open, persistent nature—in the limitless possibility it promised. Being ganked was itself a formative experience; upon venturing to the contested zone of Arathi Highlands as a low-level character, he was immediately slain by a wandering band of Horde players. It felt like the Wild West. He was hooked. Asked to describe his fondest *WoW* memory, he cites a guild-on-guild battle in the verdant woods of Feralas. A large green dragon carrying particularly valuable loot had appeared among the old elvish ruins in the forest's northern reach, and several guilds from both the Horde and Alliance were interested in its spoils: "We showed up late and there was already a Horde guild working on the green dragon." A deep moat ruled out a mounted assault. Approaching on foot, Saga's force would be seen and engaged by outriders. They needed the element of surprise.

The Twin Colossals rise above the forest floor: two earthen mounds hundreds of feet high, bracketing a slender thread of a road, offering commanding views of the elvish ruins where green dragonkin congregate. Saga summited the eastmost Colossal, and with the help of parachutes and Slow Fall spells, Max and his guildmates took a leap of faith. Gliding at a low, leisurely angle down toward the green dragon and the engaged Horde, they swept right over the patrols erected to rebuff them. In moments they'd crossed the water to land directly in the Horde's midst, laying into warriors already strained and depleted by battling the dragon. What's more,

Saga made sure not to lay a finger on the dragon—a single point of damage would turn it on their own force, and even if they killed it, the Horde would still be able to loot its corpse. Only by slaying all the Horde and leaving the dragon untouched could they claim total victory.

That's exactly what happened. Saga slaughtered their enemies with the same brutality Serenity Now deployed on the funeral, though at least these opponents were armed and armored. With the Horde players' disembodied spirits hustling up the very long way from the Feralas graveyard, Saga quickly engaged and slew the dragon before they could regroup. Max and his guildmates were thrilled. Having participated in similar tactics on my own server, I can testify to the utter elation one experiences when they work. Grown adults chirp and roar like over-caffeinated teenagers. Describing the Feralas air raid years later, Max exudes palpable excitement.

From what you've read of Max, you'll naturally assume he's a hardcore gamer. He agrees with that assessment, estimating that he played *WoW* for at least six hours per day during his two years of membership. He approaches the game's morality from a hardcore mind-set. But he hardly views his time in *WoW* through rose-colored glasses. He acknowledges he "didn't spend any time hanging out with my real-life friends and I also wasn't focused on school as much." Getting a girlfriend while attending the University of California at Davis strained his free time to the breaking point, and so Max quit. "When I quit," he recalls, "I also started doing infinitely better in school and became generally a more well-rounded person. . . . Not to be a downer, but *WoW* didn't contribute anything positive toward my life, it just put everything on hold. It was fun to play but that's it." Max acknowledges that he has "an addictive personality and that I should stay away from games like *WoW*. Now I just play games that I know I can walk away from when it's time to do something else."

These are hardly the words of an unrepentant goon, the sort of person you'd imagine enthusiastically supporting notorious online funeral bombers. This person, however precisely you conceive him, is not Max. Max is kind and thoughtful, easygoing, instinctively eager to please. He doesn't drink, smoke, or do drugs, selecting as his primary vice an unhealthy appetite for Monster energy drinks. The sugary, caffeinated brew helps a great deal with his long hours; Max is a genetics researcher at the Broad Institute in Boston, a joint research venture between MIT and Harvard. Between his work, his girlfriend, and interviewing for doctoral candidate positions, his time is spoken for. Max is the youngest of three brothers: the baby, the pleaser, the diligent student, the peacemaker. He returned my extensive written questionnaire within a week and apologized for not getting it back sooner.

I asked him if his opinion of Serenity Now's funeral bombing had changed over the intervening years. His answer: not at all. "I thought it was hilarious then, when the forum drama was going on and the video was released, and I still think it's hilarious."

World of Warcraft's many millions of players lived full lives both in and out of the game, upheld their own values, and told their own stories. These people built friendships, built guilds, populated hundreds of servers the size of small cities. Without the slightest inkling of how to build a society (nor even the inclination to try) they nonetheless blazed a path for every online community that would follow. Even an event as superficially sophomoric as Serenity Now's immortal YouTube video cast colorful characters into important moral quandaries. For the millions of players in the game's vast galaxy, each day was a new adventure with family and friends. Each week was a fresh struggle to advance, to accumulate power and treasure and prestige. So the rhythms of the game became bound up with the passage of time—those little milestones of personal triumph and tragedy that teach and change us and slowly accrete into a Real Life. We lived *WoW,* as surely as we lived our own lives. We did and felt these things, and if you think otherwise I've got a few dozen of my closest friends to back up my good word. As years passed and the game's popularity waxed and waned, as players drifted in and out of Azeroth, each of us left a little piece of ourselves anchored in that world.

For my own part, I've come a long way from Cadereyta. I've seen and done a lot in the intervening time—a decade, more than long enough to build a modest career and quit and build another, to get married, to have kids if I'd wanted them—and Ghando's still there. The puppy for whom I named my avatar grew old and passed away, but when I look at my big, black cartoon cow I can still see him. I've gone years at a time without speaking with Plastico and Slipo, with Tim or Brett or Eric, but any time we meet we're those brash young kids again, cramming lime wedges down the throats of our Tecates under Nuevo Leon's towering volcanoes: a mongrel crew of upstarts, slaying dragons and saving the world, building our little club into a powerhouse and doing whatever it took to keep that dream alive. Video games don't change the world, but they do change the people inhabiting it. The millions of us who played *World of Warcraft* wouldn't know ourselves—and cannot honestly tell the stories of our lives—without it.

« 2 »

L◊VE AΠD WARCRAFT

FEBRUARY 2005

I was laid up when the knock came. The window yawned wide and the smell of wet leaves rolled in like a fog front along with the leading edge of chill. My cleats hung by their knotted Day-Glo green laces from the latch handle and I sat in my chair pushed back from the desk, a spare chair placed off to my left as a rest for my leg, a bag of frozen peas draped over my kneecap. This is what passes for medical treatment in the world of club sports. I was glad for the extra chair's elevation, though it forced me to play *WoW* in an awkwardly reclined pose, arms stretched out straight so my fingertips could reach the number keys to cast spells.

Stranglethorn Vale is a sticky jungle stretching for mile after mile from the hills of Duskwood to the very southern tip of Azeroth's easternmost continent. Under a burning sun a miasma of vapor rises to the canopy, lending the whole reach a hazy look even from the air. It's from the air you first see it, as a Horde player at least, arriving via zeppelin from the faction's distant capital of Orgrimmar. Blue lagoons and the broad black omens of reefs under the surface lend the approach an exotic feel, like the iconic chopper approach in *Jurassic Park*, complete with velociraptors gamboling on white beaches. After your first experience, you saw it more akin to the flight from *Apocalypse Now*. Stranglethorn was a war zone; every player in the game made her way through the morass at some point. A new *WoW* character starts at level 1, almost totally helpless, and through killing monsters and completing quests gains experience points (XP) that gradually advance you toward higher levels. As you increase in power, the game naturally directs you to progressively more challenging areas, and so everyone hit Stranglethorn Vale around level 40. Prior to that point, the game's geography largely kept players from opposing factions separate. Stranglethorn dumped them all together into a roiling cauldron. So many people in a single zone meant fierce competition for every monster kill and natural resource node, and on player-versus-player servers the constant contact between factions turned the whole region into a battlefield. You could hardly step out of a town's walls before encountering an attempted murder or its immediate aftermath. Slain players resurrected with revenge on their mind, hunting down their assailants only to fall, in turn, in revenge killings of their own. There was no end to it.

Which was why I logged on when I did! Evening on the West Coast meant late night for the server, and only in those off-peak hours did the hothouse cool enough to get some leveling done. By a stroke of luck I found a mage pursuing the same difficult quest, and he'd just conjured me a cistern's worth of water to restore my mana—the finite pool of mystical energy that powers a magic-using character's spells—when I heard a knock at my door.

I debated answering it at all. Doing so would demand I disassemble my icing rig, and if worse came to worst I could later claim I'd been sleeping. But my lights were clearly on, and it was likely just someone with a message for my roommate. The frozen peas and their insulating dish towel came off my knee.

"Hey," said Rae, standing in the hall, red backpack nearly as big as she was. "How's it going?"

"All right. Just had practice. Icing," I brandished the peas. I hadn't expected Rae. That she might appear at my place (or I at hers) wasn't unusual, but there'd always been a call or text beforehand. And while under most conditions I'd have welcomed her all the same, on this particular evening I was looking forward to some *WoW* leveling. We were just about to start pulling ogres!*

---

* Monsters in most MMORPGs have two states: dormant, where they wander slowly about the landscape, and active, where they make a beeline for the nearest hostile player and attack. In order to fight enemies in the safest manner possible, players typically wait at a distance from

"Is your roommate around?"

"No, he's working next door." This would only encourage her, I knew, but I didn't want to lie. Lying to people has rarely if ever worked out for me.

"Is it cool if I come in?"

How to escape? Refusal would demand a reason, and I knew I had to avoid stating the reason. No human being has ever reacted well to being trumped by a video game and I knew this, though in no way did this knowledge alter my choices. "Uh, well," I stumbled, "you can come in if you want. But I don't know when Ryan will be back." You can see the germ of my idea.

"Did he just leave?"

"No, he's been coming in and out. He's just next door," I repeated, hopefully. Nervously I contemplated my shaman, Ghando, standing unattended and defenseless in the heart of the vale.

"We can lock the door," she smirked, putting thumbs through her shoulder straps. She wore blue jeans and a Stanford hoodie in cardinal, practical as the rest of her. "It's not like we're sneaking around."

"Right, but I don't know if he might need something for his problem set."

She sighed, scratched at her temple. "Could I come in anyway? We don't have to fool around."

"Is that . . . I mean, I just wasn't expecting you tonight."

"I wasn't expecting to *be* here tonight. But I got out of office hours and the grades were posted for my math exam and . . ." A sigh. "It wasn't good. And then I just came by."

"Ah, OK. I'm sorry."

"Yeah, well, I don't know what I'm doing in that class. Can I come in? Could you just . . . cuddle me or something?" She was uncomfortable asking.

"Yeah, you can hang out." I took a step back but remained in the doorway. "But I can't do much with you. I'm kind of busy."

---

their targets before using a long-range attack to turn the monsters active and "pull" them back to be fought under controlled conditions. "Pulling" typically falls to the hunter class, though occasionally parties will simply charge in to engage an enemy.

"Could it wait?"

"It's kind of going on right now." I use the words "kind of" and "just" when I'm being a weasel.

She peered past me. "Is that a game?"

"Yeah. I'm doing something right now, with someone else. In the game."

"Oh." Soft, simple, hurt. But I had already decided what I wanted.

"Yeah. I'm really sorry; I didn't know you were coming over." I began to worry the mage waiting for me would get bored and take off.

She looked at the floor for just a moment, then back up. "So you're going to play your game, then?"

"Yeah, I'm sorry. My friend's waiting on me."

"In the game."

"Yeah."

"OK." She left. I returned to my PC and was grateful to see my partner still waiting. *Thx man*, I typed. *Good to go now.* I punched the 1 key for Lightning Bolt.

Let that passage serve to remind you that men in their early twenties are selfish monsters. Thankfully the story ends well: Rae had the sense not to spend any more time with me, freeing her up to pursue better options and leaving me with all the time in the world for *WoW*. In the best relationships, everyone wins!

I made my choice knowing its likely consequence; she was no pushover. But it was just as clear that I'd crossed a kind of Rubicon, turning down not just personal contact but *sex with an attractive human woman* for the sake of a video game. This had never happened before. A more serious relationship might have altered the calculus (we were casual and nonexclusive), but when I thought about it afterward, I hadn't turned her away merely to play a game. I'd done it because another person was waiting on me. This mage, a total stranger, had somehow staked a psychic claim to my attention. Having committed to help (and be helped by) this person, walking away felt uncharitable, to say the least. And yes, I should have prioritized the real person in front of my face, yet in the moment these claims felt very competitive. The game had grown that important to me, just a few months after taking it up. That certainly didn't oblige Rae to agree or to continue seeing me, but not everyone would have felt the same. It turns out the world is full of people who take their gaming seriously, and there's nothing preventing those people from meeting and dating each other. In fact, online games can be one of the very best venues to do so.

Any community of young single people will foster romantic relationships. It's the nature of the young and single, after all. That the community exists only online makes little difference; more than a few modern relationships begin online (including my own marriage). But games are different from OkCupid, Tinder, Grindr, or the local bar, because people arrive in all those places with the *intent* of meeting other singles. They buy someone a drink or swipe right explicitly hoping it'll get them laid. Nobody in the history of civilization has ever taken up a video game with this hope. Yet many did, in spite of themselves, in spite of a culture that hadn't yet made peace with the idea.

By the standards of video games *WoW* is not particularly sexy. Blizzard Entertainment properties* take a unified, blandly heteronormative view of sexuality—male avatars are strapping and musclebound, female avatars thin and buxom—but nobody dresses too skimpily, and sex, if referenced at all, is never explicit. Romances are more often implied than described. There exists in *WoW* no formal mechanism for declaring romantic relationships, no marriage system as other MMORPGs have implemented, so rarely in the game outside of Valentine's Day events are players explicitly encouraged to woo. Paradoxically, many in-game couples cite this as a reason their relationships happened. Without any pressure to mingle, hook up, or evade the "friend zone," players come to know each other in more honest ways. Nobody falls in love with a *WoW* avatar—how your character looks means absolutely nothing in terms of attraction, so any wooing succeeds or fails based on who you are. "The good

---

* By which I mean the fictional universes contained in the *WarCraft*, *StarCraft*, *Diablo*, and *Overwatch* franchises.

thing about meeting in the game is that I got to know his personality first," Susana Baumann says of her husband, Pierce, in an *Entertainment Weekly* article. Talk to couples who met in-game (as opposed to couples who joined a game together, their own large and separate category) and they'll echo similar sentiments.

People don't filter their online behavior the way they do in public. When we're trying to hook up, we project the selves we think most likely to achieve this. Playing a game with other people, disconnected from the ossified rituals of dating, exposes them in a valuable way. We see how they interact with the world, how they attack challenges, how they deal with frustration and failure. What we see may be ugly, but it is more often than not the unvarnished truth. Pierce Baumann seconds his wife: "We created new characters. We created stories together." Romantic overtures toward someone you barely know is unthinkable in *WoW*, yet we expect it of each other at bars. Those who match up through games have come to know each other very well long before meeting in person. That made certain kinds of relationships easier—players who may have been gay or lesbian or trans could reveal those things at their own pace. They could seek out compatible partners without risking their physical safety, especially if they belonged to one of many explicitly accepting guilds. A quick Google search turns up the names of LGBT-friendly guilds; websites and Facebook groups aggregate their names and put gamers in touch with friendly communities. *WoW* was so popular, so big, that anyone seeking companionship of any kind never had to look far.

WoW romance served, ironically, as a kind of return to romantic tradition, with separation or impossibility as a core component. Since *WoW* is a competitive endeavor and not a dating site, expressing attraction is an awkward proposition—a combination of asking out a teammate in the middle of a slow-pitch softball game and declaring your love to a longtime pen pal. The venue makes your proposal a dicey proposition to begin with, and your preexisting relationship means you stand to lose a great deal should the other party fail to reciprocate. Romance boils slow and low, advanced one tentative step at a time and often through language with a kind of calculated ambiguity, until at one climactic point someone dashes onto that limb and makes a move. A *New York Times* story on MMORPG romances quoted a *WoW* player saying she'd confessed her love to her now-husband before promptly logging off. Rejection hurts just as much online, but it's easier to type "I love you" than to force it from a nervous mouth—and if it feels overwhelming you can just walk away from the game. If worse comes to worst and the shame really is unbearable, you can change guilds or reroll on a new server.*

CONJURATION AND CONSUMMATION

You've got yourself a sweetheart in Azeroth. What now? You can run quests together, spend long hours sequestered in private voice channels, celebrate a great piece of loot, or commiserate over the latest guild drama. Your most touching conversations you save as screenshots. You can have certain kinds of sex, albeit lacking in what Sandra Bullock once referred to as "fluid exchange." Between gaming, writing, and speaking, some deep and rewarding relationships develop. But few human beings can subsist on long-distance love for long; sooner or later everyone wants to meet. Here online games diverge in an important way from dating sites, most of which sort populations by geography. Rare are the *WoW* paramours who live convenient to each other. Meeting in person demands planning, time, money (particularly if you'll travel by air), and, most important, a damn near certainty it's all going to work out.

Love has always demanded a bit of irrational confidence from all involved parties. Love in *WoW* asked participants to go a bridge further, to make a leap of faith from a completely remote relationship to a present and physical one. This other person is made from an avatar,

---

* "Reroll" is shorthand for a player creating a brand-new character with the intention of playing it as her primary character. The term originated in tabletop RPGs, where dice rolls determine a character's starting attributes. Rerolling is a far more serious decision than simply starting a new character to play casually, or to supply one's main character with resources his skills don't allow him to acquire. Such secondary characters are referred to as "alts." To reroll is to functionally abandon one's main character.

a voice in a small digital microphone, reams of lowercase purple text and a few pictures exchanged via cell phone—until you roll up to that airport curb to receive into your vehicle and life a collection of hands and feet, flesh and bones, hair and teeth and scars and traumas and dreams and a gaggle of siblings and a transcript from a respectable state university and *holy shit* it's all real. You can't know a person, much less feel genuine attraction, until that person is right in front of you: full-featured, flawed and irksome, weight pressing on the fabric of local space-time.

Attraction abides by its own rules, so what you have online won't necessarily translate offline. This isn't a sly way of noting that people lie on the Internet, whether about their identities or their appearances. It's not the offensive and depressingly common suggestion that anyone one meets on the Internet turns out to be twenty pounds heavier than advertised. It's simply acknowledging there's no way to tell whether a pairing will "work" (however you choose to define that, from a hookup to marriage and children) until the pair meet in person. Relationships tend to follow the same loose progression no matter how the couple meet, and that progression can't begin until they really *meet*. I never connected romantically with anyone from *WoW*, but more than a few friends did, over thousands of hours of play and hundreds of pages of chat, and the first in-person meeting was always a dicey proposition, fraught with anxiety and potential for misunderstanding. *Always get your own hotel room* became the conventional wisdom. One good friend traveled from his Philadelphia home to visit a woman in Nebraska; once they met, he claimed, "things just didn't work." Since I knew them both, I queried her and got more detail. "It was pretty crappy," she agreed. "He wasn't a jerk or anything. He was the same guy I knew online. But in the same room there was just no connection, physical or otherwise. Nothing happened. I'd take my dog to the park, and he'd just sit on the couch reading." The same woman ended up dating another guildmate for a long time, meeting regularly and passionately like any long-distance couple might. The chemistry's there or it isn't. You just never know until you've already landed in Omaha.

Nobody ever tells you how to handle that first meeting. Gamers in love lack reliable stores of advice, first because online relationships are relatively new and second because our society would prefer to ignore them. They don't film well, after all—people hunched over their computers or tapping into their phones makes for bad cinema—and we derive a truly alarming portion of our romantic ideals from Hollwood. *You've Got Mail*, probably the best-known romantic comedy about two people meeting online, nonetheless relies on Tom Hanks and Meg Ryan knowing each other very well *before* they meet online. Their dissonance fuels the drama. *Hackers* lands closer to the mark, with Angelina Jolie and Jonny Lee Miller first meeting in a virtual space and bonding over their unique skills in that space, but they still attend the same high school. I'd posit that Hollywood's biggest investment in online relationships appears in the *Special Victims Unit* spin-off of *Law & Order*, where the Internet becomes a venue for online stalkers to pick out their victims. The movie *Catfish* was a queasy psychological thriller premised on deception. Healthy and happy online relationships are nowhere to be found on our screens, except when we're actually playing games.

If you *do* get past all these obstacles, through the online courtship and the practical barriers to meeting and then attraction's mercurial gamble, you're still not out of the woods. Long-distance relationships are hard for everyone, particularly when you've never been able to date outside that condition. There's pressure from the outside too; since you had to spend a lot of time together in *WoW* to reach this point, the two of you are probably in the same guild. You're almost certainly playing for the same faction on the same server, or you wouldn't have met at all. So you're going to face the same tensions any couple will when they start dating inside an established group of friends, only the natural gawking will be far worse. It'll be closer to a workplace romance, only without the legal liability. Your relationship will always be something of a novelty, the topic of one kind of conversation when you're present and another when you're not. You have to make your peace with that. Those who can't sometimes choose to move their characters to another server or find another guild where their relationship will be the baseline, the status quo. Of course, that assumes you can find a guild amenable to package deals. More than a few won't waste their time with a pair, figuring one partner (usually the male, if they're straight) is much more serious and "carries" the other. There may be accusations of bias when handing out loot or choosing rosters if one or both partners are involved in guild leadership.

If you play for different guilds, everything gets vastly more complicated. First there's the mathematical fact that you've just involved two guilds' worth of people in your personal business. However many questions and wry comments and off-color jokes you'd normally expect, double it. If you raid, you'll have different schedules and you'll always be competing with each other in some capacity. If your guild has progressed further through the game's raid content, they'll always suspect you're feeding tips to your boyfriend. You'll both be wrapped up in separate sets of politics, interguild and intraguild, and you'll be expected to take sides in serious conflicts. You'll be employed as a go-between when convenient and the subject of dark mutterings no matter how fairly you play your cards. Women in particular may encounter strange behavior from their male guildmates, spurred by feelings (recognized or not) of possessiveness—the sort of petty jealousy one might expect from teenagers working at the local pool. Yet it's real, and I've spoken to several women who noted their guilds became much less pleasant when they chose to date a "rival" player.

Yet for all the social barriers, *WoW* couples seem to have a good track record. One can attribute part of this to selection bias—the couples you can observe are by definition those still together—but when they work, they tend to work rapidly and well. Simply put, few people will go to all this trouble without tremendous affection for someone else, without a genuine connection and a will to sacrifice for it that should please any romantic. These relationships are slower, more thoughtful, more chaste (if only for lack of opportunity), and in almost every way more conservative than the general Internet-facilitated pairing. Love in the World of Warcraft is quite traditional, even if the players themselves aren't.

The Power of (Practicing) Love

If Hollywood turned a blind eye to gaming relationships, academia has at least made up some of the gap. The impact of gaming on relationships (romantic and otherwise) received a focused treatment from Brigham Young University researchers in 2012, who encountered strong feelings from their subjects. Gaming seemed to serve as a kind of fulcrum, a mechanism that damaged some relationships and aided others, and the determining factor was whether *both* partners played games: 75 percent of married nongamers cited their partners' playing habits as a source of conflict, often due to arguments over time management and in particular over disrupted bedtime routines. On the other hand, 76 percent of married couples who gamed together agreed that gaming had a positive effect on their relationship. Gaming allows couples a structured space for mutual play, a venue to have fun in a way that encourages personal expression and grants agency to both parties. You might enjoy watching TV with your spouse, but you're both just sitting on the couch passively absorbing the show. Maybe you discuss it afterward. Games push you toward constant interaction. Playing an MMORPG together ensures a never-ending stream of new challenges; you'll never lack fun cooperative entertainment on a Thursday night.

But this is about more than killing time. Playing together in a game like *WoW* pushes every member of a given party into a complementary role. There are three primary roles, often called the "holy trinity" due to their prevalence across gaming. One either absorbs the damage dealt by attackers (called "tanking"), heals that damage and keeps the party alive, or deals damage to the attackers in return (called "DPS," for "damage per second"). Just about any player can slay the average monster or duel a human opponent, but powerful monsters and battles against enemy forces ask people to constantly assist one another. If you can't coordinate all your damage on the same targets, heal incoming damage, and actively protect your healer, your group will disintegrate and fail. This kind of interplay exists across nearly every RPG ever designed, and it's why

Dungeons & Dragons groups persist for decades. The act of cooperating in pursuit of a collective goal brings people together. Even without the parties overlaying any extra-game meaning to their actions, the simple act of cooperation exerts a kind of inherent emotional gravity. Success in video games makes us happy, and people made happy by the same event bond with each other—witness strangers high-fiving a home run or embracing one another after a trip through a harrowing mosh pit.

Now imagine these cooperative deeds repeated hundreds or even thousands of times between two people. Couples who share leisure activities are generally healthier for it, so it makes perfect sense to see love germinating in online games. Play enough games alongside someone else and you'll come to know them in ways both intimate and particular. In this respect MMORPGs are no different from any game; just as you come to know that when your friend drives to the hoop with his head down, he's looking to pass, so too can you anticipate exactly when she'll disrupt an enemy spellcaster and open a window to unload hellacious damage.

These bonds are strongest in simple pairs, where each party can give the other her undivided attention. Over thousands of repetitions the simple act of healing, tanking, or even pairing up to burst a foe's hit points to zero becomes a kind of exercise in love. Whatever may happen in the course of a stressful day at work, couples can come together in the World of Warcraft and actively practice caring for each other. Of course the dishes still need to get done, but we've become a culture of consumption and few forms of entertainment actively bring people together the way *WoW* can. Ask any veteran player and you'll learn the closer joys of paired play, where the continuity of "you and I" facilitates a shared narrative. With every charge of a plate-clad warrior you can almost sense the body-on-body crunch. A lifesaving last-second heal becomes a benediction, a fluorescent burst that feels as refreshing as it looks, and with time all these special little moments accrete like stitches in a gorgeous tapestry. It's one more little vignette in a grand story you share together. Play can be a form of love—the highest form, if you ask my dog—and rare's the miserable specimen who'd disagree, especially given how far these couples go to make it all work.

A Quiet Glow

"He was the quiet one," Jessica recalls of her husband, Aaron. "I was the girl." Women play *WoW* at higher rates than most PC games, yet often feel like token oddities in their guilds. If you're female and using voice chat, everyone instantly knows it and treats you differently thereafter. So Jessica was "the girl" in her guild, raiding at odd hours on a European server along with friends from another MMORPG. Surprised and flattered at the attention she got from her fellow players, she started an online relationship with a guildmate and played along with his friends. His social network became hers, she leveled a paladin to heal him in PvP battles, and when the relationship ended she needed something to fill the void. A friend suggested raiding, and so she joined a crew then making its way through the Molten Core. There, in the oppressive cinder haze below Blackrock Mountain, she met Aaron.

"My first memory of hearing his voice was right before Garr,* where those molten giant patrols come crisscrossing your path with a thunderous stomp, and one wrong breath would bring down the wrath of doom upon the group if they weren't pulled exactly right. The whole raid is stacked into a corner, against the wall, and I see this night elf prance out into the cavern. Wait . . . wait for it . . . 'Pulling!' An arrow set loose, and he was running back towards the group and quickly feigning death and the tanks picked them up. It was like poetry, and every day I waited to hear the only thing I'd ever hear him say in a raid: 'Pulling.'

"One day after raid he goes on voice chat: 'Hey, wanna have a drink with me? I've already started!' So I did, and I think we were

---

* A giant "earth elemental" made of solid rock surrounded by eight identical minions, Garr was one of the Core's easier and more entertaining fights. The minions, when slain, exploded and launched all nearby players extreme distances. Overgeared raids had a lot of fun with these explosions.

farming elemental air or something in Silithus,* but we got to talking
and drank quite a bit. Because of the time difference, we were the
only ones awake at the time, so we'd just hang out a lot and talk. We
exchanged pictures from there. I think an attraction formed just naturally and pictures only confirmed it. He most certainly made the first
move . . . I'm glad he did because I wasn't going to." They became
an official item—a relationship very much complicated by distance.
Jessica lived and worked in Silicon Valley; Aaron was trying to pick a
career in small-town England. She started to suspect their bond was
meant to last when Aaron rearranged his work schedule to be with
her, sleeping all day to make it online at 2 AM when Jessica got home.
Separated by an ocean and a continent, they spent six hours a day
together in Azeroth, in voice chat. Jessica had a webcam, but Aaron
asked her not to use it until he could set up his own. Unfair, he said,
for just one of them to share like that.

Eventually something had to give. "We loved each other already
and had said it, and it was killing us being apart. [We didn't meet]
to figure anything out; we knew. It felt like the next natural step.
Let's just say we had done everything you can do without actually
being together. And not being together wasn't enough. It was painful to be apart." They craved each other, and about eight months
after their relationship started, Jessica took the long, lonely flight to
England. "Seeing him was surreal. I had seen him on webcam, knew
his voice, knew it was him, yet wasn't quite sure since I'd never put it
all together before." It was as though Aaron existed in several forms,
drawn through different media and stored in separate compartments
of her brain. Meeting him was less revelation than reorientation, like
waking from a long and vivid dream. "As time went on, and I mean
literally minutes, hand holding becomes normal, and looking at his
face becomes normal, and it all just catches up to you. It's really
bizarre. So this was me meeting him, and his parents, and his brother,
and it was very overwhelming. Then they took me to a castle! Quite

---

* "Farming" refers to any structured, repetitive gathering of resources from the game world.
This might mean collecting herbs, mining ore, or killing monsters for crafting supplies.
Synonymous with "grinding."

the first date. In storybook fashion we hid in a little room at the top and I kissed him for the first time because I just had to, and it was perfect. Everything just fit like puzzle pieces."

After two weeks together Jessica returned to California, but both now knew their predicament to be only temporary. They'd find a way to make things work. "From there we just decided that being together was number one, being in America [for my career] was number two, and the rest would have to sort itself out around that. The rest was a lot of work, but we did sort it out. It didn't quite hit his parents as serious until he mentioned he was visiting America for three months. He didn't tell any of his friends. . . . They weren't computer savvy and he felt they wouldn't understand. His town is small, and people never leave. I was the first American he'd ever met. I remember his dad being fascinated when I visited, that the voice he'd heard upstairs for so long was now in his house, and that I already felt like a member of the family."

Aaron hasn't lived in England since, though the couple return to visit. His three-month stay became permanent. They married not long after, in Las Vegas, where Aaron's parents could find cheap airfare on short notice. She was able to get him a job at the large company where they both still work, and that opportunity has turned into the satisfying career he hadn't found in England. Jessica describes skeptical officials at US Immigration and Customs Enforcement, but with time and money and friends writing letters Aaron was able to get his permanent residency approved. They tend to play different games these days, with Jessica trying out new MMORPGs and Aaron gravitating toward shooters, but they don't feel games were ever more than incidental in their meeting—just a venue to meet and share what they could have shared anyway. "I know he's patient," she says. "I know he's a trickster, and I know he has a heart of gold. I know all these things whether I know his *WoW* character or not."

Aaron finds it remarkable how different Jessica is from her *WoW* character. "She is not nearly as nurturing as she is to people in-game!" She agrees: "Taking care of people in real life requires skills I just don't have, so doing it in-game allows me to do that in a way I can't normally. It used to be that playing together was the only way we could be together, so we held on to it very tightly. Now we don't need that, so it's just extra, and sometimes it's too much." Playing together on top of living together can suck the oxygen from shared spaces. Games can bring people together, but everything afterward falls to them.

WORKING THROUGH THE PINCH

Of course things don't always work out in fairy tale fashion. People are messy and relationships messier; anyone telling you different is probably selling something. Playing *WoW* together doesn't augur good or ill for your relationship, just the way nothing else you share will determine its outcome. Every couple is a black box—their inner dynamics unknowable from the outside, their destiny determined only by those inscrutable workings and no external marker. My wife and I decided to meet because a dating service declared us a 97 percent match, but the instant we shook hands and introduced ourselves in person that number utterly ceased to matter. It signified nothing past the initial circumstances of our meeting. If thousands of couples like Jessica and Aaron made it work through *WoW*, thousands of others suffered pain and heartbreak and loss. The game didn't make anything work or fail, but its day-to-day realities had a way of soaking into everything around them. The game had a way of manifesting personality traits, for good or ill.

"To this day, I hate telling people that I started playing because of a relationship," says Chelsea, a public relations professional who joined *WoW* along with her then-fiancé. "As if it invalidates me as a legitimate gamer. The truth is, I introduced him to *Dungeons & Dragons*, he started me playing *EverQuest*, and that turned into *WoW*." The two of them passed through one guild and then another, finally making their way into *WoW*'s earliest raiding content, and there the cracks began to reveal themselves. "It started when I was asked to join the Molten Core raid instead of my boyfriend. He was so angry. So that night I found out how awkward it is to join a raid with thirty-nine 'friends,' and have the guy you live with, sitting five feet from you, throw a tantrum and quit the team because he was on the bench still. He spent the next week forming allegiances with certain officers, and ultimately he splintered the entire guild."

But it didn't splinter their relationship. Rare's the person shallow enough to end real friendships over in-game drama. Games don't define the connections between people; they're just venues for expression. Chelsea stuck it out with her fiancé, at least for a while, but their problems kept finding permutations in *WoW*. "My engagement was the least healthy relationship I've been in. We sat in a room less than ten feet apart, backs to one another, with headsets, only sometimes speaking in the same group chats, every night for years, playing *WoW*. We built relationships with people from across the country and ignored our own, and simultaneously became more loyal to our characters than each other. His ambition channeled 100 percent toward succeeding in the game. My attentions were on the friendships I made." At the same time, being a woman in a traditionally male space, Chelsea found herself getting attention and opportunities her fiancé didn't. Resentment welled up like filthy water in a catch bucket, and instead of resolving their issues, the young and inexperienced couple retreated further into themselves. *WoW* seemed like it was keeping them together, but in fact it had become a way for both to ignore their problems.

"It wasn't until an in-game friendship turned to flirtation, turned to what was a sincere admiration and even lust, that I realized my engagement needed to end. It hobbled on for a while after, and I ended the flirtation in an attempt to make the engagement work. Eventually, he used my indiscretion to commit his own with a work colleague, and in true gaslighting fashion, it was my fault for falling for someone I'd never met. I gave the ring back on our five-year anniversary. He moved out and directly in with his work colleague and they had a child together in less than nine months from the breakup. It was the hardest time of my life. I kept playing, but not seriously . . . instead of raiding, I'd hop around on stones in

Ironforge,* chatting with guildies. I used the support of my in-game friends to get me through, but eventually I had to return to the world of the living."

I asked Chelsea about the unnamed figure—the third party at the fulcrum of her miserable engagement. "I haven't thought about it in years, but it was this amazing friendship built on mutual aid and trust. He was a very selfless person . . . he logged on every day and helped his friend with whatever quest I needed. Taught the most helpless PvPer how to duel. And I sit here, what, ten years later and I can still remember what his character looked like. I remember how he'd bandage up my character after one of those horrible duels, and to say it doesn't provoke an emotional response would be a lie. I know he thought he was in love with a girl he never met, who poured out her heart about a failing relationship in private messages and Ventrilo channels. When the engagement ended, he reached out. I was so ashamed at everything that had happened, I told him I wasn't interested and pushed him away. We aren't even friends on Facebook. I broke his heart, he said." All the pain rendered radioactive anything in its proximity, and in the end nothing could be salvaged. It sucked. It always sucks, no matter who you are or how many times you've been through it. But nothing in life is ever guaranteed, and like a slain *WoW* avatar, there's nothing else to do but dust yourself off and try again.

FEBRUARY 2005, LATER THAT NIGHT

I told Chris what had happened, an hour later when he appeared online. *Are you serious?* he wanted to know. *You really threw her out?*

I didn't throw her out. She left.

But you told her why?

Yeah.

LMAO that's great.

---

* Ironforge is one of the Alliance faction's capital cities, home of the dwarven race and generally a fantastic piece of video game art. Very little gameplay occurs in major cities; they're economic and social hubs where players go to trade and socialize.

I thought you might appreciate my shame.

Shame nothing. I'm so proud of you.

He wasn't kidding. Chris had been serious about games for a long time, since *StarCraft* and later *Warcraft III* had provided his intense personality with an outlet. Extremely bright but uninterested in school, he ultimately made his career playing online poker. In our younger days, lacking the capital to pursue poker as more than a hobby, he gravitated toward video games. He'd read message boards and download replays over dial-up in order to teach himself every nuance and tactic, something for which I had no patience. Games for me had always been more art than science, and *World of Warcraft* pulled me in like no other title. Choosing a game over another person's feelings felt strange enough on its own; to have one of my best real-life friends applauding this decision was disconcerting. At the same time, it was rewarding to hear that kind of praise from someone who'd always been so much better at games. It also provided me the answer I selfishly sought: what I'd done was just fine, perfectly healthy. It was the sort of thing serious power gamers did. Rae found other, more worthwhile things to occupy her life. I'd officially found myself hooked on *WoW*, and my journey was only just beginning.

« 3 »

WHAT LIES BENEATH

APRIL 2005

"**P**ull him back. Pull him back!"

"Yeah."

"Start DPS?"

"Not yet. He's dodging everything. And again. Parry," Chris's voice came over the channel, audibly frustrated as General Drakkisath nimbly skirted his attacks.* Until Chris was able to land enough blows to earn the half-dragon's focused ire, attacks from the DPS players would risk distracting him from the main tank to the more vulnerable members of the raid. Flanked by two powerful honor guards, the general was at the time one of *WoW*'s strongest foes.

"Start on the first guard. Everyone away from the second, we're ignoring it. Just keep it Feared." The powerful spell called Fear was useless against mighty Drakkisath, but properly employed could keep a guard too terrified to protect his master.

"Thing with Fear is, the son of a bitch just keeps *runnin'*. Can't get range," grumbled Meaning, our ever-irascible warlock.

"Just burn the first one hard. Keep the heals coming. Just used Last Stand there." One of several emergency tools at Chris's disposal, Last Stand granted him a surge of extra hit points to survive fierce bursts of enemy damage. As a restoration shaman, a healer attuned to the natural elements, keeping Chris alive was my duty. I was doing a poor job.

---

* When anything in *World of Warcraft* is attacked, the game rolls invisible dice to determine the outcome. Without getting into the extensive details of *WoW*'s ever-changing combat system, any given attack may be avoided entirely through a lucky dodge or parry, or even a simple miss. Attacks can also strike for normal damage or "critically strike" for bonus damage.

"You didn't need to," came a chirp from our holy priest. "I Shielded you. And then there's—*shit!* I'm down!"

"What happened?"

"The second guard's loose! Meaning, what the hell?"

"It's got a DOT—bleeding! The Fear won't stick!"* A quick glance at the eggplant-colored magical miasma seeping from the loose dragon confirmed his account.

A grave error, to be sure, but recoverable. Chris, thoroughly engaged with one guard already, hauled over to the loose guard and used his Taunt ability to attract its attention. I doubled my efforts healing Chris, pumping magical energy through him like so much transfused blood, and it was barely enough. His health bar leapt between full and near-empty, his life flickering like a candle in a gale. The first of the two guards was nearly dead, though we still had General Drakkisath himself yet to defeat. As if on cue, our secondary tank (or "off-tank," as players describe all tanks who aren't the main tank) hissed onto the channel, "Conflagged!"

He'd lost control of his character, temporarily disabled by a powerful fire spell, and the general was now on a rampage. The largest of the dragonkin charged into our midst and we scattered like flies, hunters and mages pinging his attention back and forth between them for the few seconds we'd need to get him back under control. But he still lashed out, still landed hits here and there, still raked our fifteen-player raid with his fire breath. "Need heals!" came the call—a voice I recognized, a rogue in my guild—and while I knew what his character looked like, in the battle's burning chaos I couldn't find him. He died without a heal, as the first priest to fall had been his subgroup's assigned healer. My attempts to find him wasted valuable time, and so Chris died too, followed by the rest of our raid. A total wipe. We could only get up, dust ourselves off, and try again.

---

* The term "DOT" refers to spells that deal damage slowly but efficiently over a long period of time. To be DOTed is to be afflicted by a DOT—a specialty of the warlock class, alongside the Fear spell. Unfortunately, Fear is canceled when the target takes damage, even slow periodic damage. In this case, one of our warriors accidentally struck the Feared guard with a blow that both broke the Fear and applied a DOT. The DOT kept any new Fear from functioning, and all hell broke loose. These things happen a lot in *WoW*.

"I couldn't find him fast enough," I explained to the others while we slowly resurrected ourselves—"rezzed up"—and recovered for another attempt. The wipe wasn't my fault, not *all* mine at least, but smart players will always take this time to iron out their tactical wrinkles.

"You using CT Raid?" asked the dead priest, one of the server's more highly regarded healers and a good source of game knowledge.

"What's CT Raid? Never heard of it."

"It's a custom UI mod called CT_RaidAssist. Lets you see everyone in the raid if you want. Everyone should download it if you haven't."

A WORLD OF POSSIBILITY

This wasn't a problem at first. The user interface (UI) that shipped with *WoW* worked perfectly well when players first kicked off their adventures. At the start of the game your objective is simply to advance through levels, toward whatever the level cap at the time happens to be (currently 110). You're running around solo or in small parties, killing cookie-cutter monsters in the open game world or running the occasional dungeon,* and you find the UI totally sufficient. But once you've reached the game's level cap, your primary avenue to improve your character vanishes. Instead of progressing through levels by questing, you must find other ways to improve your character's equipment. It's a complete reversal of incentives, a change so jarring that some players choose to play *WoW* purely through leveling one character after another ad infinitum. To get better gear at the level cap, you have to engage with what's called the "endgame," and that means either battling ever-tougher monsters

---

* The World of Warcraft is vast but not entirely seamless. Everyone on a given realm server occupies a single persistent open world, but for some areas the game creates separate copies of the area for separate groups of players. Every group can have its own exciting tailor-made experience without intrusion from outside players. These copied areas are called "instances." A dungeon is a type of instance filled with monsters; a raid dungeon is for larger groups and includes vastly tougher monsters; a battleground is an arranged battle between two opposing groups of players. Chapter 4 contains a more detailed description of instances.

in player-versus-environment (PvE) content, or battling your fellow players in player-versus-player (PvP) content. The moment you progress past leveling, one game ends and another begins. No matter what path you choose, you'll swiftly find the default UI holding you back.

Had the dead rogue in the General Drakkisath fight been in my five-player subunit ("parties" in *WoW* have always been capped at five players, with "raids" comprising a maximum of eight full parties), the UI would have displayed his health bar in real time and made him easy to target. Being in another party, I could only target him manually. Our strategy accounted for this: each party had its own designated healer, but the priest falling early had left his party vulnerable. Wounds don't appear on avatars' bodies—the game displays no distinction between a player at full health and one near death, though certain spell effects may leave a visual trace—so I had no way to effectively heal anyone outside my party. The UI didn't allow for it.

But just because the game hadn't shipped with that functionality didn't mean we couldn't enjoy it. The history of the personal computer is one of hacking and modifying, and since MMORPGs are mostly identified with that platform, it should surprise no one to learn they've been extensively modified. Even the earliest text-based online RPGs led enthusiasts to design custom client software, sorting the game's copious text-based information into a streamlined format. From *Ultima Online* through *EverQuest* and up to the present, any MMORPG with any significant following spawned a community of UI modders to serve players' needs. If you find something in your favorite game obnoxious, chances are thousands of others felt the same and some of those others will be talented programmers. One Google search and you can benefit from all their cumulative expertise!

I didn't know this when I started playing *WoW*; I'd never modified my game before that conversation at the pinnacle of Upper Blackrock Spire, but I'd used mods in single-player games and understood the idea. Once the dungeon run was over I began my research, quickly discovering that this CT Raid was just one of several features contained in a larger package modifying everything from chat windows to the bars displaying my character's spells. What's more, speaking to my guildmates revealed many used UI mods themselves. At first this struck me as silly—investing too much time and energy in the game's most mundane details. But surveying the offerings scattered across many independent websites (none of them owned, operated, or explicitly condoned by Blizzard Entertainment) persuaded me otherwise. The more mods I read about, the more sense they all made. The *WoW* game client tracked vastly more variables than it ever displayed or any human could process in real time, but all that data was ripe for mining by mod designers. There were just so many features to be added to the default UI, so many little needs for which the designers hadn't accounted.

How, for example, to handle the game's copious natural resources? Every zone in Azeroth contains several hundred "nodes" from which players with the appropriate skills can harvest herbs, minerals, and the like to use in crafting equipment, potions, and other useful items. For most of *WoW*'s history,* an herb picked or vein mined vanished for a period before eventually "respawning" for another player to use. Since this period was unpredictable and only a limited number of nodes can be available at any time, one never knew exactly where to find a given resource. With exploration and experience you might cobble together a gathering route in your memory, as many players did in the early days, but it would never be better than approximate, the way a dog recalls spots where he's seen squirrels. Enter mods like Gatherer, which simply recorded every instance in which a user gathered resources—what he gathered and exactly where—so those nodes could be marked and displayed on the user's in-game mini-map. Through steady accretion the player would build a fairly comprehensive database of the resources in each zone, allowing him to plan efficient gathering routes.

As a more basic concern, the default UI was hideous. Years of slow iteration have yielded small improvements, but it remains grim, brown and gray, wasting precious screen space on trifles like a long

---

* Prior to the *Legion* expansion, which allowed every player in an area to loot the same resource nodes.

line of buttons to open each of the in-game menus (nearly everyone used keyboard hotkeys, opening the Character menu by pressing C and so on) and a pair of pixelated gryphons bookending the ability bars. The game made six action bars' worth of buttons available but forced players to scroll through them one at a time during combat. Additional bars could be set up at the bottom and side of the screen, but only under rigid guidelines. Character and monster portraits were grainy still images; their health bars were pinched and showed no numbers by default, and their refresh rate was painfully slow. Damage taken wouldn't be reflected on the health bar for a split second, which made healing something of a guessing game. The UI indicated when characters had been affected by "buff" spells, which augmented their abilities, and "debuff" spells, which harmed them, but these effects were displayed in no particular order and with no particular urgency. None of these rendered the game unplayable by any means, but every player of every class dealt with UI annoyances.

Most looked to custom UIs for salvation. These cosmetic mods were probably the ecosystem's most diverse, as a mod existed for every conceivable aesthetic, from brutalist gray blocks to dazzlingly ornate character frames modeled after dragons and sporting animated 3-D models of anything you targeted. Add-ons supplying real functionality were subject to the laws of mass adoption we see with popular smartphone apps: users flock to whatever they perceive as the "best" option, since the very fact of its mass adoption enhances its value (what the venture capital set calls "network effects"). Answers to your questions are easier to find with a hundred thousand other users to ask; bugs get found and fixed much faster. When it came to the most practical mods, a few powerful utilities dominated the ecosystem.

Players grouping for quests or dungeons all dealt with "threat," the common MMORPG concept governing which players monsters choose to attack and when. Dealing damage to a monster builds threat on that monster, making it more likely to attack you; healing allies builds threat on all monsters in the fight, albeit at a slower point-for-point rate than damage. Tanks use special abilities to generate bonus threat, holding the monsters' attention and absorbing their damage—like Chris on General Drakkisath—while more fragile allies do the killing. Threat is usually kept opaque, hidden behind abstractions, because to place the information front and center would confuse new players and deluge others with numbers they don't need to see. Tanks in the early days learned the system the same way the US Navy assembled its SCUBA dive tables: trial and error! If someone pulled threat off the tank / surfaced with the bends, that was too much threat / time underwater. Call the medics and try again. Eventually mod designers worked out *WoW*'s system for themselves, hammering out the arithmetic from careful examination of the meticulous combat logs kept by every player's client software. A threat-tracking mod called Omen became the most popular, beloved for its straightforward presentation and constant reliability, so long as every player installed her own copy. Hidden in *WoW*'s online data streams were secret text channels mods could use to share data, collating forty players' worth of threat into crisp colored bars in a pleasing format.

Those combat logs became the game's most precious resource. In time the modders grew better and better at reading them, at designing lightweight programs to sift through mountains of data and pluck out exactly what the player needed to see. Any flaws in their methods or bugs in their implementation drew harsh and immediate criticism; gamers, particularly PC gamers, demand a lot from their software. If a problem with a mod isn't swiftly remedied, users will abandon it within weeks. Whenever Blizzard releases a new patch updating the game itself, every mod requires some minor adjustments in order to keep functioning, and everyone expects those updates to be available within hours of the servers going live. Countless raids start late every "patch day" because a handful of players didn't bother to update their UI mods. Sometimes they'll have to restart their game software to apply updates, and there's a waiting line to log back in to Blizzard's servers.*

---

* *WoW*'s technological capacity is vast but finite; each realm server has a limit on concurrent players, and once that limit is hit a "login queue" automatically forms to check in players entering as others leave. Long queues are rare now, with the game's smaller population, but *WoW*'s glory days routinely saw thirty-minute queues just to get into popular servers.

Players forced to play without their accustomed add-ons feel crippled and confused. You can easily get by without cosmetic adornments like animated 3-D portraits, but healers (if no one else) came to need the raid frames their peers had built. Encounters were designed and balanced with the assumption that players would use extensive add-ons, rendering them ever more necessary to deal with complex fights, and over time this reliance on mods proliferated throughout the player base. Today, any player who enters a dungeon without mods to warn and guide him through each boss fight is an ignorant fool. Anyone who posts a screenshot or video on a *WoW* forum can expect at least one snarky comment about her UI aesthetic. UI discussion occupies a good percentage of guild chat and online forum discussion: *What add-ons are you guys using and why? Oh, I haven't heard of that one. What's it do?* Over years, the community's diverse ecosystem gave rise to specialized add-ons for each class, regardless of the role you chose to play, and often you hadn't even heard of the mods your guildmates were using to enhance their play. Warlocks had add-ons to monitor their DOTs on many targets at once, shamans for their totems, rogues to anticipate the two-second pulses of energy fueling their abilities. No matter what in-game problem you wanted to address, there was probably a mod for it, and once it was installed you'd immediately start to wonder how you ever managed to live without it.

All video games fundamentally represent the shifting of numbers from column to column, since software is mathematical by its very nature, but RPGs in particular operate on rigid numerical rules. The classic stereotype of a *Dungeons & Dragons* dork with his arsenal of custom dice reflects the reality of a game whose every mechanic relies on luck modified by arithmetic. *WoW* was no different; its "real-time" combat nevertheless rested on a foundation of hit points and rigidly timed weapon swings and a 1.5-second "global cooldown" throttling the number of actions a character could take. Every action in a combat context could thus be described mathematically, if you knew where to look for the data, and when the modding community asked earnest questions Blizzard's designers were almost always forthcoming.

They didn't have to be. No MMORPG developer *needs* to allow UI modifications at all. PC gamers can find a way to mod just about anything, but persistently online games rely on more than just *your* computer, and so a remote server acts as gatekeeper to your every deed. The server won't authorize illicitly modified software, and even if it can be fooled, the player operates under the constant threat of a permanently banned account—hundreds or even thousands of hours of work expunged. Whether to allow mods at all lies at the discretion of the game designers, and many simply don't permit them. These games are enormous and complicated enough without worrying about the open-ended possibilities of an entire modding community mucking through the software. An awful lot can go wrong, which is why even the developers who allow mods place them in shackles. Mods may only do certain things, the designer declares: this but not that, may use function X but only when bound to a button press and never function Y under any conditions. *EverQuest*, in many ways *WoW*'s direct spiritual forbear, allowed UI mods on a limited basis. While they organized on-screen information more efficiently, they remained cosmetic in nature. They added no real functionality. Players seeking to circumvent shortcomings in the game's design had to complain endlessly on official forums and hope the developers implemented their suggestions—which they did, however slowly and painfully. *EverQuest* was commercially successful, but the game never really caught up to the sophistication of its player base. Brilliant people labored with comically flawed tools, pulling off feats even the developers hadn't thought possible.

WoW's designers took these concerns to heart. Many were elite players in *EverQuest*, *Dark Age of Camelot*, and similar games, so they'd experienced frustration firsthand. They understood the true nature of MMORPGs—an inversion of the typical designer/player relationship, where instead of the designer creating an experience for the player to discover as a customer, players take an active role in developing online games. Developers don't spend much time *playing* their games (they're busy working on them), and so a big, obsessive community will always be a step ahead. That disconnect can be a major source of friction and verbal abuse on message boards, but Blizzard had the wisdom to preemptively hand their players the keys to the kingdom. UI mods were outright encouraged, supported with a revolutionary system that let enthusiasts program their own UIs. *WoW* has never been "open source"* but in many ways its UI was. Previous MMORPG systems had to be designed for an entire player base millions strong, deciding exactly where and when to lift the curtain into the game's quantitative complexity. Any change patched in by the developers was effectively forced onto millions of people, many of whom wouldn't like it. *WoW* stepped back from that. While striving to be the world's mainstream MMORPG, their UI paradoxically abandoned the idea of being all things to all players. Let the basic UI handle the basics, they decided. Modders would provide for the rest, tailoring their products to specialized audiences in line with their specialized needs. Players would build these parts of the game themselves. In retrospect, the calculation was daring but absolutely brilliant. It could not have worked out better, and *World of Warcraft* owes much of its success to this strategy. It allowed players to meet their own needs, freed up in-house resources for other areas of the game, and yielded redounding benefits in the modding community it fostered.

The official forums' UI-modding section had always enjoyed its own contingent of highly active moderators on hand to assist aspiring engineers in their work. Using the popular, simple, and highly modular programming language Lua in conjunction with XML, they gave their players tremendous agency in customizing the game experience. A popular menu system set up custom "macros": multiple commands and contextual triggers bundled into single clicks or keystrokes. Even a total novice could search through forums and copy-paste fabulously useful macros into her game client and stick the brand-new command right on her character's action bar. But with millions upon millions of devoted subscribers and a clientele

---

* "Open source" is a term denoting software for which the source code is made freely available for copy or modification. Many popular online tools like Mozilla's Firefox browser are open source.

including large swaths of the tech elite, it should surprise no one that *WoW*'s modders occasionally ran afoul of its developers.

A Bridge Too Far

Perhaps the best example concerns a mod known as Decursive. Released about the same time as the Blackwing Lair raid dungeon, it represented a wholly natural response to the new dungeon. Whereas the Molten Core had punished players with widespread fire damage, Blackwing Lair had a number of encounters (the two-headed mutant dragon-hound Chromaggus, to name one) in which raid members would suffer powerful and dangerous "debuffing" spells, dispellable by other players. The default UI showed these debuffs but made no attempt to discern whether any given player could dispel them, so any time a debuff appeared the healers had to perform the following routine: A) squint at the debuff icon; B) if the icon wasn't recognized, mouse over the debuff to read its category (magic, curse, poison, disease, physical, etc.); C) determine whether your character is able to dispel that type of debuff; D) determine whether it's your responsibility to cover that character's dispelling, as opposed to someone else holding that responsibility; E) determine whether dispelling this effect at this time is tactically wise (it may not be, depending on many particulars); F) target the afflicted character and dispel her. If this process takes two full seconds, your teammate has probably suffered massive damage and the raid as a whole may find itself in jeopardy. The whole chain has to happen more or less instantly; slow or clumsy dispelling has wiped untold thousands of raids over the years.

Players demanded a better system, and Decursive's authors stepped in with a radical claim: to remove the headaches and render debuff removal an automated process. *WoW*'s UI is designed to prohibit mods from unilaterally executing any kind of action, whether movement or spellcasting. Functions may be largely but not wholly automated. In order for an avatar to take an action a player must enter an input, so Decursive revolved around a single button. Any time you hit the assigned "Decursive key," the mod examined every player in your party or raid for debuffs dispellable by your class, ran checks for spellcasting range and line of sight, cross-checked with any preferences you may have set regarding dispel priorities (warriors first, personal group first, etc.) or debuff types (perhaps in a particular fight a disease debuff is more menacing than a poison debuff), and then cast the appropriate dispel on the appropriate player without even needing to target him. It did all of these things more or less instantly and with very little opportunity cost, as attempting to dispel an invalid target incurs no cost in either mana or time. If there's nothing to dispel, nothing happens. If there is, the problem instantly vanishes—unencumbered, as NPR's famous Magliozzi brothers used to say, by the thought process. The Decursive button could be mashed ceaselessly throughout any germane fight without consequence. Indeed, this became the optimal way for healers to play.

Blizzard shut it down overnight. Having designed these debuffs as fun new wrinkles to challenge players, and despite supporting Decursive's goal of streamlining a cumbersome process, pure automation was a bridge too far. One fine Tuesday, *WoW* players logged in after weekly maintenance to find their Decursive mods crippled. The designers responded to the predictable public outrage on official forums, admitting they'd decided the mod ran counter to the game's best interests. Several crucial in-game scripts, from targeting to spellcasting, were declared "protected" and thus off-limits to mods.*

The developers were happy for mods to enhance play; they just didn't want mods to do the playing. Fully automated *WoW*-playing programs existed for download, but anyone caught using one suffered a total ban on his account. The game's terms of service expressly forbid the use of any third-party software to play. While Blizzard never punished anyone for using Decursive, the fact that mods existed

---

* They remained valid for macros, but Blizzard never considered this so risky because of the limited functionality granted to macros. They must be manually entered into text fields, they can only be activated through clicks or keystrokes, and the game software insists on executing every line in a macro simultaneously rather than in sequence. Thus they lack the autonomy or decision-making capacities of a mod.

entirely within their sanctioned development space meant they didn't have to. Any mod falling outside their comfort zone could simply be disabled. If players complained—and they did, bitterly, over the loss of Decursive—their ire lasted only as long as the gap in solutions. Mod authors found workarounds and players learned to make do under the new regime. The number of players who dropped their *WoW* subscriptions because of disabled mods, while probably not zero, is very small and likely limited to the authors of those mods. If Blizzard disabled your favorite mod, you just got over it and went back to playing whack-a-mole, dispelling comrades by hand any time their raid frame lit up a particular color. Decursive made its eventual return as a limited but nevertheless useful raiding tool, though later mods like Clique would more effectively bundle sophisticated spell-casting functions into single player inputs.

But this is exactly the point: central though mods became to the playing experience, even for relatively casual players, no single mod was ever crucial to *WoW* as a whole. Blizzard cultivated a large and sophisticated ecosystem for mods, and in so doing opened new avenues for their game's growth. MMORPGs are strange organisms, both living and dead—evolving with their communities, growing as their designers release new content, yet still bound to a single piece of software too large to easily change. Update the UI, the graphics, and sound engines if you like. Overhaul the talent trees every two years,* implement first-party voice chat, and you're still just making cosmetic changes to systems too complex and interlocked to wholly rebuild. For all Blizzard's ongoing investment in the game, *WoW* remains an elderly piece of software. The dowager just wears her age well.

Whatever vision the designers had for the modding community, it's been one of the most important factors in *WoW*'s longevity and widespread appeal. Oversights in the UI didn't hamper the game's growth, because modders stepped up to remedy them. The community was able to accomplish a great deal more in the endgame, and

---

* Players allocate a character's "talent points" into special abilities and bonuses tailored to their preferred play style. They also pick a specialization, or "spec," channeling their character's strengths in a specific direction, e.g. a mage picking between fire, frost, and arcane spells.

a great deal faster, by building their own tools. Any new UI feature cooked up in Blizzard's office had to be designed, tested, and implemented in keeping with the studio's prized reputation for thoroughness and quality. Once in the game, it might be useful to only a small number of players, like elite raiders. It might confuse players unaware of the new functionality, and any new player to your game will confront an intimidating gauntlet of menus and options. Better to let the players handle it themselves—let them decide which tools they need. Let them build those tools themselves and share them over the great wide Internet. Design a deep, rewarding yet overwhelming system to let players build their own personal garrisons, let them figure out for themselves what's optimal, and sit back as add-ons like Master Plan lay out the proper path. Players have at their fingertips each solution to every problem imaginable, made credible by community sourcing and provided at no cost to either user or developer! Any problems with implementation land on the modders, any confusion is to be remedied by third-party FAQs, and no new player will ever throw up his hands with frustration because you asked him to set his own debuff display priority, whatever the hell that means.

Dumping these chores on the community may seem like a cop-out, but it turned out to be a brilliant move. It drew players together, whether to share advice on the newest mods or to post in ubiquitous "rate my UI" forum threads. It encouraged them to grow and develop mods on their own terms at their own pace, unfettered by marketing concerns or a demanding development schedule. Independent sites like WoW Wiki and WoWAce emerged to train up new modders: a focused and inspired amateur could, by drawing on these resources, their knowledge bases, and their ready-made chunks of Lua code available for copy, assemble her own simple mods. Indeed, many of the game's best add-ons started as utilities for personal or guild use. The CT_Mod collection of add-ons referenced previously, a full suite upgrading much of the UI's basic features, was built by two *WoW* enthusiasts with the simple aim of enhancing their play experience. It all started with the buff display, as developer Tucker Smedes noted in a 2007 interview: "I wanted them listed vertically with names being displayed, so CT_BuffMod was created." Smedes knew little about coding, relying on his partner "Cide" for much of it—"I'm able to edit it a bit myself, but still not able to write it from scratch"—but even Cide hadn't coded before his work with *WoW* mods.

Smedes kept a constantly updated list of mod ideas, drawing inspiration from the frustrations of his own nightly work as the leader of a raiding guild. CT_RaidAssist emerged from his guild's pedestrian needs—better debuff displays; status monitors for the entire raid; windows to show what the tanks were targeting to quickly attack the same enemy, known as "assisting"—and it was for their benefit that Smedes posted his creations publicly. Through word of mouth, like my conversation in Upper Blackrock Spire, their popularity spread. Before long, anyone serious about raiding was either using CT_RaidAssist or a mod almost exactly like it. Packages like Cosmos bundled many of the community's most popular add-ons from many different authors into a single convenient download, though the results could be unwieldy. Sloppy mods might throw error messages at users, but there were still more add-ons to hide the errors! Other users saw value in the CT mods' consistent performance, minimalist look, and low profile. Inefficient or memory-leaking mods could bog down even a powerful computer, and gamers *hate* it when their machines stutter.

CT_RaidAssist quickly became the most downloaded user-built modification in the history of video games. Millions upon millions of people used Smedes and Cide's work for hours every night of the week. "There were only a few options for worthwhile mods coming into [the November 2004] release," Smedes said. "Ours was continually being updated and worked on, and the design was dominant. When we moved CTMod to its own web server, it crashed two different servers within the first three days of its move." An enormous user base means enormous pressure to maintain the mod, to get new versions uploaded within minutes of a fresh patch release, to investigate and laser out every little bug report landing in your inbox. Server hosting costs can balloon unexpectedly; maintaining your little corner of the community becomes a full-time job, albeit one you'll never get paid for. Smedes and his partner never made a dime off their work, though more than a few of their designs (raid frames, to pick the most obvious example) have since been implemented wholesale into the default *WoW* interface. They're not building an independent product, after all, merely a mod dependent on Blizzard Entertainment's intellectual property. Everything the modding community does exists at Blizzard's pleasure, and mods exist as easily readable .LUA and .XML files—there's no way to patent or otherwise protect them. Still, a few enterprising players were able to leverage their work for the community into financial gain. They did it the same way Google does it: selling not software products but infrastructure.

BLESSED WITH A CURSE

Once we finished off General Drakkisath, collected our loot, and got back to town, I minimized the game and pulled up T K T's guild website. The site was little more than a front page over cookie-cutter message boards, since only a handful of people ever visited. We weren't much to crow about in those days—just a couple dozen players, mostly Spanish-speaking, with a friendly enough reputation but no real accolades to our name. Upper Blackrock Spire runs in the evenings were the closest we got to organized events, so who really needed a website? I hadn't even registered a user name. With that clerical detail addressed, I logged in to see a fresh post from Chris. "UI MODS," read the subject line, "FOR GOSU PROS."* Inside were links to various packages including the latest CT mods, all conveniently posted to the T K T site for easy download. More links followed, to a dozen other guilds' sites, all of them built from vastly cooler templates and packed to the gills with resources. I saw screenshots from the latest kills: impressive fire-encrusted golems and ferocious two-headed dogs from a bewilderingly huge dungeon called the Molten Core. These players were so far past myself and anyone in T K T, so much more sophisticated in their approach to the game and knowledgeable in its

---

* *Gosu* is a Korean word meaning exceptional, superior, or expert. Many Western gamers admire the Korean professional gaming scene and cribbed the term.

every aspect. Chris had always been much the same, effortlessly good at games, always up on the latest *StarCraft* builds or *Super Smash Bros.* tactics. I admired this—everyone would like to be good at things—but had never dived too deeply into any pool. Frankly, at that point in my life I had very little idea what I wanted or how to go about getting it.

I knew the guild was an ever more appealing part of that life. Without getting into trivial details, I will say I wasn't yet old enough to have acquired perspective on relationships and why they end. I also found myself, crucially, with a great deal of excess time on my hands on account of hating my classes and avoiding their associated work. *WoW* hadn't been the most important thing in my life to that point, but it maintained a connection with Chris, and fifteen dollars per month for unlimited play was the sort of deal no gamer on a college budget could pass up. The stars aligned for a deep dive into the World of Warcraft, and the revelation of this bigger, complicated world was all I needed to take the plunge. The company seemed enjoyable enough—Chris being my friend of many years, the rest helpful and sociable even if I couldn't understand most of what they said. Most spoke English well enough if I whispered them,* but Guild chat was probably 80 percent Spanish. The Mexican contingent's leader was a gregarious shaman named Plastico, who might dispense curses and insults and professions of love all to the same person inside of five minutes. He showed a boundless enthusiasm for *WoW*, frequently playing all night, chatting with anyone who'd listen before returning to his day job programming software for a major Mexican bank. Those long hours reflected his brute force approach to the game. He very much believed in the ideal of the hardcore gamer: that total investment was the highest of virtues, hours in-game numerical proof of the same. Clever tactics, judicious decision making, and precise execution mattered less than will and dedication.

---

* *WoW* includes many forms of communication, from global channels to Guild chat and password-protected private channels. It also allows players to privately "whisper" each other regardless of distance or circumstance; you can even whisper in-game with your friends playing other Blizzard games or using the Blizzard mobile app.

Plastico and I were polar opposites, in approach and temperament both, which is why we butted heads from the start. I like to play my cards close to the vest and speak little online; someone who shoots from the hip and says whatever crosses her mind will probably get on my nerves. For the entire time I played with Plastico, we fought like cats and dogs. In time we'd develop an affection—we'd even become indispensable to each other—but this elemental tension always remained. When Chris used his influence to push T K T toward bigger goals, Plastico applauded the direction but didn't really process the more professional approach. He didn't want to spend hours reading message boards and lurking on IRC channels to learn about the game; he wanted to spend that time actually *playing* the game. So he struggled with the details of raid planning and directing, while Chris assumed an ever larger role. For my own part, I was happy to take the guidance. Chris's leadership spoke to a part of me that always loved gaming but never grasped its ruthlessly competitive side. As my browser grew cluttered with tab after tab, I felt a genuine intellectual thrill the likes of which school hadn't furnished in months. But, Jesus, I couldn't help thinking, couldn't someone put all this on one website? Couldn't some enterprising soul herd all these constellations into a single viewable corner of the sky?

As it happened, someone a continent and an ocean away was thinking the exact same thing. He was Hubert Thieblot, a seventeen-year-old in France with a passion for games and a brother who'd gamed professionally, elevating his ambitions. Playing *WoW* on a European server, he founded a guild, which at the suggestion of an early recruit he named Curse. Most of the players didn't really know what the English word meant, but the name was pronounceable in French and, more important, it was short enough to stick in the memory. As Curse grew and expanded their operations, Thieblot grew frustrated with *WoW*'s fledgling modding community. They made fine add-ons, he saw, but lacked a central forum to share them—both with users and each other. Individual modders would place their work on personal blogs or free hosting sites, but these were unreliable at best, and any real success would bring a deluge of traffic to crash the servers. Word of mouth just wasn't good enough for the world's biggest and best MMORPG. Thieblot decided to do something about it.

As proprietor of his guild's website, he converted it into a central resource for his comrades. He posted the best mods, the most reliable loot databases, and guides for harvesting natural resources. Playing sixteen hours each day, raiding on a European server with one account and an American server with another, he inhaled knowledge wherever he could find it and posted everything. To that point, as Thieblot noted in a 2012 interview, "the modding community was very scattered. You had to go through these forums, and there were so many." The famous MMORPG guild Fires of Heaven, for example, maintained a popular forum for *WoW* discussion, but it was also a notorious haven for malicious trolls. Thieblot's site took the opposite approach, keeping the message board function but leading with a stream of news posts—posts that took on a steadily expanding scope. Using the Internet Wayback Machine to view the site as it appeared in the first months of 2005, one sees modest posts about the guild's first level 60 players, notices for recruitment, a few screenshots of downed Molten Core bosses. As time goes on these posts grow intermingled with articles about new add-on releases, rumors of leaked patch notes, and largely sarcastic commentary from a very youthful Thieblot on proposed features: *The caster itemization vs melee is still totally broken, melee damage is way to high when the Crowd control in WoW is so poor. This need to be fixed if Blizzard wants WoW to be a long term game for the hardcore crowd who spend most of their free time in this game, It's getting boring to replace 4-5 players per month alone because of this.*

News became a central pillar of the Curse website. On one level this made sense, as updates to *WoW* were constantly being previewed, discussed, and released; mods similarly operated on a week-to-week update schedule, if not day-to-day. Any Tuesday might bring a fresh game patch that required add-ons to be updated, and even if it didn't, modders might roll out bug fixes, new features, or badly needed menu tweaks. Thieblot did a great deal of posting himself, and the expanding community on the message boards added their own information, which Thieblot was happy to signal-boost through the front page. Modders would use his forums to announce their updates. When not updating the website, he was pounding the metaphorical pavement, endlessly promoting his site on Blizzard's official forums as a trustworthy repository of all things *WoW*. He offered straightforward solutions at a time when the game's exploding population was chafing against the level cap, starting to crave more sophistication and—like Chris and me and the rest of T K T—seeking the right tools to attack endgame content. Traffic didn't so much explode as expand, like a riverbed accommodating a doomed glacier, swelling past conventional benchmarks and swamping the original form. Thieblot became an unwitting victim of his own success when his older brother, who'd kindly footed the bills for the website in its early days, informed him they'd grown to over a thousand euros monthly. Happy as he was for Hubert's success, he told his little brother to make a choice: either solicit donations or post advertisements. An abortive attempt at the former (gamers already paying fifteen dollars per month for one subscription aren't eager to add another) led to the latter. Simultaneously, the guild's unusual practice of releasing their raid boss kill videos accompanied by pristine UIs and thumping trance music built a devoted fan base who'd stop by every day to catch updates. Curse was officially a business.

By January 2006, the changes were obvious. Curse Gaming had become entirely ad-supported, and Thieblot was contemplating a move to the United States in order to find proper venture capital for its expansion. *We have at least 2 million page views a day*, he wrote at the time. *When we opened the website, it was running on a shared server with 256 [megabytes] of ram. After 1 year, we now have 10 servers in a big data center and I think it will get bigger and bigger . . . we are now aiming for a real community website, not just an addon database.*

He also declared his intention to rid the site of all advertising that didn't comply with Blizzard's terms of service—specifically, ads for gold-buying and character-buying services. Blizzard Entertainment always vehemently opposed the practice of third parties selling gold or other in-game resources for real money. They'd do it themselves (*WoW* Tokens, addressed in chapter 7, were introduced only in 2015 after the game had been live for a decade) but wouldn't tolerate other companies in the market for *WoW* gold. Though the gaming giant couldn't forbid Curse or any other third-party site from running ads for such services, they were vocally opposed, and it remained in Thieblot's interests to maintain good relationships in the industry. Even if this choice pinched his bottom line now, he'd still benefit by focusing on stronger and more reputable advertisers. He was in this for the long haul, after all.

Once he'd ginned up millions in venture capital, Thieblot set about the work of expanding his vision. What worked for *WoW* could work in other games, he decided, given the growth of online gaming and the rise of legitimate e-sports. The world was full of gamers, and almost all of them wanted to be better at their favorite games. His company would become their go-to source for reliable, pro-level gaming tips, no matter what they played. And like the original Curse site, the beauty lay in what Thieblot *didn't* have to do: build the content! Just as he'd never coded a mod himself but merely aggregated them, a clever Curse organization could comb the web for the absolute best community resources and buy them. A look at the modern Curse website shows listings for dozens of games, but what's listed are Curse-owned community sites rather than professionally produced content. The community is the key, as Hubert Thieblot understood from a precocious age. Their passion can drive incredible progress—they just need a framework with which to work.

Indeed it was the community that performed the hardest labor, but don't feel too bad for their uncompensated efforts—they barely noticed. Hardly an exploited class, they deliberately downloaded data-mining software en masse and mailed off deluges of game data daily to player-generated databases. The first good database was Thottbot, built atop a small piece of software that extracted important information from *WoW* and uploaded it all to a central location. As the data-mining tool was a standard component in the popular Cosmos UI package, the site gained access to a vast trove of data. If you killed a monster with the utility running, it recorded that monster's name, experience level, map coordinates, and any loot.

If you mined a vein of truesilver ore, it told the database exactly where. Before too long, players had amassed resource maps more accurate than any lone Gatherer mod could create, and comprehensive loot tables on every monster in the game. If you wanted a shiny new sword, Thottbot showed you every option the game offered and told you where to get each one. For sorting its vast loot database, *WoW* has always used a color-coded system (first borrowed from fellow Blizzard property *Diablo*) so simple and intuitive it has found its way into more than a few other games. In ascending order of quality: white < green < blue < purple < orange. Typical quests and monsters yield green treasure, and sometimes superior blue items. To get your mitts on loot of purple and orange quality ("epic" and "legendary" respectively, in the game's parlance), you typically have to fight raid bosses—of whom General Drakkisath was, in the grand scheme, a minor functionary. At its most basic level, *WoW* is about getting loot, and add-ons told you exactly where to find it.

Actually *getting* that loot was your own problem. The site couldn't walk you through the game's more difficult quests, but if you knew how to ask the right question it could answer nearly any specific question, guiding enterprising players to crucial monsters or letting them know that crucial quest item was a rare drop demanding patience. This made it a less-than-ideal tool for novice users; *WoW* lead designer Rob Pardo once cited Thottbot as a resource specifically for the hardcore, claiming Blizzard directed their tutorial efforts toward those who'd never heard of the site. *WoW* never assumed its players had access to these sophisticated tools and ensured they could have fun without them.

Time devours all things, as Gollum once noted to Bilbo deep under the Misty Mountains, and game resource sites are no exception. Any operation serving a large, demanding community demands investment from its founders bordering on the masochistic. Even largely automated databases had to be monitored, their input sifted, their tables updated. As modder and game designer Adrian Finol (*Team Fortress 2*) has said, the key to making a mod or game utility succeed is executing a straightforward concept and updating the hell out of it. If a modder or webmaster lost interest in his project or otherwise couldn't keep up with the constant community dialogue necessary to keep it current, it rapidly faded away. I don't remember exactly when Thottbot fell from primacy—sometime around the release of the first *WoW* expansion, *The Burning Crusade*—but suddenly everyone was linking to WoWhead.com instead. WoWhead started as a humble but effective tool for planning a character's talent build prior to investing in the then-expensive respecialization ("respec") process, but when it added a database designed along the lines of Thottbot, it soon overtook the venerable blue-on-white site with its own distinctive dark background and Goblin rocket logo.

Needless to say, this was big business. Millions upon millions of users with disposable income, rooted to their computers all day? For anyone in online ad sales, it was like dropping sausage near a dog. In a world where nobody spends more than a few moments looking at anything, sites like WoWhead offer millions of unique users spending long stretches online, running one search after another as their gaming needs dictate. Hours of eyeball time translate to piles of cash for ad networks. That's why these sites, having reached a given saturation point, never stay independent for long. If you're running one of them, by the time you've reached that point, you're overworked and swamped with hosting costs and eager for the kind of safe harbor offered by large conglomerates. WoWhead itself sold in 2007 to something called the ZAM Network, a subsidiary of the Affinity Media Group, neither of which will ring a bell because they're deliberately faceless online media empires. The site remains the gold standard for *WoW* databases, having completely consumed its competition—ZAM already owned Thottbot and its competitor Allakhazam, giving it a functional monopoly on *WoW* database sites. What was once a concern by and for amateur enthusiasts has become a totally commodified utility for ad sales, akin to the sheafs of local coupons you receive in the daily mail.

Hubert Thieblot looms large in this arena. He raised $6 million in venture capital to launch Curse Gaming in 2007, and to date his company has received $64 million in investments from various sources,

most notably a $30 million stake from *League of Legends* developer
Riot Games. Curse has developed proprietary voice chat software
that integrates directly into online games (*League of Legends* among
them, in addition to Blizzard properties like *World of Warcraft* and
Heroes of the Storm), but its primary business remains unchanged:
it's the Internet's biggest and best central clearinghouse for online
games. Curse owns at least one fan site for every major multiplayer
game on every platform. It buys them up slowly, methodically, picking out the best and most popular community resources—whether
that means databases, add-on sites, strategy guides, or live-streaming
celebrity players—and adding them to the Curse network. Curse
presently owns wildly popular *WoW* news site MMO-Champion,
in addition to a wiki (WoWpedia), a database (WoWDB), and an
e-sports site (Arena Junkies). It lists nearly four thousand add-ons
for download. *WoW* is only a fraction of its business, accounting for
less than 30 percent of Curse's traffic in 2012. *Minecraft* resources
have become their most popular content, reflecting the industry's
seismic changes since Thieblot first founded his empire. Curse was
acquired in 2016 by Twitch Interactive, a mammoth live-streaming
video platform attracting over 100 million visitors monthly and itself
a subsidiary of Amazon. Video games have become supremely big
business, and that guarantees Curse's *WoW* sites will survive, beloved
by the community and profitable for their owners. Like *WoW* itself,
they'll be around until the last paying customers turn out the lights.

OCTOBER 2005

We made it work, in the end. In the latter half of 2005 I spent more
time playing *WoW* than doing anything else: six hours a day, sometimes eight, late into the night and first thing in the morning. Chris
was there too, for every one of those minutes and more besides. I
don't know if he had the bug worse than I, but we'd both caught it
bad, and he'd always had more of a knack for obsessive focus (he's
now a professional poker player, so the pattern held). With a battery
of mods and all the data-mined information in Azeroth at our finger-

tips, each day became a laundry list: quests to run, materials to farm, dungeons to plumb for chances at rare loot. Our occasional Upper Blackrock Spire runs became regular events, each spot on the roster coveted as we cleared faster and better than the competition. T K T, our little band, slowly accrued a name on the Sargeras server the way a local shop acquires a reputation for fantastic *banh mi*. It can't be done with hustle or swag or any other new word copywriters coin to mean "self-promotion"; you just have to do the work and trust folks to see it. We were just a little better than the rest, but that little bit makes a huge difference in online games, where inborn talent is only a minor component next to commitment and attention to detail. T K T was a good guild, but Chris and I together were something special.

There's a special link in MMORPGs between healers and the healed. The only real failure in these games is death. Characters suffer damage; their hit points reach zero; they collapse and must be resurrected before continuing. Healers keep battles from devolving into contests of finite hit points, and tanks keep the incoming damage manageable. Healers and tanks thus define the limits of possibility in the game. Good healers and good tanks are invaluable because they allow battles to be fought on the most favorable terms, and the relationship between them is—as stated above—special. Chris played a tank class, a warrior. I played a healing class, a shaman, making us a bonded pair. Too specialized to fight much of anything individually, we combined to form a deadly weapon, mobile and destructive, impossible to pin down and a steep challenge for anyone to tackle. Anyone attacking me swiftly found himself hamstrung and bleeding, desperately trying to fend off Chris's blows as I skated away to heal myself. Attacking Chris was easy enough, but all that damage directly fueled his warrior abilities, allowing him to unleash even more havoc while my spells kept him alive through anything you could throw at him. Though we'd been friends for several years going back to high school, this was the most time we'd spent together and the closest we'd been.

Before long, Blackrock Spire no longer provided a challenge, and the game's best loot could only be found in the game's first full-scale raiding dungeon, the Molten Core. T K T expanded to fill a raid-ing roster; while we'd conquered the Spire with fifteen raiders, the Core demanded no less than forty. We made our way there, then into the lair of Onyxia—once we found a good online guide to lay out the maddeningly complicated path. Chris was our leader, a role main tanks fell into naturally, and a role well suited for his even, bloodless temperament. In the midst of chaos, with stakes and tempers run-ning high, Chris never shouted. If he got angry he never showed it. At worst, he'd express just enough to let us know we'd disappointed him. Every setback was only that: a little bump on a long campaign, one we'd conquer given enough effort and time. He'd watched all the Curse videos, the Nightmares Asylum videos, the famous video of Ascent's world-first kill on Molten Core final boss Ragnaros the Firelord, with its terrible sound and painfully grainy video. He saw the whole scope of the game, somehow understood it better than the rest of us, and worked harder than anyone else to lead the way.

T K T's Mexican leadership gave me pause. They were good guys for the most part, clearly possessed of high humor even if I could only understand the curses. Plastico drove me crazy, but he was more Chris's problem than mine. If he got too obnoxious I could just mute him in text chat. On voice chat this was impossible—I'd miss important signals muting him there—but on voice chat he was a different creature. All his maddening tics and traits became adorable the moment I heard his bouncy, accented baritone. Whereas some of my guildmates flitted between Spanish and English depending on the turn of phrase, Plastico was utterly confident in his English. He would engineer some of the most agonized mispronunciations and malapropisms I've ever heard—often hilarious, occasionally insight-ful, and always pure Plastico. They even began to infect the guild's speech, metastasizing into their own convoluted galaxy of memes new recruits first found confusing but soon grew to mimic. *Haunters and chamans ready?*

His brand of leadership involved no subtlety, which he'd charac-terize as "drama"; instead he told you exactly what he wanted from you, and if you refused he pleaded and abased himself until you relented. The man knew no shame and was thus surprisingly effective as a blunt instrument, much the way anyone willing to earn the loathing of fifty total strangers can bitch his way out of jury duty. While Chris and I handled any T K T postings to Blizzard's message boards, Plastico made it his business to know everyone on the server personally, and thus everyone knew Plastico. Some of them were charmed, some annoyed, and the rest a bit confused. I thought him obnoxious. He thought me a surly gringo kid lacking any good perspective on life. His personality was inescapable, his behavior incorrigible—but for all our antipathy, in the dark days to come each of us would learn the other's worth.

THE MANTLE OF LEADERSHIP

JANUARY 2006

The green has stayed with me. When I think back to that Sunday—I'd like to pin it down on the calendar, or name it something resonant, but in the tradition of tumultuous days it left little time to process the moment—what I remember most is the green.

Dark clots of wind-warped cypresses on the left, the hills on the right a soothing mint speckled with grazing cows like still white stones. We cleared a promontory and the Pacific Ocean was exposed, a flat, darkening floor under orange sunset skies. California's Highway 101 ran under the tires. Three classmates shared the car with me, stuffed and somnolent with carnitas consumed on our way out of Santa Barbara. We'd spent the weekend there, the four of us and the rest of the Stanford Ultimate Frisbee team besides: our first tournament of the season, my first as captain and de facto coach. We'd won it, taken the whole damned thing without dropping a single game. I'd launched the last pass of the finals for an open score and chased it downfield whooping, knowing we had it won, bear-hugging the receiver, collapsing on the hot grass aglow with dusk and victory while someone passed around a joint. We drove home now in a triumphant convoy down the two-lane road. I loved my senior year of college: I had already met my graduation requirements and had negotiated a slacker's schedule allowing the most possible time for the Stanford Prison Experiment (our Ultimate team's very cool if slightly tasteless name) and my *World of Warcraft* raiding schedule. T K T was a major power; I had a great position in the guild under the leadership of one of my best friends. There was even a girl I meant to call once we got back.

It's nearly a perfect memory, and one of my favorites, but as with any memory one worries about the slow seep of falsehoods. It's been more than ten years, after all. Time has a way of telling us what we want to hear about the past, showing us what we want to be shown. I've rarely seen the California hills so green again.

We rolled into Palo Alto around nine. Exhausted from the weekend, stiff as a tin man from five hours in the car, I wanted only to stretch my hamstrings in a hot shower and then to log on to *WoW* for an hour before bed. Having been offline for three days (since Thursday night), I had resource farming to do and a powerful hankering to play. What's more, anyone who spent more than two days absent bought a round of pestering from Plastico. *Joo not gonna quit on me, baby!* Too much time out of Ghando's skin and my own started to itch. He was intoxicating. Months of Blackwing Lair raiding had yielded the kind of gear that drew awed whispers just standing around the Auction House in Orgrimmar. I was the coolest kid in school, with the shiniest car to boot. Just an hour would be time enough to log on, grind out some gold in Tyr's Hand, and broadcast my latest real-life success to my guildmates.

I logged on to pandemonium. Glaring purple whispers filled my chat window before my computer could even load the game world. I had to scroll to see them all: *Have you talked to Vier? Are you still playing? What the hell is going on?* And then from Plastico: *Ey Ghando, we need to discuss.*

What's going on?

You can go onto Ventrilo?

A weekend of shouting had left my voice ragged. Hooking up my headset and logging in to the guild's voice chat server felt like an onerous chore. *Rather not. What happened with Vier?*

We should go onto Ventrilo.

Plas, I'm tired. Just tell me.

Please, Ghando.

I dug in the desk drawer for my headset. I don't recall the exact words he used, and in any event the man's bouncing, broken English is nearly impossible to replicate in print without seeming offensive. It took him several minutes to explain the last few days' disastrous events.

Vier—*Chris*—was gone. He'd abruptly quit the game, ostensibly to focus on his coursework, and changed his permissions in preparation for selling his account. I felt a lance through my stomach, a personal wound. He hadn't told me one word. It was very late on the East Coast, and a glance at AOL Instant Messenger told me he wasn't online, but in any case I knew I'd talk to him soon. Practically, this news presented several immediate problems: first, the loss of T K T's main tank. Chris wasn't just our spiritual leader; he played the single most important position in any raid encounter, precisely positioning enemies for our safety, laying the foundation of our every tactic. What's more, his character itself held tremendous material value. High-end tanking gear is the most precious equipment available to raiders, determining to a large degree what a guild can accomplish. Aggressive competitions to deal the most DPS were not yet common in the raiding game, and a raiding guild was often only as good as the gear on their main tank.

This was a painful loss, but a loss we could sustain. T K T had a number of talented tanks, and one in particular had accumulated solid gear as our backup tank. Depth would be an issue from there, but we'd lost good players before. We'd move on, I thought, my mind working so intensely through possibilities I barely processed what Plastico said next.

"Some other guys are gone too. They left when they heard." Really? One important guy quits the game for his own personal reasons and the crew jumps ship? I found it hard to believe. We were the top Horde guild on the Detheroc server* by a country mile; any other group would be a step straight down, and serious gamers *do not* like moving down any kind of ladder, particularly of the social

---

* For the story of how T K T ended up on the Detheroc server after being founded on Sargeras, see chapter 6 (p. 152).

variety. Where would they even go? One or two of the rank-and-file, I figured, overreacting to a change and likely to beg for readmission in a day or two.

I was dead wrong. Opening the guild roster and scrolling through, I did my best to place absent names where they should have been on the list. The closer I got to the bottom, the deeper I sagged back into my desk chair. Our best priest gone. Second-best shaman *(après moi)*, gone. One of our best-geared warriors. Our best hunter and our only raiding druid. The list went on and on, sparing neither class nor role, eventually accounting for a full dozen names out of a raiding roster smaller than sixty. Every last one was a core member, a daily raider, a crucial component of the highly efficient machine we'd spent the last year assembling. They accounted for a staggering haul of high-end gear, and their talents represented some of the absolute best on the server. They couldn't be replaced. They were also, or had been until some as-yet-indeterminate point during the weekend, my friends.

"I'll talk to them," I told Plastico. There'd been some mistake; with communication and savvy politicking, this could be undone.

"Ees too late, Ghando."

"Where are they going to go? Obvious Assassins? End Guys?" I named two other raiding guilds. "They're trash. Nobody wants to play with them."

"Dey gone to joor good buddies in I.O."

"What?" That seemed impossible. Imperial Order was Detheroc's best *Alliance* guild, our closest competition. I was friendly with them, frequently spent idle time chatting on their Ventrilo server, and knew our departed raiders did the same. But Horde players couldn't join Alliance guilds—Blizzard wouldn't introduce the ability to switch from Horde to Alliance for a small fee until years in the future. "How the hell could they 'join' I.O.?"

"Dey reroll, Ghando. Dey sell their account an' go. Ees too late, I tol' joo."

I disconnected from T K T's voice chat server and flipped over to Imperial Order's. They were a much larger guild, composed almost entirely of American men in their teens and early twenties, and consequently the place was packed even late on a Sunday. Sure enough, sitting in the secure raiding channel along with the Order's officers were the bulk of my erstwhile guildmates. Before I could even send a private message, I'd been pulled into the channel.

"Hey, Ghando, what's up?" asked I.O.'s leader, a precocious teenager who ruled his band with an iron fist and had sagely decided his East Asian heritage merited the handle Rice.

"Heard you guys picked up some new members." It was a stupid thing to say, but I'd neglected to come with a plan. I don't know what I hoped to accomplish. Probably I only wanted to see whether it was all true.

"Yeah, man. Shit's crazy. Did Vier really leave for good?"

At least he wasn't rubbing it in my face. "I guess so. I've been gone all weekend. Just got home to all this."

"What's up, Ghando?" called Salem, a student at UT-Austin and until recently T K T's best priest. Several others chirped in as well.

"You guys are really rerolling?" Might as well be direct.

"Yeah, we should be level 60 in like two weeks. Rice has guys running us through quests and dungeons."

"It'll be real easy to gear them up," Rice agreed. "We're sharding half the shit we get as it is."*

While I desperately wanted to know the details, the precise and personal *whys* to which I felt entitled, there was no way to do this on an open channel without putting myself in an even more vulnerable position. So I said my good-byes, doing my best to save face, when Rice surprised me: "You want to play with us too, Ghando?"

"That's cute," I sighed.

"I'm serious. You know your shit. You're good at this game. What, are you gonna have Plastico running the show? That guy's a joke, man."

"I'm running things," I blurted out with no idea whether it was true. The present was hard enough to process; plans for the future were impossible.

---

* Unwanted gear can be destroyed by players with the enchanting profession, breaking it down into valuable components. Players often refer to the practice as "sharding." Here, Rice is saying his guild is already so well geared that their weekly raids net them little of value.

He laughed. "You sure? We've got some pally spots open."

At this early date, paladins were the one class unique to the Alliance, and shamans were unique to the Horde. My position as a shaman came with a great deal of pride. "I'm not playing a fucking paladin."

"Priest, then! I dunno, man. You're a cool guy. We're just doing what we've gotta do, you know?"

He was right. If Imperial Order's best raiders had wanted to defect, I'd have taken them in an instant. "I know."

"Offer's open if you want it. You can hang out here any time you want."

"Thanks. You guys have a good night."

My decision was made. What started as molten anger over the betrayal had quickly cooled and hardened into determination. Those guys might jump ship and take the easy route, my thinking went, but I'm not going to be one of them. I'll stick it out. On top of everything else, I loved Ghando—my whole *WoW* identity was bound up in the avatar, his menacing bulk and hunched frame, his name and high status in the server's pecking order.

I killed the connection and closed my Ventrilo software rather than jump back on with Plastico. My roommates were immersed in class projects. Playing late at night, I was used to having Salem and the others around. Guild chat was eerily quiet, the silence broken only by brief Spanish queries and equally curt replies. Connected by fiber-optic cable to hundreds of other people in a virtual environment, I nonetheless felt completely alone. Before long I went to bed, body battered to exhaustion and mind galloping over the future. I made no effort to catch up on the weekend's reading. My hardest project would start the next day. I still struggled to grasp everything that had led to that point, but I understood one crucial thing: we had a raid scheduled for Tuesday night. If we couldn't field an effective force by that time, the following desertions would leave us permanently crippled, reputations shattered. T K T would be dead and buried. We had less than forty-eight hours to save the guild.

IMPERATIVES

Every guild in history formed for a reason. The same could be said of any human organization, but people are born into their families, their circumstances, their traditions. Video game guilds (or clans, or corps, or a hundred other variations on familiar terminology depending on the game) are unique due to their doubly opt-in nature—one chooses first to play a given game, and then to join an organization within that game. So if every guild is formed for a reason, every member joined for a reason. Sometimes these are the same; picture a guild composed of two teenagers who've decided the name Beaches and Hose is totally hilarious.

Blizzard Entertainment always kept the barriers to guild formation low, making charters cheaply available in major cities. Each charter needed a handful of unique signatures, but the mechanical ease of joining and leaving guilds (with simple console commands like "/ginvite" and "/gremove") meant that total strangers could be paid a few silver to sign and then depart, charter ratified. The Guild menu's various rank options, aside from guild master, were wholly optional. Each guild was only as big or small, as serious or casual, as grim or goofy as its members wanted to be. Anyone seeking a new experience could simply opt out of her present guild and into a new one—one of many, as even a moment in unfiltered global Trade chat evidenced dozens of guilds publicly recruiting. Run around unguilded for more than a few hours and you'll start getting spammed with totally unsolicited guild invitations. Anyone who wants to be in a guild will have no trouble finding one.

With such an incredible multiplicity of options on offer, guilds had to distinguish themselves. A handsome tabard or colorful name wasn't enough mass to accrete and hold followers, since the player who joins Bloodbath and Beyond will simply up and leave at the next clever pun. For a guild to persist at all, it needed an identity, a raison d'être offering something of value to others such that they might see in that guild their own personal reason for joining. Fear, idealism, out-group resentment, and other classic motivational tools come up woefully short; in a purely opt-in world, participants must be convinced they're receiving value. The first guilds any player new to Azeroth encountered were likely those broadcasting in Elwynn Forest General chat, offering help with defeating Hogger, and with other quests too confusing or difficult for lone players. This is the guild at its most basic and essential: a source of aid in a world too enormous and complicated for anyone to tackle solo. If you didn't have friends, you needed a guild. If you did have friends, you joined a guild with them. For all the intense loyalty I eventually felt toward T K T, I joined them at first for the simple reason that my friend Chris was a member. Emotional bonds grow over time, but perks must be present from the outset.

This might be a little Zen for the context, but we are what we choose to do, and so *WoW*'s players sorted themselves through their pastimes. Guilds derived their identities from the activities they pursued. Team-based game design ensured guilds were always valuable, and the ambitions of individual players provided the fuel to propel them forward. After the social sorting, a few basic archetypes emerged:

- **Leveling Guilds:** Populated by players looking to progress toward the endgame, these guilds are often ephemeral by nature and given to names that are either quite silly (Horders) or stuffily serious (Rangers of Stormwind). Leadership is almost nonexistent, as are responsibilities. Players are invited indiscriminately and accepted regardless of skill or personality. This is a feature, not a bug—nobody is under any pressure and everyone can level at his own pace while drawing on a large pool of potential comrades. If a hundred-plus members are playing at any hour of the day, *someone* will always be around to help you through Razorfen Downs.
- **Social Guilds:** Founded by groups of friends, social guilds are similar to leveling guilds in that they lack strong hierarchical leadership. At the same time, the lack of leadership is less of a concern, since the members often share close bonds outside the

game. Whether groups of friends, family members, or coworkers, they form the guild for casual group play and a lively chat channel. Recruitment is almost nonexistent and limited to close friends, as inviting strangers would undermine the closeness for which the guild exists. Social guilds can go for years with very little turnover, even transitioning as a group from one game to another. Third-party online communities like Something Awful or Penny Arcade founded dedicated guilds on a number of servers. For all their positive aspects, social guilds are often limited in their progression by low numbers and a relatively casual approach. The lowering of manpower requirements for raids over the years—from forty-man raids to twenty-five to ten—has vastly expanded the horizons for these guilds; they've been arguably the largest beneficiaries of the game's long evolution.

- **Role-Playing (RP) Guilds:** Covered with more care in chapter 9, these groups operate like social guilds in that they rely on close relationships between members and are not primarily focused on progression through endgame content. Rather, they provide grouping benefits while maintaining a social environment the members use to immerse themselves in fantasy. Each role-playing guild has its own protocols governing behavior, so one group might never allow griping about your rough day at work while another would permit it accompanied by an "OOC" tag: out of character. Role-playing guilds also tend to be limited in terms of progression, both because it's not the members' first priority but also because the intricate and maddening process of learning a raid encounter strains any traditional notion of high fantasy to the breaking point. A serious approach to the PvP game is more common.

- **Player Versus Player (PvP) Guilds:** No other type of guild is harder to pin down. PvP guilds range from a small squad of professional arena gladiators to hundreds of neophytes looking for groups with which to run battlegrounds. Some guilds formed expressly for the purpose of running battlegrounds with low-level characters called "twinks," essentially running their own Pinewood Derby next to a NASCAR track. On PvP servers in particular, PvP guilds offer a convenient solution to the perpetual threat of ganking. Whereas a solo player harassed by the opposing faction must simply leave the area, a player in a PvP guild can anticipate a bloodthirsty mob descending to crush her enemies. Those who buy into the classic adage "Red equals dead," instantly attacking all opposite-faction players (displayed in-game with bright red character frames), will generally join PvP guilds to handle the inevitable headaches. Go into Stranglethorn Vale looking for trouble and you'll find it.

- **Raiding Guilds:** For raiders, the entire game revolves around progression. They want to make their avatars as powerful as possible, and they are relentless in pursuit of their goals. These are the kind of people who grind dungeons endlessly to level, neglecting quests and exploration, because the dungeon grind is more efficient and quests yield more gold if you save them until you've reached the level cap. Having reached the cap, they embark on a never-ending quest to accumulate the best possible gear, in part because it strengthens their avatars and in larger part simply because it is the best. Raiding guilds adhere to a weekly schedule according to Blizzard's design: every week, like clockwork, every raid dungeon in the game resets. Any dead monsters, including "boss" monsters, reappear brand new as though they'd never been touched. This can erase a raid's progress deeper into a dungeon, but it also gives them fresh opportunities for loot, as every boss can be killed again. A better-geared team makes monsters easier to kill, so each week the guild returns to work invigorated with extra power. The weekly practice of "farming" old bosses for loot in order to access new bosses, of work and reward, becomes the raiding guild's tidal rhythm. The killing of bosses and distribution of loot are their purpose. Elaborate bookkeeping systems appear to hand out loot in the fairest possible manner.

Intense competition both within and without makes these guilds high-pressure environments, in rare cases bordering on abusive. Admission demands a written application and a formal tryout process except if the player in question is vouched for by an officer. Leadership is hierarchical and possibly democratic, but not necessarily so. Poor performance or insubordination will eventually lead to removal. Positive personality traits are desired, but in the fashion of athletic teams, raiding guilds will tolerate tremendous assholes so long as they're sufficiently talented. A proven veteran member may invite some friends and family to the guild for social reasons, but those players aren't permitted to raid any serious content. To many people, this sounds insane—like the polar opposite of fun. That's why those people aren't in raiding guilds! These organizations are refuges for the ultracompetitive and demand more of their members' time and energy than any other.

These are broad generalizations. Guilds often existed in spaces intermediate to these archetypes and even transitioned from one to the other over time, but running through them should make clear what material benefits each offered and what sorts of people each attracted. Posts on realm forums and general social chatter familiarized players with the local guilds and allowed them to broadcast their characters. A natural sorting process followed. Realm servers became complex landscapes marked by self-selected factions within the larger community. Breaking up *WoW*'s player base into so many servers gave each server space to distinguish itself, but in time every single server developed guilds to serve any ambition a player might hold.

T K T, born a social guild of Latin American *StarCraft* players in the late 1990s (many of whom studied together at the prestigious Monterrey Institute of Technology and Higher Education, both literally and figuratively the MIT of Mexico) and transplanted by those same young men into *WoW*, had grown into a legitimate raiding guild. What few of the original core remained found themselves outnumbered by the players we'd taken on for the Blackwing Lair campaign. Primarily recruited by Chris and myself, the new blood consisted of young, ambitious raiders who spoke English exclusively and had little appreciation for the guild's Spanish culture (nor at that time, to be honest, did I). It was just an idiosyncrasy, the price of admission to the best Horde guild of the realm, with all the attending benefits. The defectors left because Chris's retirement, in their minds, jeopardized those benefits. They had little respect for the Mexican players and especially not for Plastico, whom they considered an ignorant windbag. Imperial Order made them an offer they thought certain enough that they were willing to spend hundreds of hours rerolling and regearing their avatars.

Those raiders who remained had calculated differently, but still the brutal math remained. If T K T did not raid, we were no longer a raiding guild. Our sudden difficulties would earn sympathy among the rank-and-file but little patience. If leadership couldn't provide a haul of epic loot by week's end, we'd see another wave of departures—enough to sink the guild. We'd always kept a tight roster with a light bench so as to concentrate loot in the hands of our best players, but with a dozen of our best now departed, we faced a steep uphill climb to raid readiness. I'd learned a lot from Chris and Plastico about how to attract and identify good players, but our last recruitment phase had lasted months. Now we had two days.

TRIALS

Walls loom around me, walls so high and primordially thick as to be planetary features, walls wounded by long fissures and high domes with yawning holes to admit the sky. Thorny vines sprout from any crack that will nurture them. This place, obviously beautiful at some point in the distant past, has become a dirty brown ruin with refuse and loose stones littering the floors. An explanation rounds the corner: a barrel-chested and heavily armored form lumbering along its patrol route. The three interconnected dungeons collectively known as Dire Maul play host to a harrowing assortment of foes, but the northernmost wing has been colonized by a tribe of ogres. Dim-witted but exceptionally strong, they're serviceable agents for my little test.

"Everyone here, with me, now. Cross the walkway and I'll pull the first one," I say into my microphone. My party complies, taking up position in a tight cluster so as not to attract the nearest ogre's attention.

"All right, Kaetau," I address the other shaman in our five-man group. "You remember the rules?"

Yes, the prospect replies in text chat. He doesn't have a microphone. This is less than ideal, as effective play is nearly impossible while typing out communiques, but under the circumstances I can't afford to be picky. This young Mexican man—I am led to believe he is all three of these things, though I will never meet him or hear his voice—understands English well enough to follow directions. He also boasts a bit of experience raiding Molten Core and has a few pieces of epic-quality gear to prove it, which elevates him immediately to a solid candidate. There's only one problem: I don't know whether he's actually good at video games. Subjecting him to what I've taken to calling the "healing test" will tell me what I want to know in less than an hour's time.

Dire Maul North is a nearly linear gauntlet of single and double pulls punctuated by several tougher fights against bosses. It's old content, easily outclassed by T K T's raiding epics and even our prospect's patchwork gear, so I've instituted a challenge for any healing recruits. They must run the dungeon as the only healer, they must never sit and drink to refill their mana, and all the while they'll be keeping me—a restoration shaman, myself specializing in healing—alive as the tank! I'm going to take punishing damage, the way a real tank might during a raid encounter, and the recruits will have to manage both my health and their own mana. All this functions as a live-fire test of many healing-specific skills, from anticipating major spikes in damage to sustaining one's mana pool over an unreasonable amount of time. Some recruits express skepticism when I lay it out, but I've found the healing test to be something like being told your five-page essay must be cut to two. With skill and dedication and a relentless pursuit of efficiency, you'll make it happen. If you can't, well . . . then, you're not someone I'll trust with forty virtual lives.

That was the theory, at least. In practice, our present crisis demanded a lower threshold, but we couldn't be telling people that. Though Chris only announced his retirement on T K T's private forums, the news almost instantly flew across the realm complete with all the typical mutations of hearsay. The mass defection was less publicized, though we couldn't deny it when asked, and the leaders of our rival guilds needled me with gleeful in-game whispers. Still, we were wounded and actively practicing damage control. Nothing scares away potential recruits like instability.

In the end, Kaetau did pretty well. I suffered two deaths, one of them my own fault, and while he wasn't *impressive* he was certainly competent. Competent would have to do. It was Monday; Tuesday we'd raid the relatively easy Molten Core to test the recruits and patch up their gear. A crew of thirty-three to thirty-five could clear the instance in a few hours, buying us another day before Blackwing Lair's stiff challenges demanded the full forty on Wednesday. Our newest member officially joined T K T as the customary chorus of fraternal welcome erupted in green text I could barely read against the verdant glow of Feralas's forest.

Kaetau did good, yes? Plastico whispered me.

Yeah he's fine, I replied.

He will be good for us. Plas's unrelenting optimism could grate, but now it was sorely needed.

If everyone had MC [Molten Core] gear we'd be fine.

Yes, but you know. These casuals. They will noob it up. But we will be okay I think.

How many friends/fam have committed? I wanted to know.

Like 6 I think? I put up the forum post to sign up. You can look at it.

I don't have it open.

LOL. Oh Ghando. What we do with you?

Just pissed at Vier. It's bullshit leaving like this.

Ghando, you know me, I always say we all quit. One day we all quit, years from now, whatever. Probably the last one, he is me. Because I am hardcore. But one day we all quit. We play other games. What is important, it's the people we know. I got friends ten years, we don't play no more. Still friends. The friends we make, it's what matters. It sucks Vier leaving. He's still T K T family. You too, even if you hate me.

I don't hate you.

Haha you love me! Everyone love the Plastico sooner or later. CMM, Ghando. The Spanish vulgarity "Chupa mi mion" cropped up so often we'd abbreviated it.

CMM, Plas.

Raiding guilds, as mentioned previously, typically allow their blooded members to invite a few friends and family. There's no real calculation to this—it keeps everyone happy and makes chat a friendlier and more human place than stressed-out raiders would otherwise have it. Our origins as a social guild made T K T more accommodating on this front than most. At any given time half the guild's total roster might have been made of these quiet souls. The bulk of our raiders didn't know them, didn't think of them, couldn't have named more than a handful or explained their connections to anyone else in the guild. I know the wider community on both realms we occupied saw them as strange, saw them representing the clutch of odd foreigners they believed us to be. More than a few correspondents had expressed shock that I, one of the guild's more visible figures and its public spokesman, was an English-speaking American.

Still, even as someone who'd known nothing different, it could feel strange to see guild chat periodically taken over with someone else's reminiscing. Logging on for an hour at a time every few weeks, they'd banter in profane Spanish with the oldest of the old guard like they owned the place, like they had no idea the guild had changed and its business was no longer theirs. The newer players chafed at it. Having built T K T into a power, did they not own it more so than those who'd built nothing? What right had they to this name, to this tabard, to this space? If it was arrogant it was also unavoidable—imagine asking the Boston Bruins to share their locker room with a recreational team who merely shared the same name. Telling the pro players "But there's enough room for everyone!" wouldn't resolve the ensuing resentments.

Salem and the other defectors wouldn't have cited the "casuals" as a problem per se, nor placed those players anywhere near the top of their personal gripes, but they laid a crucial distinction in relief. What T K T wasn't, Imperial Order *was*: a guild for and by headstrong young American males from white and Asian families. Smack-dab in the middle of that demographic myself, I certainly understood the appeal. Led along a different path to the same fork, I would have done the same. Yet having been there from the very start, as one of just three gringos among a dozen Mexican friends, I'd grown invested. What's more, the personal sting of the defections had me just angry enough to try anything. I would scour the realm for a few quality players while Plastico wrangled our back bench.

"ATTN: Tauren Resources"

Running a guild of any size or type is a question of personnel management. One's in-game skills (tanking, dealing or healing insane volumes of damage, being able to fake out a spell interrupt),* prodigious though they might be, prove to be almost entirely useless when facing any substantial crisis as guild leader—in much the same way that personal beauty or charm do very little to shepherd romantic relationships through struggle. Rarely do hard times draw upon our most developed skills. Speaking for myself, in January 2006 I was an excellent healing shaman and a clueless leader.

Running a team of college athletes in what was technically a club sport did not adequately prepare me. Athletic leadership accrues to the most skilled, the most gifted, the most productive, because all sports are at their essence abstracted struggles of individual will.

---

* Magical classes in *WoW* are extremely powerful but vulnerable to special "interrupt" effects while casting their spells—which not only cancel the spell but silence the caster for several seconds thereafter. Cunning players may trick an opposing player into wasting an interrupt by starting to cast a spell only to cancel it themselves before the interrupt hits.

Some online games (*Counter-Strike*, *League of Legends*, and so on) hold the sporting appeal of instantaneous decisions and snap reflexes, but MMORPGs are different—they're negotiations with time, with efficiency, with limitations both physical and mathematical.

Any goal in *World of Warcraft*'s universe is open to anyone! It's merely a question of time invested and help needed, transforming patience from mere virtue to the single most important skill a *WoW* player can possess, more important than quick reflexes or preternatural awareness. Patience scours whole continents for herbs; it persists despite heartbreaking Warsong Gulch losses; it corpse-runs back to the dungeon entrance, saving resurrecting healers precious seconds after the thirtieth wipe of the evening; it does its dogged duty on the fiftieth Onyxia kill just as it did on the first, long after victory's howls have yielded to the sullen grind of sharded Netherwind Crowns. A wise guild leader recruits for patience if nothing else.

Next is sociability, which I choose to define as the extension of patience to others. Conflict comes naturally to human beings, and as any citizen of the Internet knows, interpolating a computer screen between two antagonists does not improve their civility. Online guilds labor constantly against anonymity-induced assholery; it's easy to casually mistreat people, and the abstraction of text chat breeds misunderstandings. Whereas family members or coworkers get ample opportunity to build and demonstrate goodwill in a variety of settings, guild members in conflict are unlikely to resolve their differences without a third party's intervention. If I offended a guildmate during a raid—say I snapped at one for another's mistake—I'd rarely recognize the slight until someone else brought it up, at which point I'd either apologize or make a mental note to ladle out some public praise. As with any relationship, little things become extremely important. Errors are easily forgiven so long as all parties deal in good faith.

Third comes commitment. Many guilds with raiding aspirations demanded their members be available for long stretches six days a week. Thirty hours of raiding per week wasn't a remarkable workload by their standards. Hardcore raiders simply expected to punish themselves for long stretches, and those guilds naturally populated themselves with the insomniac college undergrads who could handle such expectations, but not everyone operated this way.

The smartest guilds pursued different players, seeing through the first imperative, recognizing their rosters would ultimately reflect their priorities. More than a few asserted that they were guilds for adults with responsibilities. They might raid every weeknight while working through new content, but rarely more than twenty hours per week. T K T maintained a house rule not to raid too late at night, dubbing every minute after midnight "pumpkin time." Just as Cinderella's carriage became a pumpkin at midnight, so too do raiders accustomed to forty-hour real-life work schedules. Of course, this practice has drawbacks: time being the game's primary currency, a guild raiding more hours per week will always progress faster than one raiding less. But the performance gap doesn't have to be so wide! Intelligent and efficient approaches to a new challenge can bring success nearly as quickly, particularly when you can examine what the frontrunners are doing. T K T never aspired to be the best in the world, just competitive with the best. We trusted our members to meet expectations while they trusted leadership not to make unreasonable demands. Folks will put up with an awful lot if you don't shout at them and promise they'll get to bed at a reasonable hour.

Scheduling takes paramount importance. Online organizations must constantly work for their members' attention, competing against a host of real-life obligations (work, family, holidays). These things are frankly more important than anything in Azeroth. All things being equal, they'll win out, unless the guild's demands are posed in the most reasonable terms. Tell people where to be and when; ensure that their time with you, even if unsuccessful, is neither miserable nor wasted; build trust in your ability, above all else, to start and end *on time*. Healthy, well-adjusted human beings are not "down for whatever, whenever." They want some kind of return, emotional or otherwise, on their investments. If the guild can deliver that return without demanding too much in the way of principle, they'll make time for it. Another important principle I learned from *WoW*: smart, resourceful people can find a way to make time for anything.

NONNEGOTIABLE

Well, *almost* anything. Chris and I didn't find time to speak until some twenty-four hours after everything exploded. Radioactive ash continued to rain down in the form of Blizzard forum posts—our rivals, trumpeting Chris's departure and crowing over T K T's imminent collapse. While I'm sure the sentiment was largely authentic, the posts had the practical aim of suppressing any recruitment efforts. To what degree it succeeded I have no way of knowing, though having skipped Monday classes and spent the entire day dealing with potential recruits, I felt a little better about the guild's prospects. I felt no better about Chris, about Salem and the rest. The whole episode was burning coal in my gut. To think about it was to bead sweat on my cheekbones, to breathe and taste cinder. Yet I had to talk with Chris. I had to know why. We chatted by text, not Ventrilo, since anyone who saw him active on the server would ask about it—and frankly, only with the clinical remove of typing could I check my emotions.

Hey Tony, what's up?

It's been a crazy day. Crazy couple of days.

LOL I can imagine. Crazy here too.

WTF happened, man? Plas tried to explain but he's Plas.

I had to quit. I failed a class.

Oh shit.

I failed my Chinese class.

Alone before my computer, I groaned aloud. In order to shortcut graduation requirements in his senior year of college, Chris had enrolled in advanced Chinese. This might have been a fine plan had he spoken the slightest whiff of Mandarin. "My mom is Chinese," he'd explained. "Chris," I'd replied, "your mother is from New Jersey and her first language is English." This did not dissuade him.

Dammit I told you that was a bad idea.

I know. Big time mistake.

So what then? You didn't fail that class because of WoW.

I know. But I still have to quit.

Why?

Can't graduate. Have to do make-up starting now and going through summer.

Shit.

Yeah.

A long silence. The coal in my stomach was out, just a sodden brick of defeat. Part of me wanted to argue with Chris. I wanted to tell him it wasn't too late, that things weren't too far gone, that if he changed his mind we could somehow reassemble what we'd had just three days earlier, but for all my youth I wasn't as dumb as that. Those who left wouldn't return, couldn't be taken back. And I didn't, I realized, really want them back. Chris may have retired out of necessity, but the others made a free choice—and made it without so much as a word. This hit me with an elemental smack before washing through cold and clean as a breaker at La Jolla. If Salem had been the right recruit for an earlier time, our present circumstance demanded a different breed.

You'll lead the raids now? Chris wanted to know.

I guess so. With Plas for the Mexicans.

You should.

Dunno who else would do it.

I told Plas it should be you.

My eyebrows climbed, though no one was there to see them. This I hadn't known. *You worked this out with him?*

Yeah before I made the forum post. You're gosu leet status ☺

Haha. Thanks. Couldn't he have made it clear to anyone else? I wondered to myself, still frustrated by the failures in communication, unwilling to castigate Chris at this juncture. It was late on the East Coast, so he signed off for bed. I sat in my chair for a long time, conscious of the mountain yet to climb, knowing I should log in to *WoW* to pick herbs but instead merely watching Ghando's slow breathing on the Character Select screen. I thought fourteen months back to his first steps on the Mulgore plain. I thought of my friends, all now departed.

"Pool's Closed"

I don't mean to drag down the mood. When not engulfed in chaos and suspended in perilous states, guilds could actually be a lot of fun! Exulting over the fresh corpse of a raid boss was my personal flavor, but raid guilds were only a small (if highly visible) minority of the population. Every realm server hosted hundreds, if not thousands, and I've already spent thousands of words describing their diversity. Each of their members joined and stayed for personal reasons, and much like families one can never truly understand a given guild without belonging to it. Still, we can observe from the outside.

Rarely was anything great accomplished without a dedicated and coordinated guild. So let's appreciate the amazing and hilarious things they did, the scams they pulled to get ahead, the insidiously clever prank-like undermining of friends and faction-mates known as "griefing." Even the most dedicated guilds, those insomniac amalgamations of wraithlike power gamers, could only program about eight hours of organized activity into a day where many of their members would expect to play fourteen. How did they occupy themselves?

- **Pirate Adventures!:** Back in "vanilla" *WoW*, before the expansions introduced high-speed flying mounts, travel took a huge amount of time. Even with a full complement of automated flight paths, traversing either Kalimdor or the Eastern Kingdoms took upward of twenty minutes. A system of automated Alliance ferry ships and Horde zeppelins handled both intra- and intercontinental journeys, running every five minutes from a handful of ports (the system persists, though its circuit time has since been dramatically reduced). This was both highly efficient and deliciously easy to exploit.

Zeppelins launching from the Horde metropolis known as the Undercity did so from a relatively remote and little-trafficked tower. The similarly isolated Menethil Harbor, situated in an early leveling zone and not frequented by high-level players, offered a symmetric vulnerability for Alliance players. While obnoxiously strong guards watched over the towns and towers, the transit vehicles themselves had no troop detachments. Sneaking behind enemy lines and fighting your way through bewildered lowbies onto their transports was a simple operation.

Festooned with pirate hats and other colorful accoutrements, you and your guildmates would roll up to the next port on the ferry's route and merrily slaughter the would-be passengers waiting dockside! Players would stream pirate-themed music over Ventrilo while one guildmate called out time, warning everyone back to the vehicle so as not to be abandoned to your enemies—you'd be swarmed under before your fellows came around again. A hoot and a holler, as they say, though it quickly ramped up in difficulty. Like *Grand Theft Auto*'s much-mimicked "star" system, each transgression brought more opposition. Undercity and Grom'gol Base Camp might not be too dangerous, but just wait until your zeppelin showed at Orgrimmar! Subsequent trips around the globe found each port of call loaded with progressively more and more foes, itching for revenge but usually lacking any real coordination. Massive body counts piled up all over the world until inevitably your mighty pirate coalition fell apart, but you'd kill dozens of enemies while enraging hundreds more! A win in any gamer's book.

- **The Gates of Ahn'Qiraj:** Ahn'Qiraj and its associated dungeons represented vanilla *WoW*'s third wave of endgame content. Blizzard's developers unveiled it to the public with a unique event introduced to the game world and storyline: a military campaign, pitting the combined efforts of both Horde and Alliance against an insidious insectoid menace infesting

Kalimdor's most southerly extreme. This might sound really cool, but in practice it amounted to one of the mightiest material grinds in gaming history.

First, there was a quest chain to acquire the legendary Scepter of Ahn'Qiraj. I'll spare you the specific requirements; suffice it to say they were so incredibly steep, they more or less required cooperation from every major guild across the entire server, assigning groups of coordinated fighters to harvest insectoid carapaces from enemies as fast as they spawned. This continued around the clock for weeks in order to push a single player from a single guild (agreed to by consensus between the realm's top guilds, if such consensus could be forged) to the end of the quest line. Without coordinated efforts, the campaign took *much* longer. After a series of steep trials, the scepter would finally emerge in the hands of the chosen one. With the scepter a gong could be rung to open Ahn'Qiraj's imposing black hexagonal gate.

But only a foolhardy realm would throw open the gate without an army prepared! To this end, the population of each server had to contribute a vast haul of material goods toward the "war effort." Nothing was ever truly *built* with this, naturally—it vanished into the ether in what might be gaming's greatest example of a "time sink"—but it gave nonraiding players a way to contribute to the event, or to profit by exploiting the hot new market for these materials. Personally, I spent two weeks in a frozen cave, killing so many yetis for their leather hides that I started to imagine their stench. Guilds across the realms assigned their members to producing various supplies according to their chosen professions. After a long stretch of drudging misery, the event could finally be put to bed and even smallish guilds could enjoy the excellent Ahn'Qiraj dungeon content. That Blizzard never repeated anything like this event speaks to the crime against humanity it was.* *And yet we voluntarily did this!*

---

* For the record and posterity, I here present the official totals for Horde and Alliance combined. 800,000 runecloth bandages; 800,000 linen bandages; 600,000 silk bandages; 250,000 mageweave

- **The Stranglethorn Fishing Extravaganza:** A classic *WoW* event, run weekly for years now and not much changed for all the many expansions. Initially conceived as a fun little competition for lazy Sunday afternoons, the extravaganza pits players of both factions against each other to see who can be the first to catch forty speckled tastyfish. As the coauthor of a marine biology book, I can assure you being a tastyfish is not, evolutionarily speaking, a winning strategy. These special fish are only used for the extravaganza and can't be traded, so this should be a contest of individual fishing skill.

  Maybe on player-versus-environment servers, where contestants can declare themselves off limits for combat, it is. But on player-versus-player servers, the extravaganza becomes something else entirely. Between players of both factions actively leveling, between the Horde port of Grom'gol in its south and the great city of Stormwind just a short flight north, Stranglethorn Vale is already a hotly contested PvP zone. Sunday afternoons from 2 PM to 4 PM, it's a bloodbath. Players fishing can be attacked, so guilds dispatch combat squads to defend their own fishers and gank the enemy. What's more, they may strategically decline to assist rival guilds from their own faction, condemning them to die and slowing down their fish count. No matter how many times they've won the contest or whether any member even needs its (entirely fishing-related) rewards, guilds will take any excuse to compete. I've participated in dozens of Stranglethorn Fishing Extravaganzas, but never as a fisher—always a combatant. There's nothing quite

---

bandages; 250,000 wool bandages; 180,000 light leather; 160,000 thick leather; 110,000 medium leather; 60,000 heavy leather; 60,000 rugged leather; 19,000 firebloom; 96,000 peacebloom; 52,000 purple lotus; 34,000 spotted yellowtail; 33,000 stranglekelp; 18,000 mithril bars; 180,000 copper bars; 28,000 iron bars; 24,000 thorium bars; 22,000 tin bars; 20,000 Arthas' tears; 20,000 roast raptor; 14,000 rainbow fin albacore; 10,000 lean wolf steaks; 10,000 baked salmon. Bear in mind nearly all of these items contains multiple components, representing time both in gathering and assembly. Bear also in mind that *every server* had to meet these same requirements. Try to imagine what could be accomplished were that volume of human effort directed toward actually productive ends. We could have cured cancer.

so ticklingly absurd as fighting a pitched battle while just yards away your guildmate stands placid as stone, rod and reel in hand, just soaking up beach rays.

BLOOD AND IRONY

It is after 11:00 PM on Wednesday night and in my headphones there is only screaming. With a last heave of his shoulders and a tired, rasping sigh, the beast Chromaggus slumps to the black basalt floor. Like a bull terrier crossed with a dragon and gifted a second head, he's the penultimate boss in Blackwing Lair and, this week, the hardest. We'd gotten unlucky in the dungeon's random spell selection and Chromaggus's infamous Time Lapse attack forced us to rotate between several tanks, only one of them properly geared for the task. Misfortune heaped upon misfortune as a bad combination of Time Lapse and the appropriately named Ignite Flesh slew that one geared tank. Chromaggus proceeded to butcher several raiders before a skilled DPS warrior—a taciturn orc of Quebecois extraction—wrestled him under control and back into position. Wearing cast-off tanking gear including a shield from Upper Blackrock Spire, he held on for dear life as Chromaggus fell to 20 percent health, swelling visibly in size and lashing out for an absolutely obscene amount of damage.

Toctoc's health leapt and fell like an airplane in heavy turbulence, with all the corresponding effects on my stomach. Each rapid-fire blow sheared off at least half his health; the heaviest punched him right down to 15 percent with less than a second before another came. The operation teetered on fevered throws of dice we prayed would land our way, and somehow they did. The pace was not sustainable, and yet we sustained. Toctoc kept his feet, hammering away with an orc's ostentatiously wide-shouldered swings, his avatar half swallowed by the monster. I saw Chromaggus's health tick under 10 percent and put out the call for all healers on the tank. Anyone else taking damage would have to whip out some bandages or health potions as we pushed our chips to the proverbial table's center. At 5 percent, Plastico admonished everyone to burn every last cooldown, consume every last potion and temporary boost, to *just do anything* to get this beast down. It wasn't a good idea—with Toctoc as our last tank, we were only a split second from a total wipe—but I didn't argue. I felt it too. We had to finish this now or not finish at all.

Two percent. Spanish curse words built like a pressurized storm front. One percent showed on Chromaggus's health meter—that old trickster 1 percent, seemingly the longest stretch of any boss fight as you chewed from 1.99 percent all the way down to zero and waited desperately for the first twitch of a death animation. Then the eruption. My hands fell from the keyboard to my sides as I slumped down in my chair. One boss remained: Nefarian, the dungeon's final opponent but nowhere near so taxing on our depleted tanking and healing corps. I wasn't worried about him. We'd won. We'd lived. I ran Ghando forward and crouched by the dog-dragon's corpse to check the loot. Seeing it set me to laughing out loud in my California dorm room. "Hey Toctoc, I hear you're in the market for a new shield!"

"You guys got the Elementium Bulwark?" Salem asked me ninety minutes later in Imperial Order's voice chat, where we cooled our respective heels on opposite ends of the virtual globe. I hopped circles on the roof of the Orgrimmar bank while he trudged through leveling quests in the Burning Steppes.

"Yup. Wrath shoulders too, so now Toctoc looks like a walking can opener."

"That's nice. What was he using before?"

"Might shoulders and the UBRS shield."

Salem laughed so loud it piped back through his speakers and microphone, echoing tinny in Imperial Order's otherwise empty channel. "Jesus. Time Lapse / Ignite Flesh Chromie in blues."

"All through the enrage."

"Shit."

"Yeah."

"Found some good healers, then?"

"A couple are good. A couple are OK. We'll figure it out."

"Seems like. Well, I'm happy for you guys."

"It's been a crazy week. When are you hitting 60? I want to kill your dwarf ass in battlegrounds."

"I'm level 42. Not long now." He didn't mention his present leveling zone. He knew I'd come to squish him.

"Nice. Well, I'm gonna log for the night."

"Grats on the loot."

"That's why we do it, right? 'Cause it's really not fun yelling at people for being dumb."

"Are you leading raids now that Vier's left?"

"Yeah. Which is weird because I can't pull mobs, right? I just tell someone else to pull."

"I'm surprised Plastico lets you."

"I think even Plas knows Plas running everything would be bad."

"Yeah, I guess. I just . . . I don't have the patience, I guess. Like, I'm trying to raid and kill shit and get server firsts, and I don't want to be held back by this Mexican guy and his Mexican friends. With Vier in charge it worked."

"But I'm in charge now. Nothing's going to change. Same way we've always done things."

"Yeah, but I didn't know that. He just left and there was Plastico—"

"I was away for the weekend. The timing sucked, but I talked to Vier and he said this was always the plan. He and Plas talked about it. They wanted me to take over."

"But I didn't know that."

This I hadn't expected. "So they didn't tell you anything and you guys just left?"

"Rice made the offer and it made sense. They're cool guys."

My heart thudded in my chest. Had it really been so simple? Had this all been an elementary error, compounded by coincidence and compressed time? "So . . . if you'd known ahead of time, if you'd been told, 'This is the plan and Ghando's taking over,' would that have changed anything?"

"Yeah."

"You'd have stayed."

"Probably. I mean, it's too late now."

"Yeah."

"But if I'd known, I'd have stayed. I can't speak for Krodos and the others, but I'd have stayed."

I couldn't help but chortle. "Hah, that's funny. That's really funny."

"I guess so. Just how things work out."

The mouse cursor slid toward the red X to close Ventrilo. "Night, dude. See you around." I clicked, shut down my computer, and stood from the chair, limbs bearing unaccustomed weight—a new iron girding my bones.

« 5 »
A CIRCUS OF
MASOCHISTS

Each day melted together that summer. I'd show up to work late in the morning and stay until seven at least, hiding behind drawn blinds in the cluttered studio where I spent my days editing video and marketing copy for a mobile start-up, before attempting the congested drive home. Fires raged in the wooded hills separating the Bay Area from Santa Cruz, just out of sight but close enough for the smoke to cast an eerie pall over the region. So distinctly Californian, this phenomenon, most apparent after dawn and before dusk when the sunlight takes the time to slide in from acute angles—and yet it seems universal, its grand aura reproduced and bound to a hundred different settings on as many movie screens.

Immediately after college I shared a run-down house on Waverley Street in Palo Alto with a pack of tech-worker hippies—a property oddly situated in a tony neighborhood and thus loathed by its neighbors for its presumed drain on their property values. Steve Jobs lived several blocks away, in a house whose rustic look was accentuated by an eye-rollingly obvious apple orchard. We regularly raided it to stock the house's kitchen, since the fruit was excellent and the fence low. My house was owned by an old Grateful Dead devotee who'd made himself a small fortune in semiconductors and plowed that nest egg into below-market housing. He'd named the house "Morning Dew," after a Dead song I've still never heard, and I lived in the basement. As a veteran of subterranean living I'll stick up for plenty of cellar apartments, but this was a *basement.* I shared space with giant rolls of foam insulation, ducked my head under ductwork, and cozied up next to the water heater on cold nights. A panel on the base was missing, and I'd huddle up on my side to keep my legs warm watching the pale flickering blue of the pilot light.

My other life was more rewarding. Indeed, someone devoted to the *World of Warcraft* raiding scene would hardly see a better day. That summer saw the release of patch 1.11, "Shadow of the Necropolis," opening up the forty-man dungeon of Naxxramas for general consumption. Blizzard turned the occasion into a server-wide event complete with new quests, challenges, and rewards for lower-level players across Azeroth. The necropolis itself loomed tremendous over the Eastern Plaguelands, a flat black pyramid crowned with spires and spines, immobile like a hateful mountain hovering in the diseased yellow air. The structure almost literally dripped menace, and inside waited the most brutal tests *WoW* raiders had yet seen. Without delving into the tired and nostalgia-riven debate comparing all dungeons over time, "Naxx" inarguably represented the last and most ambitious of the forty-man raids—a fittingly glorious end to the long reign of truly large-scale MMORPG raiding.

Naxxramas boasted a healthy population of thirteen bosses spread through four themed wings, with access to the final two bosses unlocked only by first defeating all the others. Early bosses like the undead stag beetle Anub'Rekhan fell to well-geared incursions in a handful of attempts, but the difficulty ramped up steeply and unevenly after the wings' first bosses. Grand Widow Faerlina could explode an entire cadre of melee DPS in moments. Even the packs of "trash" monsters spacing out the bosses dealt enormous damage, demanded quick reflexes, and demolished more than a few raids that pulled without ensuring all forty fighters were ready for action. Responding to frequent player complaints about "boring" trash in earlier dungeons, Blizzard for the first time kept all forty players permanently on their toes.

HATEFUL STRIKE AND MASS PSYCHOLOGY

It's unlikely Blizzard's raid designers knew quite what they had with Patchwerk. The first boss of Naxx's Plague Quarter, he was very simple on paper: his visual form was borrowed from the bloated, half-disemboweled "abominations" that guarded the undead of the Undercity, but inflated to enormous size, with a health pool and basic attack damage to match. He had no minions, could be pulled anywhere inside a wide-open room, and possessed only one special ability. But seven minutes after engaging, a Berserk mechanism inflated his damage to unsurvivable levels, functioning as a time limit. If a raid could not sustain some 9,500 damage per second over those seven minutes—quite a number in those days—they wiped. DPS players never had to move, administer crowd control, or change targets. The main tank had limitless rage,* so maintaining threat wasn't an issue. It was as pure a gear test as was ever devised, asking players only to output X damage and Y healing for Z time as a condition for victory. It should have been so simple.

But in practice, it wasn't. Patchwerk's one special ability was called Hateful Strike, which he would use every 1.2 seconds to deal enormous damage to a single raid member. A single such blow killed anyone but a well-geared tank, and even then extremely rapid and precise healing was needed to shore him up against the next blow. As with the DPS, healers seemed to face a straightforward problem of mathematics, but this was complicated by the fact that *nobody knew how Hateful Strike picked its targets.* They immediately started work to unravel the mystery, but without access to the game's inner workings they could settle on no answer.

Theories abounded, quarreled over endlessly in the message boards that had by this point become the game's primary medium of intellectual exchange (as chronicled in chapter 3). Threads on Patchwerk became so common that moderators had to aggressively

---

* At the time, Warriors were the only viable raid tanks. This class powers their abilities with a resource called rage, which they receive from either dealing or receiving damage, so a tank taking heavy enough damage can use as many abilities as he wants.

close them lest they dominate all discussion. Combat logs weren't then the meticulously detailed moment-by-moment accounts they became, so evidence could be found to support any theory. On one thing most guilds agreed: Hateful Strike had to involve some component of threat. It usually hit tanks, and after all, wasn't "hate" a common synonym for "threat"? If this seems terribly unsophisticated, well, we did our best with the tools at hand. The answer to Hateful Strike was never terribly complicated: as stated by Blizzard developers years afterward, it simply struck the highest-health target near the top of its threat list. The top position on the threat list was immune, so the main tank was safe, but every 1.2 seconds, whichever off-tank happened to have the most hit points at that instant got hit. The fight came at you so fast, and hard, that few realized how simple it really was. Those who did had no incentive to tell the rest of us.

Patchwerk's true challenge always lay in the DPS race, in the months of gear accumulation before anyone set foot in Naxxramas, but Hateful Strike took on an outsized role in his mythology. Its seemingly capricious nature, its sudden and terrifying violence, were bad enough, but more important, it was Patchwerk's primary wiping mechanism. Inattentive healing might lead to a main tank death every now and again, but off-tank deaths to Hateful Strike always caused the most collective misery. A wipe to the Berserk timer actually felt like an accomplishment! At least you kept the fight stable for seven full minutes. Most wipes occurred because the healers or tanks screwed up somewhere, but it almost always *felt* like capricious behavior on the part of Hateful Strike. Add to this the sheer volume of guilds who were capable of reaching Patchwerk (anyone who could clear a few challenging trash packs), compared to the relative few sporting the gear and coordination to plausibly kill Patchwerk, and you have one of *WoW*'s all-time stumbling blocks. A savage and lusty kick in the teeth. Like Vaelastrasz in Blackwing Lair, Patchwerk doled out constant lessons in humility. He became known as a "guild-killer," a boss tough enough to single-handedly turn players against each other and break down the unspoken collective will powering any serious raid unit.

Even for a solid outfit like T K T, he presented a mighty obstacle. Our rebuilding and recruiting process over that year had prepared us well for Naxx's earlier bosses, but we lacked depth at several key DPS positions and had always been a methodical, low-damage, control-the-encounter type of guild. Any DPS race we'd run uphill, through shin-deep mud. I knew we'd get there in time, through practice and gradual accumulation of gear and the quaffing of exotic potions, but first we'd have to heal through Hateful Strike and its constant psychological battery.

DPS players faced a wide-open bazaar in which to ply their trade, with only a single target to ravage and no splash-damage fireworks mandating constant movement. Convenient as this might seem, it also changed their roles. For much of Molten Core and Blackwing Lair, "He never dies" was the highest compliment one could pay a rogue. Patchwerk flipped those negative expectations to positive: DPS were suddenly held to strict and quantifiable standards of performance. If after seven minutes' time you hadn't done enough damage, you were a liability to the raid. "Damage meter" UI mods went from data-collection projects to mandatory tools. Every second of raid performance was scrutinized. Every keystroke demanded explanation. Every suboptimal enchantment or gear choice earned a patronizing lecture from the raid leader. Guildmates who were nice people and rarely made mistakes still found themselves left out of raids by virtue of arithmetic. Undead nightmare though he was, Patchwerk sowed the seeds of quantifying, gear-parsing snobbery that would only find more verdant expression in time.

Tanks found themselves in oddly passive roles, compared with the precise motion and frenetic off-tanking to which they'd become accustomed. The main tank's position wasn't important. Patchwerk never moved, so the off-tanks stood in a pile atop the main, each taking Hateful Strikes in turn, populating the boss's threat list but otherwise presenting themselves as anvils to the game's most punishing hammer. Even using every survival consumable in the game,[*]

---

[*] Flask of the Titans (then phenomenally expensive), a slew of elixirs and world buffs, and Stoneshield potions consumed religiously on a two-minute timer.

they took damage in alarming bursts with no hope of respite. Either the healers topped them up before the next Hateful Strike came or not. If not, they'd either avoid it (via dodge or parry) or die. If they died, the raid would almost certainly wipe in short order. For Patchwerk more than any other encounter, tanks sat as passive but necessary recipients of stress—galvanized bolts holding up a vast, creaky forty-man suspension bridge.*

Healers had it worst. Obviously this statement reflects my own biases, but I believe it's correct. Patchwerk healing was unlike any other fight in terms of its combination of burst damage and singular focus. Raid healers know their assignments for every fight, and experienced players will freelance outside those roles as circumstances dictate, but Patchwerk brooked no improvisation. No non-tank ever took a hit, but those tanks suffered such sphincter-clenching damage that any heal placed elsewhere was too risky. If an off-tank assigned to another healer dropped to 2 percent health after a Hateful Strike and your assignment was at 100 percent, you had to resist every practiced reflex to assist. An isolated failure might wipe your raid, but at least it would be isolated, blame easily parceled out and adjustments made. Freelancing inevitably led to a teetering house of cards, a juggling act with too many balls in the air. Instead healers dragged the tanks' health monitors front and center and focused with psychotic intensity on those little green bars. My stomach rose and fell with every Hateful Strike, with every precipitous drop and miraculous save. Everything happened too fast to process, too quickly to consciously react, forcing the healers into a kind of trance as they struggled to keep up with the punishment. Tough fights often demand this kind of concentration at several junctures, but Patchwerk forced you to sustain it for seven full minutes knowing a single error would wipe the raid.

---

* Supremely wonky aside: in vanilla *WoW* and for some time thereafter, a quirk of the combat system caused enemies to refresh their attack timers after parrying a player's attack, resulting in an instant counterattack. For this reason, off-tanks fighting Patchwerk would often deliberately cease their automatic ("white") attacks in order to spare the main tank sudden and anomalous bursts of damage.

I have never felt more stress in a video game than I did healing on Patchwerk. As raid leader on top of my healing assignment, it was the worst moment of every week. When he'd fall over dead, I'd abdicate my typical loot-sorting duty and step away from my PC for a few minutes. My stomach rolled and my head swam. I was dizzy with fading adrenaline and sick with anxiety. Even after we'd killed him a dozen times, most of Naxxramas comfortably on "farm status," Patchwerk got no easier. The fight got shorter with more gear, and the margins for error grew somewhat wider, but the fight's furious action exhausted me every single time. This wasn't fun, neither at the time nor in retrospect. Thinking back to those fights recollects a sense of duty and pride but very little pleasure. I'm left with two overriding memories: The first, silence. Playing a game with forty people over voice chat means a constant chatter, a pleasant white noise underscoring any proceeding, but during Patchwerk attempts we all fell quiet. For seven minutes the only sound in my ears was the occasional reminder for potion timers. Otherwise, aching silence. The second memory is counting the seven concrete steps up from my basement, heaving open the slanted storm door, and sucking in the cool night air to quell my post-kill nausea. In a California summer the burning hills threw off the hearth-and-home scent of a New England fall.

If you were part of this world, of this hobby better described as a lifestyle, you know exactly what I'm talking about. *WoW*'s endgame was always demanding and maddening beyond the point of material reason—so much time invested for the sake of virtual equipment that future patches and expansions would inevitably render obsolete— but it nonetheless attracted devotees in the hundreds of thousands, because the challenge and camaraderie were so damn compelling. This is true for hardcore guilds more than others, with their members specializing in patience of a masochistic sort: the patience to endure repeated failure, to the point of suffering, in the pursuit of a goal. It stands quite separate from interpersonal patience, which hardcore players do not often display. The type-A elements of their personalities leave them little patience for fools and an acute awareness of time's value. Aware more than anyone else of game mechanics and best practices, they know MMORPGs flatten out individual skill in favor of time invested. They don't want their time wasted; when venturing into a dungeon or battleground, many avoid the automatic matching features of the Group Finder and other flavors of "pickup" play, because they feel the general population will only get in their way. "PUGs [shorthand for 'pickup groups'] lead to tears," went the common aphorism.

Of course, not everyone has this masochistic tendency, and many that do have the restraint not to indulge it. Bringing a raiding guild together was an audacious act, declaring your intent to blaze a trail of glory independent of whatever guilds already existed. It also demanded immediate sacrifices from its members. Hardcore raiders shoved their way to the top of the social order and stayed there through carefully applied and maniacally dedicated effort.

RELENTLESSNESS

When I worked as a quality assurance tester for video games, the first thing I learned (besides the fact that many of my peers eschewed hygienic bathroom practices) was that it was unproductive to see my work as "fun" in any conventional way. The works in progress over which I labored were games only in the sense of economics: frameworks containing agents, choices, and payoffs. Empowering my character or advancing through a linear story was impossible; any progress evaporated with the next test build. Instead one focused on a task, whether that meant checking a particular feature or actively trying to break it, and pursued that task with psychotic dedication. Failure was not punished but rather expected. Attempt to reproduce a bug one hundred times and the hundredth failure was no more important than the first: one simply moved on to attempt #101. "Everything is possible!" proclaimeth the prophet and the game tester alike. Any barrier can be overcome with enough dedication, execution, and luck.

The same mentality inspires hardcore raiding. For those who view video games as instruments for achieving mathematical conditions, MMORPGs are the ultimate laboratory. Everything revolves around time expenditure, after all. If one deems a goal numerically achievable, achieving it is only a question of putting in the time. Twenty attempts, fifty attempts, two hundred attempts—there's no limit, so why stop short of the finish line? Your priorities may differ, but this is how hardcore raiders think. I've written in chapter 4 about the virtue of patience, and raiders need more of it than anyone else. There's no easy or expeditious way to coordinate dozens of human beings sitting in separate rooms connected by Internet voice chat. Every failed attempt is followed by a lengthy setup process as healers resurrect the fallen one by one, reapply buffing spells, and replenish their mana. Raid leaders explain and implement any changes to the guild's strategy, ready checks are made, and eventually the main tank initiates the next attempt. Efficient guilds can pull this off in five minutes or less; any dawdling represents portions of another prospective attempt, valuable raiding time, wasted. Bathroom breaks, if you must have them, occur once you're resurrected and have met your buffing responsibilities.

If this seems excessive, keep in mind the number of people involved. Any time wasted is *everyone's* time wasted, and these are competitive individuals who've put aside real-life responsibilities to attend the raid. Efficiency becomes a question of courtesy, of respect. Everything about a raider's performance is subject to the same discerning judgment. The game of *WoW*, as more than a few raid leaders have sneered, is not especially difficult. Any given raider's time in combat consists of pressing the same handful of buttons over and over again, often in a prescribed order, while moving and switching targets as dictated by the strategy posted in advance on the guild's internal forums. For this reason, it is less important that raiders be preternaturally skilled than that they play in a thoughtful manner. True greats exist; every serious *WoW* player ran across a few. Just about every serious raiding guild had a manically driven warlock who topped every damage meter even when his class was underpowered, or a virtuosic priest who'd throw his Shield spell in that sliver of time between a rogue pulling threat and the first hit landing. These people are wonderful to have around, but they don't ultimately define a guild.

In fact, when examining elite raid units, one is quickly struck by the dearth of geniuses. They're rare commodities, after all, and anyone trying to build a guild of geniuses will never have the numbers to raid anything. Competence is the key. The biggest difference between average and elite guilds lies not in the top 10 percent but in the bottom 10 percent. Good guilds don't field bad players. This simplistic maxim obscures the difficulty of not fielding bad players, as nowhere in the stars is it written that having the free time to raid twenty or more hours per week makes someone good at MMORPGs.

Filling a handful of crucial roster spots (main tank, principal healers, and DPS) with good players is easily done. From there it's a question of fleshing out a roster, providing sufficient depth and diversity to deploy a consistent mix of tanking, DPS, and healing, balancing class numbers to spread loot around, and leaving just enough flexibility to shift your raid's class composition (adding a rogue for melee damage, an extra warlock for Banish, two more healers to stabilize the raid for early attempts). Meeting all these needs *and* meeting them with good, dedicated players whose schedule matches yours? Good luck, unless your guild has the name recognition to pull the absolute best recruits from your realm and poach good players from others. Nearly every guild in the world compromises. Somewhere on their rosters are poor players, players lacking either the motivation to research and pursue optimal play or the particular game-connected sense of awareness necessary to run very quickly out of fires. "Don't stand in the fire" is probably the single most important piece of advice anyone attempting a *WoW* dungeon can receive. If the area under your avatar's feet lights up in any way, *move*.

Or don't move! Maybe that's not a lethal pit of shadow energy—a dreaded "area of effect" spell, or AOE—but instead a magical glyph increasing your damage output by 300 percent! Every fight is its own puzzle playing its own script, and it's every raider's responsibility to know everything possible about that script, including exactly how she should react to each of its events. The earliest *WoW* raids may have been "tank-and-spank" affairs, immobile nukefests enlivened by the occasional area-of-effect fireball or perhaps a squadron of lesser minions ("adds," in the parlance of our times), but modern raid encounters demand quick reactions and varied behavior from every player on the roster. (The rosters vary these days, since *WoW* now allows anywhere from ten to thirty players into automatically scaling raid encounters.)*

A druid might find himself transformed into a ghost, tasked with using unique spectral abilities to dispel four malicious phantoms before they kill a guildmate. A rogue might be randomly targeted by a boss's Charge ability, forced to sprint in a wide and prescribed arc to keep herself alive while ensuring the boss remains in range of the hunters. Any failure or even, in some cases, any hesitation will get you killed, at the very least making you look silly and at worst leading to a wholesale wipe. A bad player targeted by one of these abilities notices it once the debuff icon appears, thinking only then of how to react. A good player anticipates, *expects* herself to be targeted (even if the chance is remote) and has already visualized exactly how she will react so she wastes not an instant. Perhaps it's reasonable to fail the first time one encounters a new challenge, but if everyone fails the first challenge the guild is in for up to thirty painful wipes. Raiders must be ever aware, ever poised with lightning reflexes, reacting instantly to new developments and all the while maintaining the greatest possible throughput of threat, damage, and healing.

DPS, the most quantitative of the holy trinity of MMORPG roles, is by necessity the most rote. If ever classes were designed to sit and mash a single button, that changed years ago. Blizzard pushes every player to stay active during fights, pushing a button at least once every 3 seconds but not more than once every 1.5 seconds.† Every

---

* Hardcore raiders may select Mythic difficulty for the ultimate challenge and greatest rewards, but this game mode permits no more than twenty players at once.

† Activating most abilities in *WoW* triggers a 1.5-second period where no further abilities can be used, so players can't spam and confuse servers with multiple concurrent commands. Exceptions

DPS player cycles through a handful of abilities, typically maintaining at least one DOT spell that causes damage slowly over a long period while striking consistently with efficient medium-damage attacks and deploying special high-damage attacks as circumstances and lengthy cooldowns allow. Using gear optimized for her talent build, the DPS player uses her abilities in a basic rotation to maximize her output. That's well and good for tank-and-spank fights like Patchwerk, but most modern raid encounters involve a great deal of motion and multiple "adds" to occupy extra tanks.

DPS players hate both of these things, as they ruin optimal rotations. Certain classes can attack on the move, but boss fights demand precise positioning, and a moving raider can't focus all her attention on damage. Switching targets hurts efficiency as well, as fresh debuff spells need applying and the adds may not live long enough for a proper damage cycle. As a general rule, a player's damage per second accelerates with her time on target before eventually peaking at whatever height mathematics and latency allow. Yet even a weak boss's health bar drains at glacial pace, rendering their furious assaults slightly absurd. An erstwhile girlfriend once remarked, peering at my screen during a raid, "It looks like everybody's really busy, but nobody's *accomplishing* anything." This remains the single most accurate description of MMORPG raiding I've ever heard.

Good DPS players move very little and always with purpose, taking advantage of every loose global cooldown to shift a few steps. They bind hotkeys to target whatever their tanks are targeting, as clicking a target on the screen leaves room for error. They pan their personal cameras around, constantly alert for new threats, ignoring the numbers exploding on their screens except perhaps if a lucky string of critical strikes boosts their damage enough to pull threat off the tank. Those with cheap PCs point their cameras straight down at the dungeon floor to tone down any graphical fireworks and ensure a smoother (read: more efficient) raiding experience. If they die for any

---

are rare and typically limited to utility spells like interrupts. This "global cooldown" has existed since the game's inception and remains one of its major constants, though the implementation of Haste gear allowed players to push the global cooldown as low as 1.0 seconds.

reason short of collateral damage in a wholesale raid wipe, they are yelled at. They don't get to complain about much and are generally expected to be grateful for any loot, as their roles are presumed the easiest. Of course, if dealing top-flight damage were actually easy, everyone would be doing it.

Tanks, on the other hand, we treat with reverence. Though a casual observer would discern little difference in their keyboard mechanics, and no rational person would suggest one's choice of *WoW* raiding role as a proxy for moral value, in our collective psychology tanks assume the role of the suffering ascetic. Forgoing easy farming and enjoyable PvP combat, they exist to suffer pain. Blow after blow thuds on their armored hides, each sufficient to kill anyone else in the raiding party, and the healers ward them away from death's edge. Were this not a video game it would be a truly macabre practice, something out of Kafka's deeper depressions, but hit points are an abstraction to begin with. Even though avatars don't feel pain, the tank's role as a sponge for suffering lends him an air close to holy. Tanks, especially main tanks, don't get yelled at. They're honored and rewarded as much as possible, not only because they're hard to replace but because everything they do in a dungeon is a literal sacrifice.

Once a tank has initiated a fight and made himself the opponent's first target, he strikes it with special abilities that generate vastly more threat than their feeble damage would suggest. Building and maintaining a threat lead over the DPS is just one of his tasks. Bosses range in size from a passenger van to a large building, most are mobile, and nearly all are best attacked from the rear, so their position and facing are crucial, and it falls on the tank to place the enormous monster in exactly the right spot. But because his own survival prohibits ever facing away from his target, all positioning and repositioning and dodging of fire pits and void zones and swiveling to direct frontal attacks must be done in reverse. Tanks, like the late Ginger Rogers, do their work backward and in high heels. Main tanks also must attend every single raid, or damn near to it, because their extravagantly valuable gear is the fulcrum by which the guild leverages its strength into loot. To kill a boss you first need a player who can take the boss's damage.

To that end, a tank looks always to his own survival. If he dies the raid is probably going to wipe in short order, so this is hardly a selfish impulse. He cycles short-cooldown abilities like Shield Block to mitigate incoming damage while always keeping a watchful eye on a whole slew of cooldowns and consumables. Potions, healthstones, survival talents, and the like might not seem like much compared to the punishment he takes, but heals are constantly landing and so survival is decided in fractions of a second. Any one of these *"oh shit buttons"* may save a tank from the hit that kills him, so he guards every one of them jealously. Outcompeting DPS for the top spot on a boss's threat list used to be more difficult, particularly for early Horde players who lacked paladins' threat-minimizing abilities.

Tanking changed a great deal over the years. What used to be an arcane (metaphorically speaking) practice reserved only for the most skilled warriors was democratized—first by the introduction of viable druid and paladin tanks in the *Burning Crusade* expansion, then by the smoothing out and homogenizing of tank abilities in the *Wrath of the Lich King*. Every tanking class now enjoys reliable single-target and multi-target threat abilities, a Taunt mechanism, and a slew of emergency survival abilities on long cooldowns. All can find gear suiting their class and play style. This was not always the case! Now every tank worth his salt, regardless of his class,* maintains a diverse arsenal of tanking gear customizable for any occasion: a set for maximum hit points, a set for evasion, a set for high armor and block to mitigate sudden bursts of damage. Tanking has been smoothed out and streamlined, made accessible enough for novices to handle but kept enjoyable for longtime veterans. The appeal of shielding one's allies from harm, of snapping aggro back with a Taunt so quick the foe barely has time to turn, has never gone away.

It's that same appeal that motivates the healing classes. I came to healing out of necessity. Originally I'd planned to be a face-melting

---

* As of the *Legion* expansion, six of the game's twelve classes can capably tank given proper gear and talents: warrior, paladin, druid, death knight, monk, and demon hunter.

elemental shaman who slung lightning at his enemies, but in vanilla *WoW* it just wasn't an option. Hybrid classes, capable of playing several different holy trinity roles depending on their gear and talents, were hybrid only in name until the *Burning Crusade* expansion. Paladins, druids, shamans, and priests were good only for healing. No matter what I did, my damage would always be pathetic, and so I made the adaptation to a support role. To my surprise, I quickly learned to love it. Healing is unlike almost every other gaming practice in that it does not unconditionally reward output. Every point of damage or threat a DPS or tanking player can produce is inherently valuable; the same is not true of healing, since every character has a fixed pool of hit points. If I cast a 1,000-point heal on a character missing 500 hit points, fully half my spell is wasted. Perhaps I'm so fearful of burst damage that I'll take the loss, but every point of inefficiency carries costs in time and mana. Healers can empty their mana pools in barely a minute if they choose, so their every choice carries some question of efficiency.

It should come as no surprise that over the years they've contrived many ways to pursue this. UI mods were long necessary, as Blizzard's default UI left no way for players to see the health or status of any raid members not directly in their five-man party. What was intended to be a clear and attractive field of vision for play grew cluttered with forty distinct health monitors in addition to any other bells and whistles like tank health monitors or assist indicators. Only committed aesthetes or masters of digital feng shui could maintain attractive UIs while raid healing. Modders developed add-ons to abort likely overheals, but as with Decursive—another efficiency mod used primarily by healers—Blizzard disabled it. But players kept on innovating. There was a long period at the end of vanilla *WoW* and early in *The Burning Crusade* when healers would deliberately use lower-level versions of their spells, taking advantage of healing boosts from their gear while paying less mana.* For a long time, various ranks of Healing Wave took up half my action bars!

---

* Deep explanation of this mechanic: At the time, damage and healing spells received a boost from gear solely in proportion to their casting speed. A 3.5-second cast received 100 percent of

To heal in a raid is to be constantly presented with split-second decisions, the failure of which will result in the swift deaths of your comrades—who, once you've resurrected them, won't be happy. You learn to ignore most of the action raging around in favor of your health monitors—their healthy little green shoots shorn off to hazardous yellow, orange, red, and just as violently replenished in a deluge of healing magic. In time the abstraction becomes legible. In time you learn to discern the fight's ebb and flow in the colored language of the monitors, reading it like the vertically scrolling green glyphs of *The Matrix*. Unless the deaths are instant one-shot obliterations, there's almost certainly something you could have done to buy time, if not prevent them outright. Thus every wipe is in some sense your fault. Even trash monsters in a raid dungeon will swiftly kill a tank without constant healing, so healers rarely get to play on autopilot. For this reason good healers tend to be neurotic sorts, perfectionists who wear the weight of their awesome duty.

Healing is a constant tightrope act, keeping your raid alive through expected constant damage, unexpected bursts of damage, and scripted bursts of damage such as when a boss uses a special attack. Anticipation stands you in good stead but only to a point, as the most efficient healing spells tend to be the slowest. Speed exacts a painful price in terms of mana, and a healer must *never* run out of mana except perhaps in the closing seconds of a particularly stressful boss fight. Managing this crucial resource becomes second nature over years of raiding: the familiar rhythm of an early Mana Tide or Innervate to replenish mana and give the spell's cooldown time to elapse, potions every two minutes, the second Tide about six minutes in, by which point in any given fight things probably have gotten hairy. Raids are puzzles, and healers keep the puzzle from eating

---

bonuses from gear, with shorter spells receiving progressively less gear bonus, all the way down to an instant spell receiving only 42.8 percent (counted as 1.5 seconds in keeping with the global cooldown). A low-ranked version of a spell typically had the same casting time but a lower base strength and crucially a *much* lower mana cost. Once gear was powerful enough for the bonus to dwarf the base value, a spell that healed 4,000 hit points for 400 mana might be downranked to heal 2,500 for 50 mana. The implications are obvious, which is why Blizzard later made it impossible to use anything less than the maximum rank of any given spell.

you alive while you figure out how to solve it. When learning new encounters, every minute of survival the healers can buy is another precious minute of live-fire practice dodging AOEs, picking up and burning down adds, adjusting to the fight's particulars.

Of the holy trinity, healing might appear to be the most essential—as indeed it was in the early days, with tanking a close second. Good healers were so hard to come by, and you needed so many of them for forty-man raiding that a guild was largely defined by its healing corps (in addition to the highly visible front man figure cut by the main tank). Packing the raid with healers and turning boss fights into highly stable marathons was the safest bet. Tight time limits, like Patchwerk's Berserk mechanism, changed all that, and much for the better: DPS play became every bit as crucial. Well-geared rogues and mages, long considered disposable cogs ("Shut up and Frostbolt"), became treasured commodities.

And yet the main tank and top healers always amass the most accolades. Their roles as the wardens of life and death are just too visible. Whenever a raider takes a big hit, the surge of saving light has a name attached. Everyone learns pretty quickly which healers have the best reflexes, whose heals will be the first to land. The healers, in turn, take tremendous pride in their work. I know few feelings in video games like landing the perfect heal at the perfect moment, snatching a teammate back from oblivion and turning the tide to victory. Being on the receiving end of that save is a wonderful feeling as well, completing a powerful feedback loop. Healing in online games is a legitimately emotional experience. The experience of destroying one's enemies gets familiar in a hurry, but saving a teammate's life yields a special thrill. The gratitude that often follows cements the bond. There is no quicker route to friendship in *WoW* than healing and being healed. Any antipathy toward your teammates *must* be set aside. You cannot allow them to die; you must save even the worst asshole's life because his success is necessary for yours, and in that bond between (often) total strangers there's something beautiful. We as a species have invested too much in the symbolism of life and healing to be cynical. In the moment, in the game, this bond is very real.

THE HERO CYCLE

In an archetypal fantasy narrative common to all fiction, heroes arise through a combination of exceptional talent and trying circumstances. Either born or fated to her role, the hero can easily establish conflict with it, and the innately jealous (for they are human) audience may collectively forgive her the audacity of being exceptional. But a hero who states, "I wanted this, worked for it, and earned it, and the rest of you should make do with less," draws the same disdain as a cocky professional athlete, from whom we expect undying gratitude for his every opportunity and reward. We prefer our Sully Sullenbergers, diamonds in the rough called to action in one shining moment and then content to spend the rest of their lives trying, trying in the face of cruel fate to live anonymous "normal" lives.

Hardcore *WoW* raiders don't fit this bill. Of course they don't save lives either, but I bring up heroes to point out how the raiding game is spiritually opposed to most RPG conventions. Downing the biggest, baddest threats to Azeroth's existence *should* be thrilling, but in reality it's a matter of attention and relentless execution. Perhaps the Peter Jackson version would include breathless chases and sweeping pan shots, but raiding always reminded me of Tolkien's classic novels in that it's *not* thrilling. There's no immediate reward to be had; it's a scholar taking five full pages to describe a tree. For the right type of person, meticulous craftsmanship is its own reward. Let's imagine, for a lighthearted conceit, that a traditional fantasy narrative took a power-gaming turn! Imagine it hewed roughly to *World of Warcraft*'s timeline. It would start in roughly the same place—the beginning, a very good place to start, and like most fantasies it would be an utterly faceless beginning.

Reared alongside countless indistinguishable others in the ruddy desert of Durotar, three orclings leave their hardscrabble pig farm to seek their respective fortunes: Ichiro, Niro, and Sanyo are their names. Ichiro, being the oldest and the halest, chooses the path of a warrior and sets out from home bearing Porkplower, the family's ancestral great ax. Niro, the middle child and never able to best his elder brother in a fight, cultivates his mind for the dominion of nature. Hewing his very own staff from an ash sapling, he swears fealty to the god of thunder and chooses the path of a shaman. Sanyo is the youngest of the three, her frame lean and hard from a lifetime of fighting for scraps, and with her natural cunning she's a natural cutpurse. Sanyo resolves to spend her life in the shadows, striking suddenly with foul poisons before retreating without a trace. She becomes a rogue.

The three grow along with their peers. They labor where adventurers' work may be found, first in Durotar and then in the neighboring Barrens. Ichiro wades through quilboar and kobold alike, gleefully *thwonk*ing away with his ax though he wishes he had more interesting skills than Heroic Strike. Ichiro builds his mastery of the elements by hurling lightning bolts from a distance, converting one plainstrider after another from proud flightless birds into crisped Thanksgiving turkeys. He finds this highly agreeable, though he finds himself terribly thirsty and having to take water breaks every two minutes. Sanyo skulks through a local cave complex slicing up purple-cowled cultists, stealing their purses and selling their cowls. She's learned to brew a few poisons—simple but effective compounds that nevertheless wear off her blades and have to be replenished far more often than logic would seem to dictate.

"But why?" the trio ask, when every two levels they return to their class trainers. "Why must each rank of these new techniques be so expensive, when they provide only paltry benefits?"

"For the economy," the trainers reply, and the trio sigh and hand over their gold.

Time passes and they reach the limits of their physical power. Try as they might, some kind of externally imposed barrier impedes any further growth. Their only path to advancement lies in the accumulation of better equipment, weapons, and armor. "Where can these treasures be found?" they inquire of Google, and the legendary sage answers, "In the very deepest and darkest of dungeons."

This seems reasonable enough, but a few abortive forays discourage the siblings. The three of them haven't might enough to overcome the monsters within. Much as they'd prefer to keep their adventuring a family affair, they need help. Enlisting two confederates from Orgrimmar's back alleys, they fight their way painfully through and begin to acquire better gear. Progress is agonizingly slow, as the dungeon runs are long and the squad's spoils rarely match up with their needs. But the siblings are persistent if nothing else, and after a few months they've thoroughly subjugated Scholomance, Stratholme, and their ilk. Their gear mostly matches. Life is pretty good.

But it's not enough. What's the point in *being*, they ask rhetorically, if you're not *advancing*? Again, better gear is their only forward vector. It exists, hoarded by creatures of immense power in dungeons so deep their mouths lie at the bottoms of still other dungeons.* The young orcs don't fear the challenge, though they are queasy at the prospect of throwing in their lot with dozens of others. How far, they wonder, can their fortunes truly be advanced by union with these people? Skilled though some may be, surely others are weaker. Much as the trio chafe at sharing the spoils, without these dungeons and their epic rewards they'll have nothing else to do. The lords of the realm promise a series of official "battlegrounds" for heroes to match their strength against each other for reward and renown, but these have yet to arrive, and so off to the dungeon our protagonists traipse!

Upon arrival in the Molten Core, where heat shimmers in the air over burbling lava lakes, they find their lives much changed. Niro's lightning bolts fizzle out feebly against the highly resistant skin of the two-headed, fire-spewing core hounds; unlike a mage or warlock, his spells don't benefit from weakening curses, and so he's unable to harm them. "You should heal instead," the guild leader suggests.

---

* The original iteration of Molten Core actually did this—the forty-man raid instance was located inside the Blackrock Depths instance, which while balanced for five to ten players could accommodate a raid of forty. Anyone who died and released inside Molten Core finished her corpse run at the Blackock Depths entrance, and had to trek back through the dangerous and notoriously bewildering dungeon just to rejoin her comrades. It was madness, frustrating madness, and a prime example of flawed endgame design. Eventually Blizzard created an easy shortcut, presaging the quality-of-life changes to come over the decade following.

"Look, I'm happy to use my healing spells in a pinch, but I'm not a priest. I've got these fly lightning spells and I want to use them!" protests Niro.

"Be that as it may," says the leader, "every shaman in every top guild heals." Stunned, Niro consults great Google once more. He sees it is so. The next day he forks over gold to change his abilities, throwing points into healing talents and adapting to his strange new role in every battle. Thankfully, the gear he has so far accumulated needs no replacement, as Intellect is the only available statistic that helps shamans. He's not sure what he's doing, but there's loot to be had.

Sanyo keeps her role, as every one of her abilities represents simply a different way to stab her foes with pointy implements. She keeps her talents too, as stealth seems much preferable to the alternatives. Each battle sees her comrades drop in heavy clots. Whether a cleave or a fire breath or a terrifying roar causing the warriors to lose control of a core hound, rogues are constantly killed. A lucky string of critical strikes, far from an exciting occurrence, can spell doom for an entire raft of the raid. Sanyo learns to be patient, to carefully pick her spots, to never jump in early and always back off sooner rather than later. Survival remains her golden imperative. She isn't having fun exactly, but there's loot to be had.

Ichiro finds himself very comfortable, the happiest of the bunch. Having traded in old Porkplower for a blue metallic specimen of craftsmanship known as an Arcanite Reaper, he chews through foes as fast as Sanyo. And should he make an error, should anything go wrong, in a flash he can whip out his shield. Nearly any episode is survivable, and the guild always seems to find itself with a surplus of two-handed warrior loot. Oh, the loot to be had!

The gods announce the creation of yet another dungeon, harder yet with rewards commensurate. A fabulous idea, our heroes concur! They seek still better gear—for what is life without pursuit?—though Blackwing Lair is wracked with encounters seeming to defy the laws of physics and nature, which only some cosmic error will suffice to explain. They endure the dragon Nefarian's infamous Shadow Flame attack by wearing cloaks crafted from his own sister's scales, and even near the end of the battle, when the dark lord's fallen minions leap to life and the world grinds to near a stuttering halt, they keep their composure. Ichiro hacks away with his newest great ax, Niro peers constantly from one ally to the next, inspecting for the smallest wound to heal, and Sanyo does her best not to get hit by the dragon's sweeping tail. Nefarian's severed head is placed atop a spire in Orgrimmar, and the trio celebrate while they can, knowing the next dungeon's not far off. The three are known throughout Azeroth, feted and ogled when they step out in public, feared and respected by their rivals, but this position is by its very nature precarious. With time a dozen competing guilds conquer their own Blackwing Lairs (how each of them can fight the same fights, and do so every week, is something the gods never explain), and the trio find their advantages diminished. They eagerly await—nay, loudly demand if ever they think the gods are listening—the next dungeon, so they may collect new loot.

The Temple of Ahn'Qiraj disappoints. Fun as it might be to battle giant insects, their teeming minions are unrewarding bores. Worse still, the bosses' loot only occasionally improves the siblings' gear. The weapons are nice, but the gods' armor smiths seem to have no concept of value. Naxxramas comes as an improvement, packed with bosses and offering full eight-piece sets of armor. Attacking a new boss grows into routine, a measuring of boundaries and an inexorable boring through them. The guild asks Ichiro to hang up his ax for full-time tanking, as certain fights in Naxxramas demand *eight* reliable tanks, and with a grumble he agrees. Niro's learned to love his role with its delicate timing and grave responsibility. Sanyo's totally changed her fighting style, discarding her daggers for kludgey and boring swords. She doesn't appreciate the constant scrutiny to which her play is subjected, her every swing recorded for later evaluation. They spend their days working in preparation for nightly trials by fire, sword, ice, and shadow. All have made so many compromises, have so thoroughly adapted to the dungeons' imperatives, that their younger selves would scarcely recognize them.

Then the world shifts under their feet. The gods redraw the mystical ley lines undergirding the world. Dungeons once requiring forty heroes, they announce, will now accommodate only twenty-five. This sets off immediate infighting: who, everyone wants to know, will be left behind? Jokes about being cut from the guild abound. Anxieties build. Ichiro, Niro, and Sanyo don't worry over losing their positions, but they do worry about losing the challenge of dungeons. It's simply easier to corral fewer people, and what few twenty-man dungeons exist don't satisfy. They're lesser hurdles for lesser players. But the gods have spoken, and they promise all will be well.

Venturing through the Dark Portal into the newly discovered continent of Outland, our heroes find themselves betrayed—or at least it feels that way. Their sumptuous epic gear, desperately hard-won, begins immediately to show its wear. Simple quest rewards in Outland tend to outclass treasure from the vaults of Naxxramas itself, which strikes the trio as unfair. Shouldn't those who've worked so hard enjoy such advantages? But the gods have spoken, and Niro counsels the others that Outland's new dungeons will supply them anew. The new world's dungeons aren't too easy after all, as some had feared. If anything, they're too damn hard.

Alchemy had always aided mortal heroes in their conflicts with immortal forces. Victory against Naxxramas's strongest bosses had been possible only with dedicated use of Azeroth's most potent potions: "flasks," enormously expensive and powerful enough to be worth it. No one enjoyed using them, but defeating certain bosses was all but impossible without them. The orcish three have long since made their peace with this—Ichiro in particular, as tanks use the most flasks and struggle most paying for them—but the new regime demands them for every difficult fight. The mechanics are straightforward, but even experienced raids find themselves struggling with sheer damage output. And because this becomes the standard practice, the gods construct each subsequent dungeon assuming constant flask usage as the standard. Large portions of the day are spent collecting materials or gold to aid in their crafting, and Ichiro finds himself supremely unmotivated. This isn't why he set off adventuring. Still, he's grown fond of his comrades and the familiar routine of dungeon raiding. He sticks it out.

In time the gods hear the pleas of their people; flasks are made weaker but vastly cheaper. Twenty-five-man dungeons seem to be working well, natural attrition whittles the roster low enough, and the smaller cap gives more freedom to everyone—though Niro still can't realize his thunder-throwing ambitions. Through Serpentshrine Cavern they march, and Karazhan, and the Eye, and the Black Temple to defeat the legendary demon hunter Illidan Stormrage, and Mount Hyjal and the Sunwell besides! A dense succession of dungeons keeps our heroes sated with gear and an escalating series of challenges, broken up only by the opening of the Northrend continent to exploration and plunder.

The cycle begins anew! The guild accommodates new classes and outfits their gear using the newest crafting professions. They gear up through small dungeons to prepare for another series of long raiding campaigns, but they do so without Sanyo. She's watched the arena battle scene expand for years and no longer enjoys the grind of raiding. Loot and fame can come with less of a grind, she realizes, and so she takes her leave. Ichiro continues as the guild's main tank and Niro adapts himself to a new role. The gods have strengthened his shaman lightning spells to the point where they rival anything a mage casts, and he takes full advantage of the opportunity. Onward they push, through a repopulated Naxxramas (the particulars of its bosses' resurrection being something they've learned not to question) and the Argent Tournament and Ulduar and Icecrown Citadel, where they deliver the final blow to the dreaded Lich King and save all of Azeroth from the threat of undead domination. Lest boredom threaten, the gods have already announced their next big plans: the Obsidian and Ruby Sanctums, with fresh bosses and loot!

The world explodes in fire and chaos, the result of an evil dragon loosed upon the world and all that. By "all that," our narration means a seemingly endless series of minions and plots culminating in dungeons to raid for loot. The event comes to be known as the Cataclysm. In the course of fighting their way to the dragon Neltharion,[*]

---

[*] Father of Blackwing Lair's Nefarian and every other black dragon.

the now-duo will clear the Bastion of Twilight, the Throne of the Four Winds, and the Blackwing Descent. It's during this time that Ichiro begins to feel burned out. It's a dire affliction common to raiding heroes, and Ichiro decides his time has come—but he cannot yet retire, as his guild has invested tremendous resources in him and his gear. He is too valuable to quit, but he resolves to do so once Neltharion is defeated. After all, the gods' next series of plans and dungeons will render his treasure useless, once more as in the past.

The final encounter is spectacular. The gods have grown supremely skilled at crafting these challenges, and Azeroth's most powerful boss to date demands a show. Ichiro and his comrades assault the corrupted black dragon in midair, leaping from an airship to forcibly pry the elementium scales from his spine. After crashing into the sea, they finish off his broken and maddened form for good. Tucked into the haul of loot is a sword of incredible power, which the guild immediately agrees should be Ichiro's. As their main tank, their physical and emotional anchor, he has more than earned it. But he can't accept their gift, and he cannot explain why without explaining everything, and so that's what he does. He is leaving, he says, retiring to help rebuild the sundered and brutalized Durotar of his youth. The rewards must go to his successor, to help the guild going forward. There is always the next dungeon. There is always the loot it holds.

We are left with Niro at last, Niro alone along with twenty-four of his guildmates forging ahead to the lost continent of Pandaria and then through time itself back to the reconstituted world of Draenor. He senses the world around him changing. New adventuring heroes appear every day, rising, accumulating power and gear, slapping together undisciplined bands nonetheless able to achieve great power through raiding. The distinction between ten-man and twenty-five-man raids has collapsed—one simply zones into a raid with any number of comrades between ten and thirty and it scales itself appropriately. The truly bold attempt Mythic challenges with twenty, conquering the final bosses and then for months after selling the copious loot to strangers for piles of the gold that everyone seems to have these days. Raiding is no less rewarding than it ever was, but it no longer confers special privilege. Niro is unsure what that means. Though he knows the gods will continue to produce exciting dungeons to plumb, he no longer enjoys their exclusive favor, and so his life's pursuit feels less valuable. A sacred calling, a discipline for which he's strived and suffered, is now one choice among many. A campaign through the Broken Isles in pursuit of the ancient Tomb of Sargeras sees him acquiring an "artifact" weapon, a tool of unspeakable power and majesty, but every single one of his guildmates can say the same. They raid a few hours a week, nudging their gear up to the point where it is powerful yet utterly uniform, for who can really get excited about upgrading his boots from item level 810 to level 815 and then to 820? So much work for such fleeting reward. Niro still enjoys his adventures, particularly in those frenetic months after each new continent opens for plundering. They just don't seem to mean much anymore.

Always an Ending

We all leave the game eventually, as I can't help reminding you. High-end raiding is a paradox in that it labors to retain players while at the same time driving them away. Blizzard's designers are experts in player retention, pacing out new content and ever shinier rewards on an invisible but remarkably consistent internal schedule: major updates at least every six months and expansion packs every two years. Building every new raid dungeon as an outgrowth of established storylines, they leverage the work you've already done against the promise of conclusions. Each final boss they engineer as a show-stopper, showcasing never-before-seen mechanics in a grand assault against some edifice of Warcraft lore. You stand ever at the precipice of satisfaction, of a peace that never comes. In Azeroth, it is always the End Times.

That this is a kind of pyramid scheme scarcely needs stating. Leave aside the question of hours invested and the human capacity to rationalize almost any further investment given enough principal already paid, logic says it's not sustainable. Pushing for one late night after another through a brand-new dungeon thrills like few other gaming experiences, but you do it knowing you'll be doing the exact same things in four months' time when the next dungeon drops. Add to this the malaise I ascribed to Niro in the preceding section, the self-interested (but fair) dissatisfaction with a game that no longer puts raiding first, and it's easy to imagine veteran raiders leaving the game. Indeed, "burnout" exerts constant pressure on every guild's roster. Smart guilds are always recruiting, as a healthy roster keeps raids painless and helps avert further burnout. Raiding is failure, after all—masochism in the pursuit of pixel riches—and most of us already encounter enough rejection in our day-to-day lives. It's why I don't own a cat.

So it's not uncommon for raiders to take breaks, when their work schedules ramp up or the hours on the treadmill get to be too many. Doing so used to be difficult; anyone who missed a tier of raid content would need to be carried back through it (wasting the guild's time) in order to gear up enough for the following tier. Thankfully Blizzard has been diligent about catch-up time, making gear progressively easier to get until anyone can be made ready for endgame encounters in a matter of weeks. From a practical standpoint this is fantastic, though again it devalues the achievements of those on the cutting edge. But those players have alts to level in addition to their main characters, and they may want to take breaks themselves. Any hardcore raiders badly wounded by concessions to the casual left Azeroth long ago, as the developers have been pushing (at glacial speed) in this direction for the better part of a decade. More than a few quit in a huff to later return, profiting by the same systems they scorned, returning to the fold having found no better vessel for their gaming ambitions.

Because there's nothing else quite like it, after all. The world abounds with MMORPGs of many stripes, some more hardcore than others, and while some enjoyed success, many foundered precisely where *WoW* succeeded: the late game, that nebulous universe of content past the end of the leveling curve. You can build your leveling process around a compelling narrative like *Star Wars: The Old Republic* or you can stretch it out with endless grinding like *Aion* or you can add mini-games and fun platforming sections like *WildStar*, but eventually players will reach whatever arbitrary cap you've set, and then they'll need something else to do. They need some other way to continue enhancing their avatars, and most games on the market simply don't have a good answer beyond PvP arenas and a handful of small dungeons. Rarely do developers invest in large-scale raiding content, because it's time-consuming (read: expensive) to produce and only a fraction of your customers will ever see it. Most of the raid discussion in gaming the last few years revolves around the first-person shooter *Destiny*, whose MMORPG-inspired "raid" encounters accommodate only six players at a time. The style of raiding popularized by *EverQuest* and perfected in *WoW* is just too ambitious for margin-savvy modern publishers focused on mobile gaming. This means that if you're a raider by past and inclination, and if you want to scratch that extremely particular itch, *WoW* is the only real game in town.

So why bother? Why build raid content at all, if it's just going to be a never-ending treadmill for a small tribe of quirky masochists? In the case of *WoW*, it may have been a product of personnel: early in the game's development, Blizzard hired Jeffrey Kaplan (alias: Tigole Bitties) and Alex Afrasiabi (alias: Furor), who were famous for their leadership and commentary in the *EverQuest* raiding community. They were also infamous for campaigns of online harassment and unrestrained misogyny, as Kaplan's childishly offensive nickname suggests. The *EverQuest* guild Afrasiabi helmed, Fires of Heaven, solicited nude pictures from female applicants and circulated those photos among its membership.* That Kaplan and Afrasiabi's pasts never became an issue during their years at Blizzard is a testament to the blinkered, back-scratching nature of video game journalism—no reporter given access to Blizzard developers would jeopardize it asking after years-old discussions from the web's benthos. Perhaps Kaplan and Afrasiabi have grown in the past fifteen years; perhaps they enjoy

---

* I was told this by two former Fires of Heaven members along with one of their wives and shown the image archive.

excellent rapport with their female colleagues. In any case, these individuals (along with designers Rob Pardo, who played *EverQuest* with Kaplan, and Tom Chilton, who worked on *Ultima Online*'s legendarily punishing player-versus-player system) were instrumental in *WoW*'s early development, championing the value of endgame content and catering to the relatively small portion of players doing it. As the game's most invested players, they'd stick around as paying customers year in and year out.* Their consistent presence would mitigate the inevitable churn of more casual players.

What's more, those hardcore players yield downstream benefits to the community. Raiding demands a great deal of material investment, from precious metals for crafted armor to herbs for potions, to cloth for bandages. Some enterprising raiders farm these components themselves, as I typically did, on a squad of alternate characters diversified like a stock portfolio into every region of the economy. A death knight with mining and herbalism skills to gather materials, a mage with alchemy to process the herbs, and a monk with enchanting to break down any incidental gear might back up a druid main character who uses jewelcrafting and inscription for their attendant gear-enhancing benefits. Leveling those alts and developing their professions takes a great deal of time and money in purchased materials (as with so much else, the grind is now more humane than it used to be), but for serious raiders it's often worth it over the long haul, preferable to paying volatile Auction House prices for consumables. Any savvy merchant knows to place useful raiding materials for sale Tuesday evening, when the lazier raiders are logging on for a fresh dungeon clear following the weekly reset. No matter your approach, raiding provides a necessary avenue for consumption, fueling demand for important supplies across the server. Even the leveling of alts helps the community by populating cities and leveling zones. Underpopulated MMORPGs find themselves trapped in a downward spiral,

---

* Even if you're taking a break from *WoW*, the fifteen dollars per month is a relatively minor expense, and many active, paying accounts aren't being played on a consistent basis. Outright canceling one's subscription is enough of an existential statement that few are motivated to do so. My *WoW* account remained active and paid for almost a year after I stopped playing.

where empty zones come to feel like tombs and the game's social element withers away. Raiding guilds are just the highest link in an ecological chain distributing resources throughout each server, maintaining the health of this odd colonial organism.

Speaking of organisms, one of *WoW*'s most notorious incidents started in September 2005, when raiders did the field of epidemiology an inadvertent favor. A new raid dungeon called Zul'Gurub contained a boss named Hakkar the Soulflayer, because the self-aware humor that characterizes *WoW* has never extended to its hilariously overwrought names.* Hakkar afflicted players with a spell called Corrupted Blood, which caused heavy damage over several seconds and, more hazardously, could be spread to any adjacent comrades. It was never meant to leave the raid instance, but an oversight on Blizzard's part left the pets of hunters and warlocks vulnerable. If a player dismissed his pet before Corrupted Blood expired, he could resummon it later in the open game world and thus pass on the disease. Players would die quickly, but a second programming oversight made computer-controlled NPCs into asymptomatic carriers. They took no damage themselves but passed the disease to any player who drew close. Through a mix of accidental and intentional transmission (using pets to deploy raid debuffs in major cities was an occasional hobby with hilarious results like blowing up the Auction House), Corrupted Blood spread across entire servers in a matter of days. Players avoided population centers where they might encounter tainted NPCs, and ultimately only a series of server restarts and bug fixes from Blizzard annihilated the plague. Mainstream news sources leapt on the story like few others in that first year of *WoW*'s existence. Researchers broke down the spread of the plague and players' reaction to it, their struggles to isolate and protect themselves in a deliberately social game.

But nobody blamed the raiders for this. I can't imagine any kind of collective misbehavior that would honestly threaten raiders' position at the top of the social hierarchy. Everyone, put bluntly,

---

* Personal favorites include Razorgore the Untamed (who dropped a tanking mace called Spineshatter), Firelord Smolderon, and Teron Gorefiend.

wants to be the coolest kid in school—wealthy, surrounded by friends, decked in the newest style. Our race of adolescent apes can't help but invest in social currency and hierarchy, particularly in a game that's social by nature. A new player walking into Stormwind City will be drawn to the highest-level characters in the most impressive-looking gear the same way tourists to a museum swarm around its most prestigious attractions. For all the complaining über-players do on forums, their mere existence provides a guide to aspiring new players. If you joined an MMORPG and all the only other players you saw in its greatest cities were wearing shabby gear little better than your own, you'd assume that was the game's ceiling. To shamble, a pauper, into Ironforge and see characters clad in spectacular, dramatically crafted epic armor vastly eclipsing your own is to get the inkling that you too could be wearing that armor one day. You too could be downing raid bosses or winning "Gladiator" titles in the arena and crushing lesser-geared players in battlegrounds. Just about anyone with enough spare time can work her way to epic gear these days, but the absolute best loot will always go first to the game's elite. When I raided, any spare time in Orgrimmar was spent politely answering queries about my gear: *Where did you get it? How? What's raiding? How does someone get into raiding? Is there any space in your guild? I promise I won't annoy anyone!* One guild has some success in the raiding game and others follow, competing even if they don't intend to fully catch up. This is on one hand a simple thing, almost juvenile, but it's how small things grow large. It's how an admixture of jealousy and admiration inspires games (online or off) to grow into cultures.

And it's culture you need, if you're an online game developer and you want to keep your job for more than a few months after going live. New games come out at a dizzying pace, and online gamers are a fickle crowd, often flitting from one game to another in order to play with friends. Convincing players to stick around takes more than responsive combat or a fun crafting system; it takes a genuine human connection. If a player's friends leave the game, he'll probably leave as well unless something else in the game can reliably provide that connection. He needs a guild of people to play with, to bond with. Raiding provides guilds with the kind of structured, scheduled activity they need to stick together—which is why purely social guilds rarely thrive. Working for hours every night on collaborative puzzles while socializing—is it any wonder these organizations grow so tightly knit? This is more time than most people spend with their friends; if you and a friend play an MMORPG together it's a guarantee you'll see each other more online than off. You'll spend more time with them than you do with anyone except the people living in your own home. What's more, you'll spend that time helping, supporting, and saving each other, building and reinforcing those bonds on a nightly basis.

From a certain perspective raiding is a strain of masochism, but from another it's a form of practiced love. I mentioned love as part of healing earlier, but everyone in a raid environment is in some way emotionally bound by it. Sage observers of humanity have long noted the relationship between practice and belief, and raids are always steeped in ritual. The weekly server reset filling dead and empty dungeons with fresh life and loot in a cycle of rebirth; the raid leader marking targets with abstract symbols before each pull; the pull itself, the hunter's use of her Misdirection spell before the twang of her bow and the lumbering surge of her enemies into motion; the repetition of spells, tactical calls, the casting of Bloodlust for a final burn; the rolling of virtual dice to divvy up loot. Each guild performs these rituals in its own way, with its own superstitions. Fitting into a new guild becomes a matter of repeating the practice until it feels natural, asserting you belong until one day you do.

BYGONE DAYS

If today you ask longtime raiders their opinions of the raiding game, they feel conflicted. On the one hand, they'll acknowledge, encounters are better designed than ever before. They demand more from players, intellectually and mechanically, than their ancient forty-man forebears. Raiders invest fewer hours for vastly more loot,* and the farming requirements become trivial through repeatable quests (see chapter 7) and a battery of alts, easily leveled and maintained. The superelite still treat raiding as a job, putting in sixteen-hour days with mandatory meal breaks and seven hours allotted for sleep, but these pushes only last about two weeks at a time or, as the European superguild Method has claimed, until they run out of vacation time. But they do that because they love the intensity of the experience; they love the masochism of relentless failure followed by giddy screaming triumph, much as veteran political operatives crave the caffeinated insanity of the campaign trail. Some only enjoy the game in binge form.

Countless other guilds work through exactly the same content at their own pace, happy for the loot and the challenge and unconcerned with the race for world firsts. The game belongs to them now, and who's to say it isn't richer? It's hard to get an exact number, but by the best estimates only about thirty guilds—which is to say, only twelve hundred people on the planet—killed Kel'Thuzad, the final boss of the original Naxxramas. Even if that elite raiding is important to sustaining an MMORPG community, such exclusive challenges probably aren't healthy, and they certainly aren't good investments of developer time. Now raiding is broken up into clearly delineated difficulty levels, so even those unready for the hardest fights can accumulate gear and train on versions with easier mechanics. The first time a raider sees a fight in twenty-five-man Heroic mode, he's already beaten it a half-dozen times. The game's changed, not grown corrupted by casuals or any similarly tired formulation. But by the same token nobody's obliged to prefer the new. By this writing, most of the old-school raiders are gone, and there's nothing on the gaming horizon even claiming to offer the same experience. Those who remain have made their peace with a long, pleasurable twilight.

---

* In vanilla WoW, the typical raid boss dropped two pieces of epic loot. By *Wrath of the Lich King* that number had grown to five pieces—impressive even before you consider the change from forty-man raids to smaller twenty-five-man raids and later to flexible raids as small as ten players. Add in the weekly loot hauls from easier ten-man raids and you can see how a fresh *WoW* avatar can be geared for cutting-edge raids in less than a month.

Back in the old days, I'd stand at the mouth of my cellar door and suck in cool air to quiet my stomach. We scheduled Patchwerk for early on Wednesday nights and there'd usually be just enough sun still out to turn the clouds on the hills bloodred. The neighbors would arrive home from work in their BMWs and Lexuses (Teslas were a few years off), easily spotted down the block by the blue LED glare of their automatic headlights even if it wasn't yet dark, and if they looked to me at all it was with thin-lipped contempt. I felt like I deserved it, unshaven in sweats outside my basement dwelling, but it didn't hurt the way that kind of feeling had hurt all my life. I was Ghando, after all, restoration shaman of accomplishment and renown, leader of the world's top Spanish-speaking raid guild, privy to a universe they couldn't begin to understand. At this moment in my life, sneered at by successful people, the idea of a career feeling elusive in the best moments and impossible the rest of the time, I stood at the top of my own little profession. And if you told me it wasn't real, I'd have pointed to the forty people waiting on direction for the Grobbulus pull. It was as real as we made it, and good God was it fun. When the discomfort subsided I unlatched the door and gently pulled it closed, padded down my cold concrete steps, and settled into the warm throne of my desk and its stuffed black rolling chair. I'd strung white Christmas bulbs down the rafters and over the ductwork, and they lit the room like gauzy little stars.

« 6 »

THE BUSIΠESS OF ΠURDER

MAY 2007

"**R**ez up. Rez up and we'll go again."

"Man, it's late."

"Still twenty minutes on flasks. We'll have this fucker dead in fifteen."

"It's *late*, man."

"It's late because we've been fucking up," I clucked back into my microphone. "Should've been outta here an hour ago. Here we are. Rez up."

I couldn't hear a sigh—push-to-talk buttons conveniently mask your least convenient emotions—but the collective disappointment of twenty-four other people was palpable. We'd staggered all night through Serpentshrine Cavern, a vast dank underspace with proud vaulted ceilings and shabby wooden plankwork assembled in walkways from one monster-infested pylon to the next. The dungeon was brutally difficult, infested with both unforgiving bosses and a tremendous volume of their snakelike naga henchmen who slaughtered raids for even momentary sloppiness and yielded no rewards to speak of. It also featured a sequence of bosses demanding tight execution and high DPS, each of them linked to his own slavering legion of trash. We'd meant to clear the bulk of the instance, saving the savagely entertaining Lady Vashj* for the next day, but ran into

---

* The final boss of Serpentshrine Cavern and a major character going back to *WoW*'s single-player forebear *Warcraft III: The Frozen Throne*, she featured a phase where special "core" items had to be looted from water elemental minions around the edge of the room and transported

snag after snag and now faced the prospect of having to reclear an hour's worth of trash. I was desperate to salvage the night, and a kill of Morogrim Tidewalker (a purple carbuncle of a sea giant who, as part of his idle animation, would occasionally fart a rancid green bubble into the air and pop it with his index finger) would set up T K T for a solid raiding week. We might, if we were lucky and worked our tails off, earn ourselves the privilege of a dozen progression wipes on cutting-edge content past Serpentshrine. It was a mean reward, and my guildmates weren't keen on pushing past midnight for it.

"Once again," I keyed my mic. "If you've got any extra hit point gear, put it on. Anyone above 9,000 will be safe from the Grave and Quake combo." I finished a resurrect spell, picked a new corpse to target, and began the next cast. The ten-second spell crawled along its lime cast bar and I thought about the next night's raid: would we have the DPS for Vashj? Four rogues at least to quickly slaughter water elementals, with as many affliction warlocks spaced about the arena as relays for the cores and efficient melters of the powerful swamp striders Vashj would summon in the fight's second phase. Our tanks and healers would be there, I knew; it was just whether the damn DPS would appear—not even in terms of numbers or precise class balance but experience. Anyone new to the fight became a liability— never got on the elementals quite fast enough, couldn't be trusted to handle a core without passing it to the wrong comrade or losing track of it in a clogged, disorganized inventory screen. I thought to check the online raid signups, but I'd checked them just before the prior pull and they'd look no different. Any given lineup became not a collection of friends and fellow gamers (many of whom I'd personally recruited) but an ever-shifting heap of actuarial tables representing variously painful degrees of risk.

"Ready check," I announced, and instructed a mod to query everyone. Responses blotted blue and red on my raid monitors. "All

---

to four central altars. However, possessing a core paralyzed the bearer, so the item had to be tossed from one guildmate to another in a chain, with the final link standing adjacent to the altar. A single fumbled exchange usually wiped your raid. It was the sort of mechanic that, while conceptually fun, makes you want to reach through the screen and throttle your guildmates.

right, should be good once Savena's back," I named our current main tank, a sardonic young man I'd met in Mexico, with ghost-pale skin and a head of long, straight black hair like you might see in a conditioner ad. He was a fabulous player, a true pillar of our guild, and I'm sure I drove him crazy. "And if you let him die, I'm just going to have Plastico disband the guild."

And then I rename us Sex Machines, Plas typed in Officer chat, beyond the sight of the guild's rank-and-file.

Seriously though, I replied. *We can't kill fucking Tidewalker. Easiest boss in the instance and he's wrecking us.*

But we one-shot Karathress, yes? Tell him chupa mi mion!

Three-shot. Two wipes. You were there, Plas. Jesus Christ.

Two wipes, no wipes. We got his loot, what's the difference? :D

Difference is it's pumpkin time now, I replied, employing our term for late-night raiding. At the stroke of midnight, our otherwise intelligent and capable raiders had turned into pumpkins.

You worry too much, Ghando, said warrior officer Angelus. *We get this fat asshole tonight.*

If we don't it's a bad clear tomorrow. My stomach knotted just thinking about the psychological drag it would exert. Guilds thrive off momentum, week to week and raid to raid; what you do Tuesday determines what you can schedule Wednesday, and every hour becomes precious. T K T just couldn't put together enough good hours to make them all count, and as a consequence we were stuck in the mud. With our progression stalled at the final boss of the Eye, Kael'thas Sunstrider, the Black Temple was due to open any day, and we wouldn't be able to set foot in it. We were falling behind the curve, and on a relatively small server there was no proven raid talent not already spoken for by us or our rivals. These problems all felt like my fault, and I had no way to fix them.

It had begun bleeding into the rest of my life too. Still employed at the mobile video start-up, editing footage and writing white papers for the executives at Sprint to ignore, I'd spend long stretches of my day mentally and emotionally mired in *WoW*. Not wanting to play it, not looking forward to logging in at night, but dreading everything that might go wrong. Everyone who might not show up. The loot our tanks needed that might not drop. As you might guess, spending every hour of the day gnawing neurotically at yourself over video game responsibilities isn't healthy. I spent long stretches at work learning anything I could about the game, watching videos of Nihilum and the rest of the world's best guilds beating Kael'thas. This phenomenally complicated and creative fight demanded so much from every player at every moment, and for the first time since the very end of Naxxramas I honestly didn't feel T K T could reach that level. My browser home-page, even at work, was ElitistJerks.com. Elitist Jerks was and remains to this day one of the better guilds in North America, but they'd also built the world's foremost site for intelligent *WoW* discussion. Aggres-sively moderated, populated by the smartest players in the global community, it was required reading for anyone serious about the game—including Blizzard's designers, who acknowledged its impact on their thinking by including Elitist Jerks members Gurgthock and Wodin as quest-giving NPCs in each of *WoW*'s expansions starting with *The Burning Crusade*.

Elitist Jerks' site (now defunct) became my personal oracle. I read hundreds of posts every day and integrated myself into the community by commenting on my own experiences as a raid leader, on shaman play, on healing in general. I'd played for years, but here I developed my first real fixation on *WoW*; it consumed my daily thoughts, repre-senting the classic pairing of obsession and bane. Thinking about it, reading about it, discussing it all made me happy in a way that actually playing the game no longer did. My identity as the leader of a hardcore raiding guild felt important as ever, but it also felt like a burden. I didn't like where I was, and I didn't know how to fix it.

I started to think of quitting. There was a world of other games to play, after all, though unlimited online entertainment for fifteen dollars per month was a hard price to beat. Still, I kept these feelings to myself. I couldn't tell T K T or my fellow officers; the MMORPG player constantly threatening to quit is a painful stereotype I wasn't eager to embody. If you're talking about quitting, you better do it or shut up. I couldn't tell my girlfriend either, as the prospect of my quitting would excite her a little too much. I'd managed to keep my frustrations with raiding from spilling over into our relationship, but nobody could totally overlook all those evening hours in a head-set trance. For the first time in my life I confronted the question: how the hell was I supposed to have fun in this video game?

FINDING THE FUN

Over the years, more than a few mainstream media outlets have snarkily weighed in on the idea of games as work. But in elite gaming communities, the issue of burnout is very real. Hardcore MMO raiders, professional *Counter-Strike* gunners, and platinum *League of Legends* players are all people who've made a serious commitment to a craft. However much they may enjoy the game, their commitment to it takes on its own weight. The investment of time and emotional energy makes it hard to step away; what's more, the player's identity becomes bound up in his in-game accomplishments. Goals unrealized keep players sticking around—I once naively swore I'd never quit *WoW* until I saw the Lich King, Arthas, dead at my feet. Most important of all is the commitment they feel to their teammates. Years of teamwork, struggle, and shared memories forge powerful bonds even between those who don't know each other in real life.

To contemplate quitting *WoW* was to contemplate abandoning some of my closest friends, to say nothing of the guild itself. T K T was mine, after a fashion—something I'd worked for, suffered for, built with digital if not literal blood, sweat, and tears. I couldn't separate myself from it without pain and tremendous loss.

But not everyone felt this way. More than a few serious players took a radically different approach. Rather than tackle the raiding game with its endless progression cycle and Sisyphean pursuit of better gear for tougher monsters for better gear (and so on), they stripped *World of Warcraft* to its competitive core. If the first video game emerged a Planck instant after the first computer (as tell the scrolls of our people's history), head-to-head gaming followed the invention of the network by the same margin. The classic shooter *DOOM* owes its hallowed place in the canon not to a moving story or particularly fine mechanics but to the fact that two PCs linked by a cable could play *DOOM* against each other. Head-to-head competition is the raison d'etre for online gaming. You can meticulously craft a great single-player game, but to a certain mind-set computer opponents will always disappoint. They're predictable, after all, especially in MMORPGs where every round of combat falls under the same simple rule book. Attack a monster from range and it will rush directly at you and begin mindlessly swinging away, using any special abilities as soon as their cooldowns conclude. The toughest raid bosses are no smarter, operating according to rigid rules; raid guilds progress by learning and exploiting these rules.

Even the weakest human opponent, by contrast, offers (by her unpredictability) a challenge. She fights according to her impulses and ambitions in the moment. She may not fight at all, instead employing any manner of tricks to flee. She may have a comrade idling nearby or hidden in stealth. One engages a fight with monsters knowing exactly how it proceeds, but when fighting against players anything can happen.

These are the two types of combat in *WoW*: player-versus-environment (PvE) and player-versus-player (PvP). Though nearly every player who ever opened an account engaged in both types of play, they have always stood at either precipice of a seismic divide. Running from the top of *WoW* to its very root, the divide raises crucial questions about how and why people play video games—whether for fun or profit, love or compulsion.

Whether she'll play on a PvE or PvP server is one of the very first decisions a new *WoW* player makes. PvE servers do not allow PvP combat in the open game world unless both participants explicitly flag themselves for battle—you're safe from other players unless you choose to fight. PvP servers allow players from opposing factions (Horde and Alliance) to freely attack each other in all but a few low-level zones—even in your faction's capital city, you're almost always vulnerable to enterprising killers. Everyone on every server

has access to special instanced areas called battlegrounds and arenas*
if she wants to battle her fellow players, but those are instances apart
from the open game world. PvE and PvP servers offer exactly the
same content, experienced very differently by their players.

Playing on a PvE server offers a safer and more scripted experience. A series of leveling quests can be tackled at your own
pace and leisure, disrupted only by the possibility of other players
crowding out your quest mobs (an inconvenience you can avoid
simply by grouping with them). Any answer you'll ever need lies
in an online database. You'll compete with the opposite faction for
resource nodes in contested zones, but only in a finders-keepers
sense. Combat with that faction happens only at the places and
times of your choosing, which is to say in strictly recreational contexts. On a PvE server, you are always doing more or less exactly
what you want to do.

On PvP servers, by contrast, hunting season lasts 365 days a year.
Gamers naturally avail themselves of any opportunity to virtually
murder each other, so bringing two factions into simple proximity
is enough to induce violence. How much proximity they encounter
has varied through *WoW*'s ages; vanilla *WoW* used geography to seg-
regate players between Orgrimmar on one continent and Ironforge
on the other, but *The Burning Crusade* congregated everyone into a
single continent around a single capital city (Shattrath City, labeled
a "sanctuary" and thus off-limits for all combat). Subsequent expansions tinkered with the formula but always made sure to throw the
factions close together in at least a few zones. Questing in a contested
zone, one always keeps both eyes open for trouble. Even a few seconds taken to gather herbs may prove fatal if a stealthed rogue or
druid lies in wait or an enemy party rides by. Put simply, anyone who
plays on a PvP server is going to get ganked. It's going to happen a
lot, especially if you don't regularly play with friends, and you're
going to spend many extra hours of your life viewing the game in

---

* A footnote in chapter 3 (p. 47) explains the concept of an instance in depth, but both
battlegrounds and arenas can be thought of as dungeons where instead of fighting monsters,
players fight each other.

grayscale, running back to your corpse in ghost form. You'll spend even more hours warding off gank attempts, fleeing from them, or initiating them yourself instead of questing or gathering or whatever else you had planned.

This drives some people up the wall. More than a few of my *WoW*-loving friends refuse to play on PvP servers because they hate the inevitable culture of ganking. It's not the combat itself, or the lost time; it's the *anxiety*, the constant state of alert, the ceaseless sweeping of the camera back and forth, the game audio cranked up to hear the distinctive whisper of a player stealthed nearby. Never allowing your hit points to dwindle below half or your mana to drop too low, lest you need to fire off a Polymorph and run. Nobody enjoys being ambushed out of the blue and killed in a game, but for some people it's truly upsetting. Just as some folks love horror movies and others refuse to watch a scene, it's a question of temperament. Still, nobody familiar with gamer culture would be surprised to learn that PvP players frequently look down on PvE players.

Temperament goes a long way toward explaining why active PvP persisted through the early days of vanilla *WoW*, when the game offered literally zero incentives for it. Blizzard had promoted *WoW* through much of its development with promises of fierce PvP battles, with special PvP content and accompanying rewards. They promised a ranked system to reward player kills and structured battlegrounds to organize combat past mindless mass melees. The Alliance / Horde conflict was supposed to be a central pillar, as it had been going back to the original *Warcraft* strategy games. But at the time of the game's North American retail release in November 2004, none of these systems existed. The developers' promises wouldn't materialize for months, and yet a vibrant PvP scene appeared across the servers. It was one of the early game's most impressive elements, and it happened purely because of the community.

"LFM TARREN MILL, PST FOR RAID INVITE"

It emerged at peculiar points across the game world, where the continents' subtle geography ran opposing forces together, as depressions in soft soil erode over ages to raging rivers. The placement of towns and cliffs, roads and caves, ore veins and herb sprouts, quest givers and quest objects and mob spawning patterns—though every element was meticulously designed by the gaming industry's finest professionals, layer upon layer of interlocking systems led to unpredictable results. Swarms of low-level characters laid siege to Hammerfall in the Arathi Highlands; the stretch of road between the Alliance town of Astranaar and the Horde's Splintertree Post often boasted a fine dusting of bleached skeletons like a morning frost. Parties moving through the narrow passes in and out of the Searing Gorge watched constantly for ganking parties: high-level players mustering for runs through the nearby Blackrock Spire. Traveling to Stranglethorn Vale as a Horde player (as I've written elsewhere in this volume) felt like choppering into 'Nam. Chaos seethed under every inch of that steaming jungle canopy, where barrel tree trunks and thick vegetation cut off sight lines and encouraged ambushes. The moment Grom'gol Base Camp's mighty stockade walls faded from sight, you knew you were in terrible danger. Players memorized the paths back to the gates, where powerful NPCs waited to come to your aid, if you could just reach them in time. Even on a run back to base you risked stumbling into roaming monsters or still other enemies, but you might also encounter an ally with a mind to help.

Then there was Tarren Mill. In vanilla *WoW*, this Horde town south of the Undercity was placed near the Alliance town of Southshore in a zone packed with low-level (20ish) quests.* These quests weren't only fun—they were poignant and well paced with excellent rewards, and packed with the area's classic *Warcraft* lore. For fans of

---

* The *Cataclysm* expansion remade the entire zone, combining the Alterac Mountains into the Hillsbrad Foothills, wholly destroying Southshore, and consolidating Horde rule in the region. It no longer includes an Alliance town.

the series there was a real sense of treading the footsteps of history, and the zone was a kind of crossroads for the northern half of the continent. Traffic had a way of converging here, at the halfway point between two towns separated by only a few wide-open pastures and a ruined old watchtower. It was here that players who truly loved PvP congregated to do battle. How a fight started wasn't important— one low-level character ganked another, the latter's high-level guild-mates rolled over to crush him and camp his corpse,* the camped player logged on to his high-level alt—because they all ended the same. A gaggle of fighting players turned into dozens, then scores. As word spread around the server, through guild chat and whispers and all-caps announcements in Trade chat in the factions' main cities, hundreds might pile into the melee, pushing back and forth between the towns in a tug-of-war lasting until the wee hours of the morning or until a world server crash knocked everyone in the zone offline. If the servers were up and you wanted a fight, you could always find one in Tarren Mill.

Only someone who played in the melee can truly appreciate its gleeful madness. Though players might band together in parties or raids, organization and strategy were all but impossible. Your allies might be level 22 or level 60, decked in epics or garbed in greens, serious players or college students on the verge of blackout drunk. They had nothing to bond them, no real inclination to play together, and (unlike an actual conscripted army) they held no fear of death to inspire teamwork. The opposing forces would mass like two angry hornet swarms, standing just out of the standard forty-yard spell range, buzzing and stewing until at last a critical mass worked up the nerve to charge.

---

* For those unfamiliar with the term, "corpse camping" is the practice of killing an opposing player and then waiting near his fallen corpse. WoW (and some other MMORPGs) obliges dead players to run in ghost form back to their bodies to return to life, so a corpse camper intends to kill his opponent once again while weakened immediately upon resurrection and thereby to prevent him from playing or accomplishing anything in-game. Camped players can either engineer an escape, arrange assistance from allies to kill the camper (and then to camp him in revenge), or resurrect at the graveyard and incur a severe ten-minute Resurrection Sickness penalty.

As they charged, every single player's computer locked up. Buying a nicer rig wouldn't help; the servers weren't meant to handle open-world combat in large numbers, particularly in the early days, so at the moment of contact everyone involved saw the game's intricate animations just *stop*. You'd see one or two frames of action per second, characters popping in and out of vision, spell effects hanging frozen in midair or detonating explosively on empty air. You'd mash your abilities, try to target enemies or heal friendlies, fail for the most part, and eventually the game would tell you (without preamble, warning, or even the perception of being damaged) that your character had died. It always seemed as though you were the only one suffering this terrible lag, only you struggling to cast while everyone else battled freely, but of course that wasn't true. It didn't work for anyone. When you fell, you'd make the corpse run, pop up next to an enemy healer, and try to drop her before dying once again. Each death increased the amount of time before resurrection was allowed, so after a while most players ended up just standing around in ghost form waiting on extended, five-minute resurrection timers, unable to coordinate anything beyond the occasional mass rez and a frantic pile-on following.

It was not, by any traditional metric, *fun*. And yet the chaos was intoxicating, the battles thrilling for their sheer scale if not their mechanics. It was also the only game in town. Anyone who wanted to fight the opposing faction in any setting other than individual gank attempts—anyone who wanted on-demand PvP play—had to go to Tarren Mill. If it was frustrating, it also represented a kind of purity. In its very silliness and disorganization, the total absence of any material incentives, the Tarren Mill melee was spontaneous and authentic and free, assembled by accidents replicated across every server in the world. The players created and owned and maintained it even at the cost of crippling lag and server outages. This dysfunctional free-for-all was play in its purest form.

As an alternative, weekends and evenings saw gank squads roaming in and around Blackrock Mountain, seeking each other out for tight tactical battles. Enterprising folks used message boards and voice chat to organize five-on-five tournaments with their enemies. Friends partied up and adventured out into the wilds with no other plan than "looking for trouble." That sounds great on the page, and I'm on the record with my affection for unstructured play, but in practice you'd often spend hours poking around fruitlessly.

April 2005 saw the release of the Honor System, Blizzard's first attempt at codifying PvP into a genuine game system as opposed to a charming quirk of the rules. Suddenly players received "contribution points" (CP) for killing members of the opposing faction, so long as they didn't outlevel their targets by too much. Killing players far below your level gave no honor, though it also incurred no sanction. The time-honored MMORPG tradition of slaughtering lowbies without consequence remained intact. Harshly punitive "dishonorable kills" were handed out only for kills of certain NPCs stationed in enemy towns—quest-giving NPCs, whose deaths stymied players' ability to quest and play even if they chose to avoid PvP. Honorable kills earned you a few CP while dishonorable kills cost you thousands. At the end of every week, when the server reset for maintenance, every player on each faction was assigned a rank based on her total CP and number of kills. There were fourteen ranks in total, starting at Private (Alliance) and Scout (Horde) and culminating respectively in Grand Marshal and High Warlord, each granting access to a higher tier of PvP-themed rewards. Blizzard's designers had learned a great deal about players' equipment needs, and so the Honor System's rewards were quite appealing from the outset. Superior-quality armor at the lower ranks yielded to epic gear at higher ranks, along with special rewards like a 10 percent discount from friendly vendors (rank 3) and discounted epic mounts (rank 11). Sitting at rank 14 was an assortment of the best offensive weapons in the entire game. If you were a class heavily reliant on damage-dealing weapons (warriors, rogues, hunters), you swooned at the thought of wielding one.*

---

* Even the best raiding weapons didn't measure up. Molten Core and Blackwing Lair offered fine weapons with higher headline DPS than their PvP equivalents, but the rank 14 weapons had the advantage of speed—or rather, the lack of it. Warrior, rogue, and hunter special attacks

The trick was getting it. The Honor System wasn't an objective grind, where gradually amassing a set number of kills and CP unlocked rewards. When it came to PvP, Blizzard graded on a curve. A player's weekly CP was compared to everyone else on her faction, and new ranks were handed out based on that comparison combined with a flat 20 percent weekly decay rate. Only a certain percentage of the total player base could hold a given rank at a time. This made climbing to the top a measure less of skill than raw dedication. Outplaying your opponents was neither sufficient nor even necessary; you had to *outwork* them. You had to continue outworking them, day after day, week after week, gradually sifting your way toward the top of the enormous heap. Reading this, you might guess competition would simply push everyone toward more and more grinding, more and more hours, sweeping up entire servers into a brutal race to nowhere. You would be correct.

THE ULTIMATE GRIND

Reaching rank 14 in the vanilla Honor System (reigning from patch 1.4.0 in April 2005 to patch 2.0.1 in December 2006) was the single most difficult accomplishment in the history of *WoW*, and nothing else came close. Even the most difficult raid boss can be dropped with fifteen minutes of intense focus, provided you've got the gear for it. If you haven't, farm easier bosses until you get the gear and then drop the hard boss. PvE goals, as I've asserted more than once already, are made to be reached at your own pace. Every guild on the server can kill a raid boss if they want to, but the vanilla Honor System allowed in most cases *only one rank 14 player per faction!* Blizzard gated the ranks so harshly that it forced players into relentless competition with everyone else on the server. Take a week off (say, for a family vacation) and you lost several weeks' worth of progress. Take even a single day off and you'd fall behind everyone who hadn't taken that

---

were largely calculated based on the damage of a single weapon swing, thus favoring slower weapons dealing more damage per swing. Later patches normalized these calculations against a relatively fast baseline speed, making fast weapons more competitive.

day off, which might be OK for a rank 11 grind but would *never* get you to rank 14. To reach rank 14, you had to amass more CP than absolutely everyone on the entire server, but that wasn't enough. The system also gated the amount of rank players could gain in any given week, forcing them to slowly grind past every single player above them at every single rank. Progress might be faster or slower depending on how much the competition played, so you never really knew when you'd worked enough until the moment of truth Tuesday morning. Competitive PvPers stood their ground at Tarren Mill until the last moment, hacking away until the servers went down. Neither death nor victory swayed them; there was only CP.

Those ascending the ranks found the going ever steeper the higher they climbed. Though Tarren Mill offered on-demand action any hour of the day or night, you never got more than a fraction of the credit for any given kill, because so many others were involved. What's more, successive kills of the same player suffered diminishing returns: a 10 percent drop in CP ending at zero. It didn't pay to hunt in the same place for long. PvPers spent endless hours ganking, catching other high-level players alone on their way to dungeons and slaughtering them before help could arrive. Needless to say, most who advanced were the powerful damage-dealing classes already attracted to the rank 14 weapons. A skilled warrior or rogue could consistently take down other players one-on-one and handle the occasional two-on-one. A healer made her even more deadly; the pair of them might even, under the right conditions, ambush a full five-man party and walk away victors. Often the healer, so as not to siphon off CP, would operate un-partied and would avoid launching attacks at their target.

This state of affairs persisted for only two months, until June 2005. Nobody had yet reached rank 14 when PvP was upended forever by the release of *WoW*'s first two battlegrounds: Warsong Gulch (10 versus 10), tucked at the border of the Barrens and Ashenvale, and Alterac Valley (40 versus 40) up in the mountains above Tarren Mill. Arathi Basin (15 versus 15) followed in September. Instead of contestable open-world battle zones as the designers had first conceived, battlegrounds were instanced, like dungeons. PvP underwent an instantaneous and fundamental change in character: no longer was it linked to the game world. What had occurred exclusively in the persistent, open world now raged in countless private instances. Though each battleground ostensibly involved a pivotal conflict over territory, no territory ever changed hands. Nothing was ever truly resolved.

Alterac Valley in particular could barely be described as PvP, since it revolved around the killing of NPCs to claim objectives, and matches could drag on for hours. It replaced the Tarren Mill tug-of-war for the most part, though die-hards could often be found tussling in the fields. But it wasn't good for grinding CP, because you were stuck killing the same forty people over and over.

Warsong Gulch and Arathi Basin offered better prospects. Diminishing returns applied just the same, but these battlegrounds (the former a capture-the-flag format, the latter a contest for control of five strategic points) ran much faster. A practiced unit could snatch and capture three flags or secure five points in a matter of minutes, earning a fat stack of bonus CP in the process. In fact, the bonus honor from a victorious Warsong or Arathi match usually doubled the honor from kills in that match. Quickly banging out victories in the smaller battlegrounds became the best strategy for amassing honor. An arms race was on, not only to develop the best tactics but also to simply outproduce the opposition. It wasn't enough to be a great player with an iron will to grind sixteen hours per day. Anyone seriously attempting rank 14 needed a crew of similarly dedicated players to help him win battlegrounds. The grind revealed an organizational angle, forcing players to win the loyalties of other talented PvPers so they could rise through the ranks. At any given time on any given faction of any given server, there might have been a half-dozen contenders for rank 14, each with his own team, banging out battleground wins as fast as possible and dashing from the battleground exit to try to pick up a few ganks before the next round. Every hour and every minute were precious, twenty-four of the former never enough if everyone has access to them.

Top PvPers spent more time grinding than anyone else, and their grinding was the hardest kind. Raiders spent their downtime on resource harvesting, gold farming, and other pursuits that ultimately came down to knowing where to get these things and possessing the patience to kill and skin each and every one of a thousand yetis if you needed to. PvPers fought other human beings of equivalent level, with only the advantage of talent and perhaps superior gear. If anything a pure PvPer was at a gear disadvantage compared to PvE raiders, unless he himself raided on the side. Even so, once he reached rank 12 or 13 he'd probably have to stop raiding, committing totally to the battleground grind. Someone else was always working harder.

I had one guildmate make a serious attempt at rank 14—Slipo, our guild's *patron* and a man relentless in pursuit of his goals. Normally he didn't play much, but rank 14 became an obsession. After every raid we'd band together with him and fight a dozen rounds in Arathi Basin, winning every one with our coordination and Blackwing Lair gear. When the last of us went to bed Slipo would keep on playing through the night, logging eighteen to twenty hours per day. He took vacation from the company he'd built to focus on this singular chase. His commitment was almost painful to watch, and that's why the rest of us worked so hard to help him, to honor his very real sacrifice. He succeeded after months of agony, so burned out that in the year following he barely played at all, leaving those spectacular weapons to collect dust.

With the stakes so high and the demands so steep, top PvPers on many servers recognized the endless, fruitless race they'd gotten stuck running. It was a bit like the Internet writing economy: a gaggle of talented individuals engaged in such intense mutual competition that they burned themselves out without actually getting ahead. Needing to break the cycle, community leaders on more than a few servers hit on a brilliant solution: they'd form a cartel.

A cartel is an association of businesses formed for the purpose of controlling asset prices or otherwise restricting competition within a market. Both the economics profession and the general public hold the concept to be generally negative, the former because of market-centered ideology and the latter because of the word's association with murderous Central American drug lords. *WoW*'s PvP cartels, let me assure you, did their murdering entirely within the game. Their leaders used the publicly available honor rankings to contact their faction's top PvPers and offered them simple terms: everyone ground a set quota of CP every week, descending according to her place on the list, ensuring that everyone gained rank without upsetting the overall structure of the list. When the number-one player on the list hit rank 14, she picked up her rank 14 rewards and immediately stopped grinding, ensuring she'd drop back to 13 the next week. This wasn't exactly a hard sell once she'd reached the mountaintop and earned the rewards— almost nobody who reached rank 14 held that position for longer than a few weeks anyway. The number-two player became the new number one, ground out the appropriate quota of CP, and waited for the following Tuesday. Number three became number two, and so on.

In this way, the cartel ensured a smooth and orderly line of succession. Players weren't left grinding twenty-one hours a day to beat out someone grinding twenty. Instead they produced their weekly quota of CP (still very substantial to stay above anyone outside the cartel) and waited their turn at rank 14. Finishing below your quota was fine—if you lost ground on the list, you'd just wait a few more weeks—but exceeding your quota was grounds for an immediate blacklisting. Nobody associated with the cartel would group with you for battlegrounds anymore, cutting you off from the skilled teammates necessary to succeed. Not every server had honor cartels and not everyone abided by their rules, but they went a long way toward civilizing what had become a genuinely inhumane process. The simplistic appeal of Blizzard's early Honor System should be obvious, but they badly underestimated their players' competitive fervor.

OFFENSE: A TRAGEDY IN THREE ACTS

The server Detheroc opened along with the original flight of PvP servers at *WoW*'s launch. Named after a demon from *Warcraft III*, it never attracted many players. However capriciously players picked their servers at the launch, an accelerating dynamic soon emerged: those servers with established and successful guilds attracted more players, fueling those guilds and further waves of fresh rerolls until Blizzard had to lock them. Detheroc suffered from the opposite effect: nobody ever put together a really successful organization, so ambitious players rerolled elsewhere. It was an invisible little backwater.

That very fact made it an appealing destination for a particular clutch of friends. They'd started playing *WoW* to do battle with their fellow players and found a home in the Alliance guild Retribution on the Arthas server. In time Retribution became famous for their hardcore raiding exploits, and this group of friends felt disenchanted. They weren't having fun anymore, spending all their time on PvE rather than PvP. Rather than quit the game entirely, they rerolled to Detheroc for the opening of battlegrounds with a plan: assemble the greatest PvP guild on the server, an unbreakable squadron of elite badasses capable of dominating the realm. Shunning PvE pursuits, they promised each other never to go back to raiding. A warrior by the name of Intrepid led them.

It worked. Naming their new guild Offense, the friends quickly leveled to 60 and began accumulating PvP gear. They found their Horde opponents spirited but woefully disorganized—an ideal combination, as they were easily defeated but continued to gamely queue up for the massacres, feeding CP to Offense. As for their fellow Alliance, they deferred to the acknowledged finest players on the server. Offense won so much, they needed no cartel. Though his character hadn't even existed on Detheroc at the Honor System's inception, Intrepid became the server's first Grand Marshal. The next seven Grand Marshals and ten of the Alliance's first twelve were Offense players. It was a viciously efficient engine for minting rank 14 players. Offense hummed along, harmonious, universally victorious, and might have remained so for a very long time had it not been for the unforeseeable intrusion of outside forces. Detheroc's low population status inspired Blizzard to name the server as a destination for free character transfers from the high-population Sargeras server. Many players, sick of the crowding and latency and login queues that came with life on a popular realm, took them up on the offer. Hundreds immigrated, including entire guilds who'd debated the possibility for months beforehand. One of those guilds was T K T.

We landed on the shores of Detheroc as conquerors. That was half the appeal: after the cutthroat competition and overcrowded cities of Sargeras, Detheroc promised a whole new world to ravage. The first night, we stood en masse atop the broad-roofed bank in Orgrimmar's central plaza bedecked in our finery, dancing or hopping in circles around homemade campfires.* The "natives" could barely believe their eyes. Nobody on Detheroc wore raiding epics, certainly no one in the Horde. To settle in we assembled our best ten PvPers into a Warsong Gulch squad; after a few easy victories over randomly assembled pickup groups, we hit a snag. These Alliance were geared like the previous PUGs—PvP reward armor, crafted weapons—but they were clearly superior players. Their leader, a night elf warrior, wielded a modest Arcanite Reaper, yet under his ferocious lunging attacks we suffered our first casualties of the night. The moment we showed distraction they pounced, snatching the flag from under our noses and using a swift-footed druid to cap it before we could respond. This was no PUG; it was a premade group made up of members of Offense.

We won in the end, using Chris's raid-earned tanking gear, rendering him effectively immune to their melee-based attacks. We faced them again, and in the next round they brought a swarm of mages using superbly coordinated Pyroblasts to fry Chris in his armor—that is, until we switched to the fire resistance gear we'd spent months farming for use in certain raid encounters. Anything they threw at us, no matter how inventive or exactly executed, we could counter

---

* For those who didn't play *WoW,* know that the roof of a bank was a perfectly normal place to host parties. It may not be permitted in your municipality.

with gear. I posted obnoxious trash talk on the realm forums; Offense responded with all appropriate venom, and a rivalry was born. It was a fun night.

Of course, the rivalry was hopelessly one-sided. Even T K T's second-string Warsong Gulch squad could work Offense like a speed bag, again by simple dint of gear. They'd still have no problem out-grinding the rest of the Alliance faction, securing their Grand Marshals, but overnight their dominance over the server had ended. Epic PvP rewards only took them so far. Blizzard's focus on the PvE scene had created an environment where even the best PvP gear couldn't keep up with raiding epics. One side of the game was built around constant measured progression as rewards for specific tasks; the other, unstructured fun. Unfortunately, neither could be extricated from the other. Where both met, PvP was clearly the lesser.

So Offense started raiding. The activity they'd rerolled to get away from, the one thing they swore they'd never do, they did. Without better gear, they'd always live under our boot. They had no choice. Having already cleared the Molten Core in their previous lives, they advanced quickly, but divisions immediately surfaced. Not everyone agreed with the choice to raid. Even those that did chafed at the surge of recruitment—diluting what had been a small and tightly knit cadre—and the new recruits, once they felt they'd proved themselves, looked none too kindly on the officers' habit of awarding themselves the best loot. Skins and patience wore thin. How could it be otherwise? The guild was operating counter to its very purpose. What they envisioned as a temporary catching-up project stretched longer into Blackwing Lair, and those of us in the Horde watched with a mix of amusement and pity as one core member after another took his leave. While their roster spots were easily filled, Offense was hemorrhaging talent. We awaited, then received, the inevitable news: the great warrior Intrepid had retired from *WoW*. Barely six months after Detheroc received the transfers, the finest native guild she would ever see, Offense, was dead—beaten from without, driven into extinction like flightless island-dwelling birds.

"Are You Not Entertained?"

Offense's story isn't unique. More than a few awesome guilds found themselves forced into the PvE raiding business for the sake of loot and were irrevocably warped by the ensuing compromises. Those tragedies reflected not flaws of the guilds or their players but the fact that Blizzard had promised two games and delivered only one. A huge portion of the player base picked up *WoW* specifically to play PvP, and yet exactly two years from launch (November 2006) that side of the game remained frankly incomplete. The Honor System rewarded those of high rank, but few players could stomach the grind and many others didn't find the rewards compelling. Even the vaunted rank 14 weapons aged poorly, as Ahn'Qiraj and Naxxramas offered new and better rewards, while the PvP weapons stayed just the same. Normalizing weapon speeds rendered them even more obsolete as faster PvE weapons gained ground. If ever the grind had been worthwhile, that time was past. Serious PvPers grumbled, played endless battlegrounds, and bided their time for the promised arena system.

The Burning Crusade, the game's first retail expansion, introduced players to a brand-new continent and raised the level cap to 70, bringing with it a slew of balance changes, redesigned spells and talents, new professions, and everything else typically associated with a forty-dollar MMORPG expansion, including PvP arenas. For the first time, there existed a formalized system for small-group combat—one that emphasized skill, reflexes, and tactics over gear and application of numbers. Sorted into two-versus-two, three-versus-three, and five-versus-five brackets, the arena system matched teams of roughly equivalent skill and placed them into one of several small, confined instances. Teams had a short while to prepare and buff themselves before two gates opened and each spilled into the arena proper. The resulting battles could last fifty seconds or more than an hour, though most finished in ten minutes or less. Once one team was entirely defeated, the match ended, awarding rating points to the victors and subtracting them from the losers.

Blizzard also made subtle yet fundamental changes to *WoW*'s PvP gameplay. Every expansion brings big changes, but for PvP *The Burning Crusade* brought totally new mechanics. First and most important was "resilience," a stat attached to gear like critical strike chance or haste, but one that *only* applied in PvP. Resilience reduced both a player's chance to be critically struck and the damage done by those critical strikes; since monsters in *WoW* cannot critically strike, resilience was useless in a PvE context. At the same time, resilience was an obviously and immensely valuable stat in PvP. A character in full PvE gear might deal incredible damage, but against a PvP-geared opponent she'd find her attacks falling short while he tore right through her. Raiding gear now performed poorly in PvP, and the converse was also true. Blizzard had solved a huge problem that had been dogging their designers for years, but in so doing they had introduced an artificial divide to their game world where none had previously existed. It used to be that gear was gear, regardless of its provenance, but now for the first time its power depended explicitly on where your character was, what your character was doing. Artificial borders appeared in what purported to be an open world. Arenas were subject to other rules not present in either the game world or battlegrounds: potions and just about every other kind of consumable item were outlawed, along with certain trinkets.* Abilities with cooldowns longer than ten minutes were disabled entirely. Players from the same faction, for the very first time in *WoW*'s history outside a declared duel, could battle each other. Arenas were their own separate universe, divided and treated apart from the rest of the game. This was a big departure, because instances to that point (battlegrounds and dungeons alike) had all been subject to the same rules. For arenas, competitive balance trumped all. If world PvP suffered as a consequence, the designers were willing to live with it.

---

* An avatar in *World of Warcraft* employs armor on her head, chest, legs, hands, and so on. She also wields a weapon. She wears a necklace and up to two rings. She may also equip up to two "trinkets," which are essentially minor baubles with major powers. Trinkets don't boost your stats to the degree of armor or a weapon, but they often include unique and useful powers. For most of *WoW*'s history, the single most popular trinket was the so-called "PvP trinket," which allowed players to remove disabling effects imposed by other players. If a rogue stunned you or a mage turned you into a sheep, a PvP trinket allowed you to turn the tables.

The experiment worked. Arenas were wildly popular from their introduction, and Blizzard's new PvP reward system impressed everyone from casuals to the most hardcore. The new gear was *good*, the weapons in particular. Playing a mere ten arena games per week in a given bracket qualified you to receive arena points, a currency redeemable for the aforementioned excellent gear. Higher rating yielded more arena points each week, but even a low-ranked player could eventually hoard enough to buy epic items. Blizzard also introduced better gear with time, coordinated to regular resets of the leaderboards. They called the periods between resets "seasons," in keeping with traditional sports jargon, and each new season brought improved gear. The newest and best gear (weaponry in particular) was always restricted to high-rated players, but anyone could buy the prior season's gear. Even if you were terrible at PvP and only played a handful of arena games each week, you could slowly accumulate a set of competitive gear. If you were really good, you'd enjoy the finest rewards on a comfortable schedule, and at the end of the season you'd get one of several highly prestigious "Gladiator" titles to stick in front of your name.* Arenas established the PvP side of *WoW* as every bit the competitive equal of PvE raiding—parity they've maintained ever since.

And yet from a certain perspective, that's the whole problem. Head-to-head gaming has always been about competition, not achievement. Competing against another human being yields a kind of pure, guiltless joy that reaches across almost any human divide. No matter your preferred play style or activities in *WoW*, at some point along the way you engaged in PvP. It may have been a gank attempt, but the moment you rezzed back up you went looking to get even. PvP was about feelings, about pride, about competition. Prior to *The Burning Crusade*, nobody did it for gear; except for the

---

* No sarcasm here. Gladiator titles were coveted like few other rewards in the game, and winning one accorded you instant respect with anyone you met. People paid hundreds of dollars under the table for great PvPers to help them reach that lofty height. I missed "Gladiator" by the smallest of margins during season 2, and falling short was so devastating I never seriously played arenas again. It haunts me to this day.

early days of the rank 14 weapons, there were no fabulous rewards to get. In a game built around the treadmill of constant gear acquisition, PvP always stood apart. Pushing players toward standardized sets of PvP gear ran philosophically counter to everything else in the World of Warcraft, which may be why the developers keep tinkering with the reward system. From rank-based gating in vanilla to tiered currencies of honor and arena points in *The Burning Crusade* to conquest points in *Cataclysm*, through countless tweaks to weekly quotas and rollover policies between expansions, Blizzard has never seemed satisfied with their PvP system.

Cataclysm's "rated battlegrounds" livened up a small corner of the community but never amounted to a major change. A dragon dropping a chest of mystery loot is a satisfying end to an epic adventure. Waking up Tuesday morning to find you now have 1,812 conquest points and turning in 1,750 of them to a vendor for a new pair of gloves . . . well, it doesn't feel quite the same. Grinding endless battlegrounds against faceless foes from other realms becomes a miserable slog. It's especially frustrating when competing against others with superior PvP gear, as they slaughter you without much effort. The only way to accumulate a functional kit is to get flattened over and over again in arenas and battlegrounds, scraping together enough weekly points to trudge your glacial way to respectability. It is not fun, or anything close to fun, especially given that *WoW*'s roots in PvE created permanently terrible conditions for PvP. Whether via stun, fear, snare, or root, just about every significant ability in the game involves removing avatars from their players' control. Crippling the only part of the game world you control is like losing mastery of your own body. It's viscerally unpleasant; it's atrocious game design. When attacked by a rogue, for example, a player can expect to spend the first five to six seconds of the encounter just watching himself get pounded on. If the rogue makes a mistake, he may have an opportunity to respond, but more likely he will die without ever mounting anything like a functional response. Needless to say, this is fun only for the rogue. Attempting to use most classes in *WoW* PvP feels like being a participant in a game for someone else's amusement.

The *Legion* expansion brought yet another overhaul: this time, an attempt to mitigate the advantages of gear. As in the past, PvP instances (battlegrounds and arenas) would simply be subject to special rules. Once *Legion*'s changes took root, players who zoned into PvP instances found that the statistics on their gear were automatically adjusted for the duration of their stay—enough to render players at the top and bottom of progression roughly equivalent in power. The game even redistributes the certain stats to match preset values; a player who tries to stack Critical Strike or Haste may find her gear instead provides Mastery and Versatility, which she may not value as highly. At the same time, the progression system is based on popular online action games like the *Call of Duty* and *Battlefield* series: PvP play unlocks small but functional perks, along with ascending ranks based on experience. Additional perks can be earned by reaching the top rank and then voluntarily resetting back to the bottom; doing so repeatedly thus feeds (the designers hope) an endlessly rewarding cycle of effervescent, lightweight competition. Unscripted world PvP all but died out in the age of ample quick-travel paths and flying mounts and empty leveling zones. *Legion* refocused players on open-world content, and cross-realm zoning automatically brings players from different servers together in open areas. Certain quests directly encourage PvP outside of battlegrounds and arenas. The expansion served as an honest attempt to return this side of the game to its simpler roots.

SUPERSTAR ATHLETES

Blizzard's arena designers always had the e-sports scene in mind. They knew, from the mammoth and ongoing success of the professional gaming scene behind their real-time strategy game *StarCraft*, that e-sports were big business with international reach. And while a few raiding guilds managed to get themselves sponsored by this or that mouse manufacturer, you can't build an exciting entertainment product off twenty people collectively solving a puzzle. You need head-to-head competition between the very best players, at least some of whom (you hope) prove to be marketable stars. Teams of two, three, or five in a single arena fit all the action at once in a single frame, as opposed to many other e-sports that force the camera to jump around constantly. Arenas let audiences focus on individual play while also keeping a single unified field of vision, the way live sports are filmed with cameras distant enough to show all the players at once.

The community instantly took to them. Play at the highest levels was ruthlessly competitive, every advantage pursued relentlessly, every win and loss shaking up the standings. Vicious flame wars played out on the official forums. To win among the elite you had to run the right team compositions with the right gear and the right tactics—anything less and you'd get smoked. Websites like Arena Junkies broke everything down, sifting through team records and compositions, hosting endless debates over the finer points of rogue talent builds. After Blizzard divided their hundreds of realm servers into roughly a dozen "battle groups" for matchmaking purposes,* competition emerged both within and between them, each jostling for the title of the most elite battle group, until the Internet's hive mind collectively decided on battle group 9. At that point, the server cluster's reputation attracted a continuous stream of aspirational PvP rerolls and transfers until many of the game's best individual players *were* in fact in "BG9." They tended to congregate on the Tichondrius server, and it was from this crop of players that *WoW* promoted its first wave of stars.

In March 2007 North American pro gaming outfits Team Pandemic and Check-Six announced their acquisitions of the world's number-one and number-two rated five-versus-five teams. *WoW* as an e-sport was officially born, and even more sponsors were drawn to the action. Those who played at the time will doubtless recognize

---

* This change was made late in vanilla *WoW* as a solution to the lengthy battleground queues that had emerged on many low-population servers. Cross-server matchmaking offered a healthy population of opponents no matter the time of day or night.

names like Noktyn, Nitrana, Kintt, and Sck—the anchors of Pandemic's squad, who dominated at the World Series of Video Games in Wuhan, China. In three-versus-three games they won just the same, clearing their way through early tournaments before ultimately losing at BlizzCon 2007 to MoB Turtlebeach following the disqualification of crucial priest player Kintt.*

Competitions outside of BlizzCon's restrictive rules saw Pandemic back on top. Just when the community had started to question itself about a future dominated by a single team, the WSVG organization imploded. It simply couldn't make ends meet. Planned events across North America were canceled overnight, and the professional scene went briefly quiet. No tournaments took place until the end of the year, when the European gaming gathering DreamHack hosted a three-versus-three tournament.

In a strange turn, only teams from the old WSVG could qualify, and so DreamHack saw spectacular matches between Turtlebeach and Pandemic. The former beat the latter in early rounds, but the double-elimination format allowed Pandemic to claw their way back up through the loser's bracket for a rematch in the finals. Pandemic's classic rogue/mage/priest squad beat MoB's attrition-based hunter/warlock/shaman team and reclaimed the number-one spot. I watched it streaming live and was riveted. Every match was a delicate balance of crowd control, pulverizing damage, and miraculous escapes as characters squeaked behind cover to avoid killing blows. Their coordination was magical to watch, all the more so because it *seemed* so accessible. This was the same game I played, after all, the same software with the same spells and gear. When LeBron James or Cristiano Ronaldo does something incredible, it makes sense. They're chiseled titans, winners of the genetic lottery, and so naturally they should do these things. A pro video gamer's anticipation and reflexes—learned

---

* Kintt, as a non-US resident, was not eligible to participate in the tournament. This kind of oversight was fairly common in the early days. For example, though one of the key skills available to hunters is the ability to train a wide variety of pets to aid them in combat, the tournament only permitted them to use a bear as their pet, despite the bear being terrible in PvP.

behavior, really—denies the rest of us the easy excuse of talent and genes. They simply *decided* to be better at something, then went out and did it.

In early 2008 Blizzard announced all ongoing professional arena tournaments would be confined to the three-versus-three bracket. Five-versus-five was too chaotic for viewers, too prone to one-sided games. Two-versus-two was simply boring, a victim of *WoW*'s perpetually imperfect class balance. Every team ran one healer and one DPS; every match dragged on and on until one healer ran out of mana or committed a fatal error. So three-versus-three it would be, spread across four summer tournaments to be hosted by Major League Gaming (MLG). The promised money and attention attracted a fresh crop of sponsors eager to sign the winners. Entrants would not be selected battle group by battle group as before but by a series of qualifying rounds on a special Tournament Realm accessible for a one-time payment of twenty dollars. The Tournament Realm represented another fundamental leap for *WoW*: it divorced competitive players from their personal avatars.

Since time immemorial, MMORPGs bound players to avatars. You had access to one in-game representation of yourself at a time. Alts and rerolls had to be leveled and geared by hand, making them authentic if nonexclusive representations of the self. A max-level character existed because a real human being poured hundreds of hours into it, and that gave every one you saw in-game a certain weight. They left a wake in the game world, tracks on the road, depressions in local space-time like marbles set on a freshly made bedsheet. The Tournament Realm vaporized that idea, at least for competitive PvP. Arenas had already taken the first conceptual step by attempting to standardize gear, but the Tournament Realm let anyone create a max-level character of any class with a full set of epic PvP gear and jump instantly into combat. Players were limited only by their personal capability. For hardcore arena players it was ideal, but it represented another step away from the traditional MMORPG model of open and persistent worlds. Faction, geography, role-playing—everything but the meta-game* went out the window. Someone might play a certain class more than others, might even be renowned for playing that class, but the moment he felt a different matchup might better help his team, a new max-level character with full epic gear was just seconds away. These characters weren't avatars. They served as nothing more than precisely manufactured instruments.

Ultimately, *WoW* as e-sport never caught on to the degree its promoters hoped. The three-versus-three arena bracket has persisted to this day at BlizzCon and Major League Gaming events, but by the release of the fourth expansion, *Mists of Pandaria*, the scene had largely died out. Exactly why this happened has been the topic of much theorizing online, centered most compellingly around *WoW*'s intimidating entry barrier. Someone wanting to play *League of Legends* can download the game and be playing in minutes, and it will be immediately recognizable as the same game the pros play. Someone wanting to play *WoW* has to buy the game, pay for a subscription, spend weeks leveling a character and months gearing that character before even setting foot in a competitive arena. So the pro scene has continued in its diminished form as the arena seasons roll along on the live servers—eighteen by this writing, with many more to come. Professional gaming careers are short, and anyone with that inclination starting today will pick another game.

E-sports stars often struggle for recognition. Traditional athletes appear on our televisions in the flesh; protective gear may hide their faces but still we can picture Adrian Peterson's pulverizing runs, his upright gait and windmilling arms. We are only bodies, after all, and our brains are built to recognize the human form. Video game competitions obscure the body in favor of the avatar, the camera cutting only occasionally to shots of the human participants, no voices heard except perhaps some paltry postgame words, mumbled and rote. If you're an e-sports star, millions of people instantly recognize

---

* Since online games exist in a state of constantly rebalanced flux, "meta-game" refers to the Internet-accepted best practices at any given moment. Open up a game's sub-Reddit and you'll figure it out in a hurry.

your handle, but you will never be recognized (outside of South Korea) on the street, and even serious fans couldn't pick you out of a lineup. For the few who reach a higher level of fame, whose face and personality supplant their avatars in the public mind, it can be more curse than blessing.

THE STORY OF HAFU

Rumay Wang was born in 1991 to immigrant parents in Massachusetts and for some sixteen years enjoyed an unremarkable suburban upbringing. The event that catalyzed her development into one of the world's most recognizable gamers was itself painfully normal: a bout of mononucleosis her freshman year, inflaming her spleen and laying her up for months. As she explains, "I started getting these really high fevers, and my parents—the Chinese way is to sweat the fever out, so they put like six comforters on top of me . . . and they all went out to dinner, and when they came back they drove me to the emergency room. And they just put an icepack on me and said, 'She should take a *cold* shower,' and my parents are like, 'Oh, that's the opposite of what we did.' I think they said I was half a degree from having brain damage. They figured out it was mono and I kinda skipped two months of school. I just stayed home and played *WoW*." She sunk her ample time and limited energy into a druid named Hafu.

For all the hours invested, she still saw the game as little more than a venue for having fun with friends from school. That changed when she found herself suddenly and rudely excluded from a friend's two-versus-two arena team—in part, she suspected, due to her gender. Arenas hit her as a rude awakening: "It was really sad. The first week, they actually ended up being second in the battle group, and I got like two hundredth with random people. . . . I couldn't have been that bad, but I wasn't great, and I definitely remember them being second and me being way back there at two or three hundred. And I was just so *salty*, about them not letting me play with them, and I was like 'I'm definitely going to beat them.' Which meant I had to be number one. I didn't know I was that competitive a person, but from that point it was just the mission."

It wouldn't come overnight. "I knew exactly what druids did, but I didn't know that [much] about the other classes, and I didn't know what they were trying to accomplish when I played them. So I started dueling every single class to figure out what their spells did, what their combos were . . . I just dueled everyone until I stopped losing to everyone. Like, no one could kill me. I learned to [chain the actions] PvP trinket–Kidney Shot instead of Cheap Shot, PvP trinket–Intercept instead of Charge. There were no streams back then," she recalls, referencing the popular and lucrative phenomenon of watching high-level players do their work online through streaming video services like Twitch. "There were, like, really shitty guides online . . . once I did actually piece out what every class would do against me specifically, I could really figure out in a 2v2 setting what was going wrong. And from there I just stopped losing. I enjoyed winning and getting better and every time I lost figuring out what I can do better to beat this team next time. It always felt mentally engaging, and I never really got that from school, so it's the first time I felt challenged."

She was hooked. Before long she found herself at the top of her battle group, and after a transfer to the infamous Tichondrius server of battle group 9 she summited its rankings as well. Restoration druids were enjoying a *moment*, as they say, having been massively buffed since their feeble vanilla days. Their mobility and resistance to spell interrupts made them the best all-purpose healers in every arena bracket, but in professional *WoW* everyone had access to the class. Hafu was just a teenager and still better than the rest, though she felt she benefitted from early attention by virtue of being one of very few women in the scene.

Her team's success on the Tournament Realm led to her first paid gig in gaming—Hafu's first real job. Team Orz, her warrior-warlock-druid trio, became the e-sports story of 2008. Alongside teammates Rhaegyn and Glick, the unproven squad took first place at MLG Orlando in July and third at the Intel Extreme Masters tournament in August. They rode the hype to a phenomenal October, finishing first at MLG Dallas and third at BlizzCon, and Hafu garnered much of the attention. Much as she tried to share credit with her teammates and professional as the broadcasters were, e-sports are creatures of the online audience, and those people wanted to talk about Hafu. If her team won, it was proof her teammates carried her to success, that anyone could win in her place. If they lost, it was all her fault—the plays she could have made but failed to make, every one of them evidence she'd never deserved her lofty perch. In either case the fandom reached conveniently identical conclusions: she was there only because of her gender. *Because boobs*, as it went on the message boards. These people weren't sexist, they insisted; if their highly meritocratic process for adjudicating value just so happened to conclude the most prominent woman in the sport was a fraud regardless of her record, it was just happenstance.

It was all more than a bit ironic. Hafu was the youngest of her team and let them do most of the talking—the classic healer, preferring a background support role. In an interview with SK Gaming's website she admitted she didn't even enjoy the live tournament atmosphere: "I don't want people to watch me play, I make a lot of mistakes." She recoiled from accolades, didn't like being the center of attention, and yet the attention came. Other women played in the competitive scene and went to tournaments, but for many fans Hafu had become a fixation. Popular PvP bloggers scrutinized her play for post after post. One in particular tried to make a name for himself distributing photos of the teenage Hafu, claiming she quit her team to play with him and insinuating she slept with other members of the arena scene. Needless to say, these posts junctioned nicely with the idea that the e-sports media promoted Hafu solely for being a woman. All the basic elements of the latter-day "Gamergate" saga were in place, but in 2008 nobody in the mainstream media paid any attention to that particular nook of the Internet.

Amid the doxxings* and hackings and flame wars was lost Orz's quiet genius. In a hypercompetitive scene seeking every imaginable edge, they kept things simple and eschewed shortcuts. Most teams stopped queuing the moment they started losing games, attempting to avoid their vanquishers and thus save precious ranking points. Orz plowed through undaunted by defeat: "This new rogue-mage-priest showed up and they would shit on us seven or eight times in a row. And I actually didn't realize how good a team I had. Their attitudes were so good compared to some of the people I see today, where they start losing and start blaming everyone else and get really salty and start making excuses. But my team never really gave up. We just kept queueing into them and trying new things and we lost over a hundred points . . . eventually we learned to keep the priest Hamstrung, so I would never get feared. I could crowd control the rogue and we could work from there. And that worked out, and I think we beat them once or twice, and they started dodging us after that." Orz would face the same opponents (Frag Dominant Duelists) in the grand finals of MLG Orlando, rolling three rounds to one and more than doubling their prize money.

When warlock–shadow priest–shaman teams emerged as specific counters to teams like Orz, Hafu learned to kite and pillar-hump for the precious seconds necessary to survive their Bloodlust-fueled spell damage. "We had it down to a science, and we could still only win like 50 percent of the time." But their hard work paid off in live tournament environments, which forbid UI add-ons or mods of any kind. "They all used add-ons, and they relied on them. But none of us used in-game add-ons; we actually played perfectly fine on LAN. And we actually beat them at [North American Regionals in Boston] even though they directly countered us. And it was only because we queued against them nonstop, right?" If Orz only fought their opponents to a draw online, they could win in live competition. They didn't win every match or every tournament, but for a long while (by the standards of pro gaming) they stood atop the heap.

---

* "Doxxing" refers to the malicious online practice of revealing someone's personal information (address, phone number, place of employment, etc.) for the purpose of encouraging abuse.

Nothing lasts forever, least of all in *WoW*. The game's development frustrated many of the arena scene's top players. All sports, electronic and otherwise, need stability in their rules. Coaches and players compete, craft new schemes within the rules, and the game slowly advances. But imagine a basketball league where everything about the game itself, from the intricacies of fouling to the size of the ball and court, saw major overhauls every two years. It would struggle, yes? It would confound fans, who'd develop strong attachments to some features and despise others and bicker endlessly over them all—for Pete's sake, we're still having acrimonious discussions about the designated hitter rule. It would frustrate players, who'd find their capacities yoked to seemingly capricious changes. Well, *WoW*'s pro arena scene is exactly like that. Blizzard's never-ending development puts players at the mercy of every new patch. Nobody whose income is on the line appreciates that kind of uncertainty.

Hafu herself left competitive *WoW* early in *Wrath of the Lich King* for exactly this reason. "They never really supported PvP as a whole. I remember one tournament they literally had us play on a new patch where it was just a joke . . . suddenly we're playing with level 80 talent trees on level 70 [characters], where no one's tested anything. So it's like a brand-new game! It's not even competing . . . no one has any practice on this stuff. And I didn't expect that a tournament would be run that way, and I didn't realize back then tournaments could be unprofessional."

"Unprofessional" is the operative word. Competitive arenas attracted audiences due to *WoW*'s huge and rabid following, but Blizzard refused to allow the e-sports scene to interfere with their long-term plans for the game. They sought to retain subscribers over the long haul, and if muddled, inconsistent pro tournaments were the price, they were happy to pay. One can scarcely begrudge the developers their ultimately successful strategy, nor the players their frustration.

Fast-forward most of a decade and May Wang remains a force online. The teenager who named herself Hafu grew up and quit *WoW*, though she kept the handle and now broadcasts a popular live video stream for online games like *Hearthstone* and *League of Legends*.

She's moved from game to game and won at all of them. Though it's been a long time since she's actively competed for money, fans from across the globe tune in to watch her ongoing exploits. Their donations pay her bills, which you can manage when five or ten thousand people at a time are glued to their monitors watching you play. For someone who felt like a specimen on display at tournaments, streaming is a more controlled environment. She's more comfortable there—nearly silent during competition, Hafu chatters and laughs and curses and sings along to the music in her high-end headphones (the manufacturer is a sponsor).

But look her up on Twitch or YouTube, scan the comments, and notice people are still saying the exact same things. She cannot Tweet without incurring, within five minutes, responses leering at her teenage sex life—at least, as it exists in the fevered imaginations of awful creeps. Being quiet and deferential by nature has gotten her nowhere; Hafu's habit of verbally double-checking her choices with teammates becomes proof she knows nothing about games. Her sensitivity and open devotion to her friends (she once broke down in tears at a *Hearthstone* tournament after eliminating a teammate in solo play) feeds the sad fantasy of her sleeping around, the tired tropes of women as emotional and clingy under pressure. *Because boobs*, again, as an easy reduction. She's learned, slowly and agonizingly over many years in the spotlight, to tune it out and keep perspective. "I wish people treated other people better online, period. I see it not just toward women but, like, if someone is overweight on stream they get shit for it. And it's not just a little bit, it's endless. . . . I've heard and read the nastiest stuff, all of it, and I've never had anyone say anything close to that in person, and I've been to many, many events. There will always be people who appreciate what you do, and [I try to] focus on this."

The Internet hasn't changed a bit, it's just gotten bigger. Like a cracked ballpoint, it's bled ever more into the rest of our lives, because what began on now-defunct and largely inconsequential arena message boards is now on Twitter, on Facebook, on any number of the services we use to unify our many persistent selves. When an online identity no longer makes us happy, when it has become actively corrosive to our lives, how are we supposed to escape?

LEARNING TO WALK

Everyone leaves home in his own way. For me it started like lunar tides. I would find myself frustrated with the game and uninspired to play, logging on each night only out of obligation to my guild. The most logical response to a game you're no longer enjoying is to stop playing it, but years of investment made that difficult, and I found that if I only waited, the feeling passed. It never lasted longer than a few weeks; at some point the passion returned, ebbing up imperceptibly slowly, until I was back in love with *WoW* and playing every free moment. The down spells passed and the good times returned. After a while I stopped worrying about it.

This time it didn't pass. I was miserable and couldn't pin down exactly why. I have something of a gift for pinpointing what to complain about—to the ongoing delight of family and friends—but here I was stumped. What was making me so unhappy? It wasn't the game itself; I enjoyed arenas, battlegrounds, leveling alts, and so on. It wasn't the farming; while *The Burning Crusade* suffered terribly from an overemphasis on flasks and other consumables early on, Blizzard had by this point scaled back the busywork. It was something to do with raiding, which disturbed me, because raiding had always been my favorite part of *WoW*. Had I just burned myself out, raiding too many nights over the last few years? When I really pondered, it wasn't that either. The mechanics of healing, the pressure it packed into each global cooldown, the ruthless decision making of who gets healed and when, the thrill of interceding to save a teammate at the last possible moment, the downing of bosses and divvying of loot—it was always fun. Progression on Kael'thas or anything new felt good as ever.

The problem was, I realized at last, that there wasn't enough of that. My time was consumed not with the game itself but rather with the burdens of leadership. Marshaling twenty-five people every weeknight and organizing ten-man raids on the weekends, stressing constantly over T K T's advancement (or lack thereof), forced me to spend all my time dwelling on others' mistakes. As raid leader I was playing through other people, occupying their skulls, and it had worn me the hell out. I wasn't tired of *WoW*, just my circumstance. I didn't want to be in charge anymore, but neither could I simply step back and remain in T K T. The burdens would find their way back to me unless I swept the trail clean.

« 7 »

"TIME IS MONEY, FRIEND!"

SUMMER 2007

Principles are tricky things.

We'd all like to believe we hold them. Pop culture and cable news teach us that virtuous people live their lives according to iron-clad moral codes compromised only in the gravest of scenarios, in which case Jack Bauer is allowed to torture people. Large portions of our society are given over to the signaling of virtue, to social competitions over who can prove herself most in tune with the pre-vailing moral sentiment. For such a depraved place, the Internet is *very concerned* over who is a Good Person and who is not. Which goes a long way toward obscuring the truth that we're all just navigating circumstances as we find them: opposed to piracy until we really want to watch *Labyrinth* and it's not on Netflix, ardent advocates of public education until we spawn and find the local schools are awful. The universe makes fools and liars of us all.

For my own part, I'd always told myself I wouldn't play MMORPGs. Spending hundreds (if not thousands) of hours on digital ephemera seemed wasteful until it became the best method to keep in touch with friends a continent away. By the same token I'd told myself for years that I'd never play for another *WoW* guild besides T K T. Having rejected tempting offers during our period of strife, when my presence felt like the only thing holding the guild together, sticking it out became a point of pride. I had a pretty clear conception of myself outside of *WoW*, but I didn't know who Ghando was with-out the only guild to which he'd ever belonged. So I'd either play for

T K T or I wouldn't play at all; that was my line. But now, after more than a year of leading raids, the strain was making me miserable. It wasn't getting better on its own, and so continuing as normal wasn't an option. I'd have to quit the game.

Something kept me from doing it. I'd go about my daily raiding chores with half my mind on the after-beyond, desperate to reach it but petrified to actually say that aloud. Nobody in an MMORPG guild is more exhausting than the long-faced Eeyore always threatening to quit. If you want to quit the game, the sentiment goes, just do it and spare everyone the bellyaching. I never pulled the trigger because of the elements I still enjoyed: the fights themselves, the learning of new encounters, the frustrating but tantalizingly tangible progress from one wipe to the next. I loved the mechanics of raid healing, the ebb and flow and pulse of health bars, the furious gymnastics necessary to hold together a fight spiraling out of control. I was *really* good at what I did. I had some raiding left in the tank, I thought. I owed myself the opportunity to find a new home.

By sheer coincidence, it was at this very moment an opening emerged. As an avid reader of the Elitist Jerks forums, I kept abreast of the eponymous guild's progress via short posts on the front page. Guild leader Gurgthock, the community tribune whose incisive commentary on raid tactics and game design had already attracted acclaim and a named in-game NPC, would on rare occasions recruit through these posts. *We're looking for one Shadow Priest*—that sort of thing. As it happened, in the midst of my ennui one such post appeared: *Needing one or two healers to finish out Black Temple progression, Shaman and Priest in particular. Exceptional candidates of any class will always be considered.*

Much as I loved T K T, Elitist Jerks represented a higher standard, especially to Horde players. Without ever recording a world first, they came close enough, and did so without a heavy raiding schedule. Their contributions to the global raiding community were beyond dispute, and I'd always told myself that if I were to play for anyone else I'd play for an outfit like EJ. I wrote up an application, several pages' worth, sent it off, and returned to the staggering grind. When

I apply for anything, from schools to jobs, I try to ignore submitted bids. I assume I'll never hear anything back one way or another—in the Internet era, you're rarely worth a rejection. But two days later, Gurgthock wrote me back. He wanted to talk.

So at a prescribed time on a prescribed evening I made a fresh level 1 character on EJ's home server of Mal'ganis—the name Ghando was available—and logged in for a chat. Alone and half nude on the plains of Mulgore, hopping in circles and speaking only in whispered chat, I would have cut a strange figure for the other new characters just starting out. Gurgthock was gracious and professional throughout, agreeing to take me on while making clear that the risk and cost of transferring servers fell on me alone. If I came to Mal'ganis, there'd be no going back. I would have a chance to prove myself, but nothing was promised; EJ could reject me at any moment. I told him I understood, signed off, logged back on to the original Ghando, and did some farming before bed. I'd finalize the paid server transfer in the next few days. After a career dedicated to dogged and irrational loyalty, to the ideals of family and home, I was officially a hired gun. The only business remaining was the last post—the official announcement, the last good-bye. It made me nauseous to contemplate.

Principles, as I've said, are tricky things.

WILL HEAL FOR INTERNET PRESTIGE

We're all mercenaries of a kind. Capitalism permeates every facet of our lives, and like the proverbial fish who asks "What the hell is water?" we've ceased to question the premise. Our video games accept it tacitly—games like *EVE Online* may maintain a libertarian ethos, but nearly every MMORPG in history includes such advanced capitalistic features as banking and fiat currency. *World of Warcraft* features a straightforward and fairly controlled economy premised around classic specie: copper, silver, gold. One hundred copper coins to a silver, one hundred silver coins to a gold. For all the innovations since 2004, this has never changed. Gold enters the economy through the actions of players, who acquire it in two ways: 1) killing monsters and looting the bodies; 2) completing quests, nearly all of which offer a cash reward in addition to experience points. Non-gold resources like weapons, armor, and crafting materials accrue by similar means, and sometimes (in the case of ore and herbs) from the nodes scattered across the game world. These nodes respawn with time, as do slain monsters, so the game world provides its players a functionally infinite flow of fresh goods. Players may freely barter among themselves, but their wares must necessarily derive from the game world—they cannot conjure permanence from the ether. Most items can be sold to NPC vendors for modest sums,* but nowhere near what other players might pay for them. Individual players' incomes are limited only by their characters' ability to rapidly kill monsters and their reservoirs of free time.

Any closed system generating infinite resources eventually produces a glut, and in such a system the worth of gold over time naturally approaches zero. Older gamers may remember a world such as this in Blizzard's own *Diablo*, where every player had so much gold that it became worthless as means of exchange. To prevent this, the developers instituted a number of sinks in the system. First there were repairs: every death from monsters or the environment (excluding deaths at the hands of other players) damages a character's equipment. If sufficiently damaged it breaks, rendering the gear useless until repaired at an NPC vendor for a modest sum of gold. Even without dying, combat slowly wears down your gear and thus costs money. The amounts are small at first but can really add up, particularly if you're a raiding guild wiping over and over on new content. Players often refer to repair bills as a "raiding tax," and tanks despise the toll constant battery takes on their armor (they pay about 10 percent more as a result). Provisions like food, water, bandages, and certain crafting reagents are also bought from vendor NPCs,

---

* The price paid by a vendor NPC for any given item is more connected to the item's classification than any sense of value. Vendors pay only slightly more for rare and epic items than for mundane items, so anything valuable is best sold to another player, if possible.

and all that money vanishes permanently from the game world, as do the repair bills.

From *WoW*'s inception, rideable mounts were its biggest cash sinks. Fresh characters had to cross Azeroth's broad continents on foot, an agonizingly slow process alleviated by the introduction of the Riding skill at level 40. Moving 60 percent faster than standard foot speed was an incredible convenience, one obviously worth paying for, which is why Blizzard set its price at 90 gold coins. That was quite a figure in the vanilla days, considerably more than anyone had on hand upon reaching level 40. Personally I spent two full days at level 39 grinding monster kills to accumulate cash on top of a 20-gold loan from a friend. And I'd been frugal! After weeks of seeing higher-level characters scream by me on their cool-looking mounts, it felt amazing to join them.

A mount was more than a major convenience; it was a status symbol, setting you quite literally above the teeming masses while broadcasting to all of Azeroth that you'd been around the block. This went double for the "epic" Riding skill, which at level 60 unlocked 100 percent speed-boosted mounts for a whopping 900 gold. Saving up so much took weeks if not months of dedication, at a period when players badly needed money to upgrade their gear. *The Burning Crusade* introduced flying mounts for the Outland continent, which cost only 250 gold to fly at 150 percent speed but a whopping 5,000 gold to fly at 280 percent speed.

It was worth every penny and more. Epic flight felt like operating a jet fighter, faster and more direct than any flight path, allowing players to hover high and (mostly) safe in the sky, where no ganker could reach. It was the ultimate status symbol this side of a Legendary weapon, and probably fueled the illicit gold trade more so than any other development in *WoW*'s history—about which more later. *Wrath of the Lich King* allowed 280 percent flight on the continent of Northrend for a paltry 500 gold but made special 310 percent mounts available as rewards for cutting-edge achievements and then later charged players without those mounts another 5,000 gold for the marginal upgrade. *Cataclysm* held no big-ticket gold sink for mounts (just 250 gold) and *Mists of Pandaria* allowed flying mounts in Pandaria for 2,500—quite cheap by that point in a character's adventures. Rare mounts are now traded as vanity items, but the days of forking over your life savings for the privilege of riding at a comfortable speed are over.

Other, subtler gold sinks permeated the game in order to keep server economies from decaying under deflationary pressure. Until *Mists* allowed characters to acquire spell upgrades automatically upon leveling, they had to exchange heaps of gold every two levels in exchange for stronger versions of their spells. *Warlords of Draenor* drained thousands for upgrades to various structures in the player's new personal garrison and introduced a many-headed hydra of alternate currencies like apexis crystals and abrogator stones and seals of inevitable fate, none of which are interesting enough to explain. This comes on top of PvP honor points and PvE valor points and "badge" tokens of every description. They just offer the game's developers a host of different ways to dole out rewards, in precise increments by the hour and the day and the week. They attempt to gear you up at high speed while also carefully throttling the volume of resources you can collect, so you always have something rewarding to do but still feel you've worked for the rewards. Those who post valuables for sale on the Auction House pay a percentage tax for each successful transaction on top of flat fees just for listing. *Mists of Pandaria*'s Black Market Auction House offers highly prized vanity items, including rare mounts and old legacy gear for cosmetic transmogrifications,* for prices in the tens of thousands. All that gold vanishes from the economy, representing a vast if wholly voluntary gold sink.

But Blizzard giveth as well as taketh away! They've pumped money into the economy as well, first by increasing the gold rewards for quests and then by converting XP rewards to gold. Once a char-

---

* Transmogrification allows players to change the appearance of their gear, copying any other gear they already own. This lets your character look however you want without sacrificing power or stats. It's also pricier than you'd think, acting as a slow gold sink on top of repairs and travel costs.

acter reached max level, completing leveling quests awarded healthy sums, and players were thus incentivized to continue exploring the game world at the level cap. Daily quests awarding gold or crafting materials, repeatable every day, became commonplace. At first Blizzard permitted only ten "dailies" per character per day, but the cap was later raised to twenty-five, before being removed altogether. Sticking to a consistent, efficient routine performed every day at about the same time became the best way to stuff your pockets, and it remains so to this day. *Legion* introduced "world quests" spread across the Broken Isles that reappear every few days, pushing players to travel the game world and tackle new challenges in exchange for more diverse rewards. Recognizing *WoW*'s place as a stabilizing force in many players' lives, Blizzard encourages them to stay connected and materially rewards them for doing so. Repeatable quests contribute to gold and resource glut by an expansion's end, but they also keep players engaged and help populate the outdoor zones with active, socializing players. Distorting the market makes sense in the service of a happy, active community, particularly since nobody's taxes are going up.

Soulbinding is probably the biggest single element of economic manipulation. Since high-end gear represents the absolute most valuable items, it obviously possesses great potential to warp the game economy. With a few exceptions, *WoW* affixes powerful items to their wielders the moment they're picked up, like a benign curse preventing the item from ever changing hands. You may disassemble or destroy these items or sell them to NPC vendors, but you may never trade them to other players,* and thus for all their power their monetary value is negligible. Without this safeguard in place, entire servers would quickly become hand-me-down exchanges, and players behind the bleeding edge would face little incentive to explore new content. If you want awesome gear, you must get your own.

---

* Certain items are soulbound to player accounts rather than specific avatars and may thus be sent to other characters on the same account via in-game mail. Players who acquire bind-on-pickup loot while in a group may also trade it to their comrades in that same group for a limited time thereafter.

Sort of, anyway. Your avatar must be present for raid bosses and arena victories, but nowhere is it written you must do the hard work. Finding teammates sufficiently geared or skilled to pull your under-geared or underskilled ass through high-end content is typically just a question of money. Trade chat abounds with many such promotions. Scare up enough gold and it's easy to buy your way into a Mythic raid dungeon, where an experienced guild will do all the killing as you do the looting. Of course, nobody can guarantee any given piece of loot will drop, and the guild will declare certain items reserved for their raiders, but for the most part the customer may loot whatever he desires. The thousands of gold in proceeds are split between the raiding guild's war chest and the guild members, as compensation for their time.

These kinds of arrangements have existed since the moment top players were powerful enough to easily clear endgame content—to have it "on farm," in the game's parlance. T K T routinely engaged in the practice, selling loot from old dungeons to fund our own raiding operations. After raids we'd escort customers through difficult timed Stratholme runs, clearing the dungeon inside forty-five minutes as part of a long quest to upgrade their blue-quality armor to purple. An hour of work (including transit time) yielded a fee of 300 gold split among four raiders, courtesy of one happy customer. I offered a 100 percent success guarantee—no charge if we failed the run. Enthusiastic referrals meant more business than I could handle, sent along to guildmates eager to cover their own repair bills.

It was a fabulous system for all involved, sadly ruined by a rival guild. They started their own paid runs, which wasn't threatening on its own terms, as demand far outpaced supply. The problem came when, for reasons unknown, they decided to drop their price from 300 gold to a measly 50. *Fifty!* Split four ways, 50 gold wasn't worth an hour of a raider's time, but our rivals somehow talked themselves into it. Naturally the bottom dropped out of the market, nobody wanted to pay T K T prices anymore, and even our competition closed up shop. I was too disgusted with the whole episode to bother reopening, and frankly recalling it still makes me angry. There is, as the saying goes, no cure for stupid.

WORKIN' DOWN THE PIXEL MINE

Of course, all this discussion of the gold economy masks *WoW*'s one true currency: I speak of time. Any *Warcraft* enthusiast knows the phrase "Time is money, friend!" usually blared in the rusty-trombone rasp of a goblin NPC. Indeed, it serves as the mercantile goblin race's unofficial motto. It's a recurring theme of MMORPGs and therefore of this book: given sufficient time and motivation, a player can achieve anything she desires. Gold, as the game's most fungible resource, becomes its closest analogue for raw time, for the clock's ticking and for the sequential churn of atoms in our body cells. We recognize this in the real world too, since nearly everyone participating in Western civilization exchanges his labor (that is, his time and the presence of his body and the devotion of his mental bandwidth) for money. Modern games accept this fungibility. It is baked into their bones. Witness the extended phylogeny of "free to play" games, where players either grind slowly for free or progress quickly for small but cumulative payments. There's no shame in this; we all pick and choose how to spend our entertainment dollars. So it should come as no surprise that some *WoW* players chose to expedite their hobby by buying in-game gold with hard-earned cash.

The problem was that Blizzard expressly forbade it. From retail release, Blizzard attempted to erect barriers between the real economy and *WoW*'s. The developers didn't want their game to devolve into a marketplace controlled by and for the benefit of shady outsiders. Certainly those entities would exist and work their way into the game—it's the nature of the Internet, after all—but they'd meet active resistance at every turn from a well-funded corporation determined to curtail their activities. Per the game's terms of service, any real-money transactions through third parties were (and remain) grounds for immediate and permanent bans from *WoW*, buyer and seller both. But they couldn't stop everything, and sites offering gold for US dollars proliferated online. Despite Blizzard's best efforts, Trade chat teemed with ads for gold sellers even during the game's beta testing phase, and the same remains true today.

A bigger game naturally means more customers for gold sellers, and so *WoW* by itself powers a strange illicit corner of the online economy. It is at its core a business of resource extraction: how best to extract gold from the game world for resale? Automation would be ideal, but "botting" programs aren't terribly reliable in a big, open place like an MMORPG. More important, Blizzard has developed its own algorithmic methods for detecting and punishing automated behavior. Gold sellers may cleverly open and close all the throwaway "burner" *WoW* accounts they like, creating and discarding untold thousands of characters with gibberish names, but they still need to maintain some accounts in good standing, because fundamentally someone needs to go out and kill the monsters. Even a level 55 rogue in questing greens represents time invested, so it's bad business having your farm accounts banned for botting. The gold sellers needed human labor of the cheapest kind, and they found it in limitless quantities across the developing world.

There's not a huge amount of publicly available information about these operations; their illicit nature, distant remove from the actual centers of *WoW* operations, and lack of formal organizational structure makes accurate journalism a struggle. Suffice it to say that anywhere low labor costs and reliable high-speed Internet met, one could find *WoW* gold-mining operations. Most of these locales were in East and Southeast Asia—China, Vietnam, Malaysia, and the Philippines. Due to China's sheer size and bustling *WoW* community, it accounts for the vast majority of gold farmers. Thousands of workers, overwhelmingly poor young men, toiled long hours per day, hot racking through bare mattresses on the floor behind their stations, for very little pay or sometimes none at all. The *Guardian* reported in 2011 on Chinese prison inmates being forced to farm *WoW* gold. In that story, a former inmate describes the scheme: "Prison bosses made more money forcing inmates to play games than they [did with] manual labor. . . . We worked 12-hour shifts in the camp. I heard them say they could earn 5,000–6000rmb [$800] a day." As one might imagine, the suffering didn't end with eyestrain and headaches. "If I couldn't complete my work quota, they would punish me physically. They would make me stand with my hands raised in the air and after I returned to my dormitory they would beat me with plastic pipes. We kept playing until we could barely see things."

The practice of using forced labor in these operations is probably common though by no means universal—a *New York Times* article from 2005 describes scores of young men farming *WoW* gold in the basement of an old factory, at a workplace fundamentally like any other. The workers received competitive pay and considered themselves lucky to play a video game for a living, rather than waiting tables or risking their safety in manufacturing or construction. The *Times* estimated a hundred thousand full-time gold farmers in China alone. Chinese government policy forbids the exchange of virtual currencies without explicit licenses, but small outfits are obviously hard to track. Lacking coordination or formal leadership and relying on a bewildering range of different tactics and techniques, the gold-farming industry cannot be stamped out. As a PhD student at the University of Minnesota, Muhammad Aurangzeb Ahmad analyzed gold-farming networks and compared them to drug-dealing networks. By working only with known associates and delivering product through middlemen, they limit their organizational exposure to risk. Attacking portions of the network leaves behind isolated but active elements, and those attacks have an order of magnitude less impact on the so-called "affiliate" networks of distributors and customers. Given the volume of economic transactions in *WoW* (high-population servers exchange upward of 50 million gold per day through Auction Houses alone), even large illicit transfers blend into background noise. Detecting and punishing the individuals connected to those transactions, let alone their suppliers, consumes a developer's resources without ever truly disrupting the trade.

Which isn't to say folks didn't try. Blizzard has banned hundreds of thousands of accounts connected to the gold industry over the years. Their enforcers swept untold millions of gold from the records in so doing, each purge sending severe if ephemeral shocks through the system as the price of gold skyrocketed overnight and gradually settled back down. Blizzard's developers and community managers spoke out forcefully against the gold industry, contributing to the players' ongoing sense of vague disapproval—which didn't, in practice, keep them from being regular customers. In the vein of vice prosecutors everywhere, Blizzard came down harder on the sellers than the buyers. Buyers, after all, are the customers. They're the constituency. Ban fifty thousand buyer accounts from the US servers and you'll face an immediate avalanche of complaints from customers and the friends they play with. Ban fifty thousand Chinese-based seller accounts in one fell swoop and nobody makes a peep. The sellers find another way to do business and the buyers find a way to get what they want. They're *WoW* players, after all.

Why exactly players despise gold farmers is hard to pin down. It's a noxious cocktail: distrust of outsiders, particularly the foreign variety; resentment at the valuable monster spawns stolen from more deserving "real" players; fear of shady third-party groups trying to manipulate the game economy; and the difficult-to-quantify but very real suspicion they see the rest of us as marks to be scammed. That most gold farmers weren't in guilds and didn't vocally participate in the community meant they were even easier to demonize. Players developed keen eyes for the signs of gold farming: hunters or rogues, unguilded, usually with gibberish names, endlessly grinding humanoid monsters for their gold and valuable cloth drops. When they saw these farmers, they killed on sight. If killing wasn't an option, whether due to faction or to PvE server rules, they'd drag extra monsters to the farmers—whose incidental attacks would draw the arriving creatures' attention and get them killed (a common MMORPG practice called "training," as the monsters chase the aggroing player like a line of rail cars). Of course, the farmers could train monsters right back at you, and often did. Though instructed to keep grinding no matter what, if their routines were sufficiently disrupted they had no choice but to fight. T K T would regularly farm Tyr's Hand in the

Eastern Plaguelands for gold after raids, and murdering Alliance gold farmers was an implicit component of our own farming. It was the fun part! The fact that we were disrupting the work of poor people thousands of miles away, some of whom may have suffered corporal punishment as a consequence, flitted weakly in the shadows at the backs of our minds. Best left unconsidered and unspoken, though the common epithet "China farmer" made the stakes clear enough for anyone wanting to see.

As game critic and *WoW* fan Stephen Winson once suggested, this kind of animosity was always misplaced. Gold sellers surely affected the economy, but not in the ways or to the degree popularly assumed. Players fretted about the inflationary danger of gluts of gold, but Winson roots this more in a political and historical fear of inflation (Weimar Germany! Greece! Wheelbarrows of cash to buy bread!) than in actual economics, where inflation is defined by rising prices. In *WoW* prices didn't consistently rise over time; in fact they dropped, spiking only for the release of new content like expansion packs. Each expansion overwrote its predecessor, making those old resources obsolete and introducing new resources that were always scarce and wildly expensive at the start. As players reached the new level cap and harvested the game world's bounty, scarce items became common and prices fell. When gold farmers turned their gathered inventory into cash through the Auction House, they aggressively undersold their competition and contributed to further deflation.

Winson made another excellent point on deflation: Consider why players buy gold. It's not simply to have, sitting in a bank account or used to seed some other investment. Again, gold doesn't represent money, it represents time—time devoted to obtaining in-game rewards. That means whatever gold they buy, they're likely to spend almost immediately, and in ways that remove it from the economy. I bought gold only once in my *WoW* career, to help finance the 5,000-gold epic Riding skill early in *The Burning Crusade*. It was $300 for 2,500 gold, delivered by hand at a meeting point on the coast south of Orgrimmar. (Transferring gold via in-game mail leaves too many traces that linger too long in Blizzard's archives.) Within an hour I was penniless again but screaming over the Auchindoun wastes at 280 percent speed and extremely happy. That gold would have taken at least two weeks of hard nightly grinding, on top of my raiding obligations. I was happy to spare myself the time. This was a perfectly normal transaction, and it goes to show how most of the farmed gold vanished from the system almost as swiftly as it was made.

The player base's animosity toward gold sellers was always misplaced, though certainly the hailstorm of gold-seller ads pumped into Trade chat was annoying. For crafters hoping to make money through their professions, the downward pressure on prices meant only the finest products were worth selling. Gold sellers also caused minor disturbances in major cities: to circumvent ad-blocking chat mods, they used illicit software to spawn level 1 characters high in the air and drop them to their deaths in precise patterns before logging out (leaving the bodies inert but intact). Visitors to Ironforge might see, on the plaza just outside the Auction House, several dozen gnome corpses arranged in giant letters, spelling out the name of a popular gold-selling website for all the server to see. Removing them took a long time, as Blizzard's teams had to individually ban each and every burner account, expunging them from the server's database entirely before the dead avatars would vanish. Even more costly to the customer service team were player accounts hacked by gold-selling networks. Using any number of tactics running a long gamut of sophistication, these outfits sussed out passwords, took control of accounts, and locked out their proper owners. By the time the customer regained access to her account, her gear had been vendored and every gold coin on every character mailed off through an inscrutable network of middlemen. This took a lot less time and labor than farming for gold, and it was understandably far more nefarious. Blizzard made available a series of authenticator devices and even included them in the physical packaging for *Cataclysm*, so most *WoW* accounts are now safer than their owners' bank accounts, but security is never perfect, and hacked accounts have caused tremendous grief to thousands of players over the years. Guilds must be very careful about who receives access to the guild bank, since a single compromised officer could empty out the whole vault in minutes. Blizzard customer service has grown grimly adept at handling these situations, but they are always playing catch-up.

In the end the solution was simple: give everyone more money for less work. Daily quests were more than chores to keep players occupied. They also dramatically improved your gold yield despite taking far less time than traditional grinding. Since players were paying gold sellers to save themselves time, the developers reduced their incentives. The pattern continues from vanilla *WoW* through the present, always leaning toward giving more, to the point where *Warlords of Draenor* allowed players to make thousands of gold just by running their newly introduced collections of followers and naval vessels through trivial missions. The missions took time too, but they ran persistently even with players logged out, and upgrades could multiply each haul several times over. Countless players earned millions of gold without leaving their garrisons. Blizzard eventually recognized their error and removed the *Warlords* gold-earning missions from the game prior to *Legion*'s launch. Even so, anyone focused on earning gold has no difficulty with it. I cannot imagine anything that would inspire me to exchange real money for gold under the current regime. But then, even if I did, I wouldn't have to go to the third-party sellers who still spam advertisements all day long. I could just get my gold from Blizzard themselves.

March 2, 2015, marked a tectonic shift in *WoW*'s economic philosophy: the day Blizzard announced the *WoW* Token. Players could use the in-game shop* to buy a twenty-dollar Token, an in-game object redeemable for a month's subscription to play (regularly fifteen dollars). The Token isn't designed to be used by the buyer, nor can it be traded by hand; it can only be sold on the Auction House for a predetermined quantity of gold set by the current supply on the

---

* The *World of Warcraft* shop is an extension of Blizzard's online retail operation, allowing real-money purchases from within their game clients and extending across their many online games. Most of the products available in the shop are purely cosmetic in nature, allowing players to exchange real money for game items like special pets, mounts, or decorative armor.

realm server. Any Token purchased at auction binds to the purchaser, rendering further resale impossible. In this roundabout fashion, one player exchanges cash for in-game gold, while another exchanges gold for a month of game time.

This formalized the bond between gold and time and dollars, rendering all of them liquid within the *WoW* economy. Picture two *WoW* enthusiasts, player A and player B. Player A is a partially disabled US Army veteran with plenty of time on his hands but not a lot of cash. Player B is a young attorney balancing a demanding career with a young child; she's got disposable income but very limited gaming time. Player A levels a crew of alts, each with complementary professions and a circuit of repeatable quests each day.* This yields more than enough gold for him to buy Tokens from the Auction House and pay for his own *WoW* subscription. He enjoys hundreds of hours of entertainment per month essentially for free. Player B pays for her subscription out of pocket, occasionally throwing some cash at Tokens that she can then flip on the Auction House to player A. She spends the tens of thousands of gold the auction yields on new gear and other upgrades. Everyone gets his or her needs met, Blizzard injects no artificial resources into the game economy (every gold piece is farmed by a customer and the Auction House fees mitigate inflation), and third-party sellers are cut entirely out of the equation.

Blizzard made its reasoning explicit: "Buying gold from third-party sources negatively impacts the game experience for everyone. The overwhelming majority of the gold these services provide comes from stolen player accounts. . . . On top of this, gold selling companies often farm resources using hack programs, sell fake product codes as a scam, and spam entire realms with ads to buy gold. . . . The *WoW* Token allows players to exchange real money for gold in a secure and sanctioned way." It almost makes one think of drug pol-

---

* *Warlords of Draenor* introduced personal garrisons, which at low levels functioned as cash sinks but by the endgame became absolute gold mines. Even an undergeared alt could pull in hundreds of gold every day simply by sending NPC followers on timed missions. Blizzard wisely stopped awarding gold for *Warlords of Draenor* garrison missions near the end of that expansion, but many players had already stockpiled millions of gold with minimal effort.

icy: years of failed, trudging prohibition yielding to transparency, dialogue, and ultimately sensible regulation.

But like any policy, even the sensible kind, its successes were incomplete. Gold sellers persist. Accounts continue to be hacked, though it's impossible to divine any trend, as Blizzard has never released any numbers about hacks or resolutions. Compensated human labor is rare for today's gold farmers, who rely on what Winson dubs "automation, theft and slave labor." They've stripped down their labor costs to stay ahead of Blizzard's long offensive, and to this day gold sellers are able to offer lower prices on gold than the house. It's riskier to buy than *WoW* Tokens, but some margin of players will always chase any discount.

Here Blizzard acknowledged that purity isn't the highest virtue. Developers of online games would, by and large, prefer to create a world entirely severed from the real-world market. Games should reward skill and tactics, after all. Placing players at disadvantage by virtue of their household income leaves a sour taste in most mouths. But is that really so different from the standard MMORPG approach, which favors players with the most free time and online social capital? I fail to see how. If the game's central objective is to entertain through gradual gear progression, why reward players with a surplus of time over a surplus of funds? "We've earned it," the former group would argue, "through our greater commitment to the game." This is fundamentally the same argument hardcore players use to delegitimize everyone else. Better to keep both competitive, so everyone can enjoy the game and feel they're progressing.

"Free to play" video games across the world have embraced this ethos, recognizing that their products are just components of their customers' lives—components players should be free to arrange however they wish. Online games need paying customers to function, but so too they rely on healthy and active communities. A player who pays his subscription in gold and spends six hours a day running battlegrounds can be just as valuable as a casual player who pays fifteen dollars per month but never logs on. *WoW* Tokens let players choose how they want to contribute, either through dollars or sheer volume of activity. They provide a universal if tightly regulated medium of exchange—as well as an objective real-life barometer of value in Azeroth for those with bigger financial ambitions.

MASTERS OF THE MARKET

If an online video game features tradeable currency of any kind, you can bet a class of players will spring up around it. Of course everyone accumulates money, uses it, plans purchases in advance—but these people are different. To them, the economy is the game. In *WoW*, they consider the Professions menu and the Auction House to be the fields of play; everything else is a gaudy distraction. These players call themselves traders.

At first blush, *WoW* isn't the best game for trading. It places stringent controls on capital like the measures described earlier (soulbound gear, mount fees, and the like).* Trading in most MMORPGs hinges on two tactics: either you sell a few big-ticket items at insanely high margins, or you sell large volumes of simple materials at low margins. *WoW* makes both a struggle. For the former, the very best items soulbind when picked up and the only valuable bind-on-equip items in the game drop only through dumb luck. As to the latter, the Auction House's listing fee and 5 percent commission on every sale slash into any profits. Since prices for materials useful in the most recent expansion face constant downward pressure, buying and reselling large volumes within the Auction House becomes difficult to sustain.

What does that leave for the traders? Quite a bit, as it turns out, and it all starts with capitalism's oldest question: what will people want to buy? *WoW* is designed to furnish neophytes with

---

* In addition, the game sets a hard limit on the amount of gold any one character can possess, but this "gold cap" has climbed steadily northward over the years. Through the first two expansions it stood at 214,748 gold, 36 silver, 47 copper; money was saved as a 32-bit integer, and this seemingly random figure represents a volume of copper coins equal to 2^{31}, less one coin. *Cataclysm* raised it to 999,999 gold, 99 silver, 99 copper, and *Legion* to 9,999,999 gold, 99 silver, 99 copper. Hitting the gold cap on one or more characters is a common goal in the trader community.

everything they'll need through the leveling process, so there's no necessity-of-life market like groceries or fuel. You can only offer them what the game doesn't. The average *WoW* player, the kind of person whose day-to-day transactions fuel daily market volumes in the tens of millions, buys a few select types of goods. First, he buys materials to advance his trade skills (leatherworking, enchanting, jewelcrafting, or the like). Most players lack the patience to spend hours farming all the materials necessary to max out their skills. They'd rather throw a thousand gold or so at the problem and save themselves the time. This makes trade reagents, for both present and past expansions, the Auction House's best investments.

Supplying the raw materials for these impulse buys are various traders, though you'll typically see just one name at a time. Traders hate competition and try not to sell anything unless they can be sure they're the only seller listed on the Auction House. Too many players in any corner of the market swiftly tanks prices and profits, so like high-order predators they try to give each other wide berths. When selling these materials they want to ensure their product is the cheapest on the market while also turning a profit. They need to control prices, but how to accomplish this in a huge and highly volatile market?

Using online forums, traders invented and popularized the "price reset." Imagine a trader wants to unload a heap of true iron ore. He checks popular Auction House–tracking websites like the Undermine Journal and WoWuction (yes, "uction" without an *A*) for the global price for a stack of 10 ore and finds that it's currently going at 120 gold. Checking his server's Auction House, he sees several hundred true iron ore already listed at 95 gold per stack. If he undercuts this price he won't turn the profit he's seeking, but if he lists at even 96 gold per stack, none of it will sell until his competitors' stock is out the door. So he simply buys it—all of it, every piece of ore listed on the Auction House below his preferred price. Any trader worth his salt has the liquid capital to render these kinds of purchases trivial, and he'll quickly make back his investment when he relists his new stock at 120 gold. In one fell swoop he resets the price and neither the other seller (whose product sold, after all) nor the casual buyer (who's been bilked but only sees one price) is any the wiser.

Other opportunities appear from time to time on the "sniper" UI mods all traders run while sitting idle, informing them when anything gets listed above or below certain prices—much the way stock traders have automated their own operations. If lucky and alert they may even catch other players attempting to transfer goods cross-faction through the Auction House, snapping up rarities for as little as a single copper coin.*

Traders who choose to invest heavily in their own trade skills can sell powerful epic items, but this market decays as successive waves of content give players easier and cheaper access to better gear. Pieces are more valuable for their appearance than their statistics, since transmogrification is so popular. Leveling gear is an even better bet—epic weapons and armor made from cheaper materials, designed for characters below the level cap, whose constant churn (*WoW* players love their alts, after all) powers the market. Older items and materials, scoured from the bright but empty catacombs of prior expansions, yield more consistent profits than many of their new world equivalents. Crafters looking to make big profits turn to products with churning markets, like enchanting and jewelcrafting (any time players get new gear, they need to enchant it and fill any available sockets with stat-enhancing gems). The latter is especially popular in the trading community, because jewelers can craft rare and expensive mounts. Mounts stand as *WoW*'s ultimate prestige items, the coolest cosmetic baubles in a game full of them. Widespread transmogrification means a character's visible gear rarely reflects its true worth, so if you're inclined to loaf around capital cities looking fly, you've got to do it with a slick ride.

---

* Because the warring factions are prohibited from swapping items in person or through the mail, the Auction House system is the only way for a player to convey goods from an Alliance character to a Horde alt, or vice versa. Originally such transfers were conducted at one of several remote and little-trafficked Neutral Auction Houses, but *Warlords of Draenor* merged the Alliance, Horde, and Neutral Auction House offerings into a single pool, rendering this trick much riskier.

Mounts derive their value from a few sources. Some players have an eye for art, for size and color and panache like *Warlords of Draenor*'s house-sized Gronnlings or *Mists of Pandaria*'s wonderfully stylized Cloud Serpents. Others prefer ostentatious displays of wealth, like the Grand Expedition Yak, which carries three players in addition to NPC vendors and costs 120,000 gold. Some pay huge sums for rare mounts like the Thundering Ruby Cloud Serpent, which is looted from a powerful boss only accessible through hours of farming. The most valuable mounts in the entire game are connected to the *World of Warcraft* collectible card game, awarded through the in-game shop for codes printed on certain rare cards. On large servers the rarest of these, like the Corrupted Hippogryph or X-51 Nether-Rocket X-TREME, routinely sell for six figures. Acquiring them for sale is a trickier process involving real-life eBay auction sniping, but once in-game they're commodities until soulbound through use.

Advice abounds for those looking to become traders, in part because gold holds interest for even the most casual player. Every economy is different and any conditions of supply and demand unique to their moment, but generally newcomers are advised to pick out just a handful of different items for exclusive attention. Dominate the market for five or six products and you'll crank out a healthy living every week—enough to pay your account costs, if you're diligent with your sniping and reset the prices whenever they start to dip. From there you expand slowly, one scrap of market territory at a time, learning the server's landscape as you go. If competition gets tight and you're not an established power with the back stock and liquidity to throw your weight around, you back off and find other ways to bolster your war chest. Deeper pockets means more investment capital, and profits can expand geometrically without much risk. The economy never suffers recessions, and most entities in the market are buyers of convenience with ample income, whose purchasing power fades little in the face of higher prices. The market is so big, the pool of players and the sum of their collective needs so vast, that there's enough bounty for

everyone. *Warlords of Draenor*'s merging of the Horde and Alliance
Auction Houses guarantees healthy economies even with badly
imbalanced populations.

THE JUBILANT SCIENCE

As I made my own way through Azeroth and came to know the
landscape, the Auction House hawks tossing memes back and forth
in Orgrimmar General chat to pass the time, the belligerent gold
farmers in Tyr's Hand, and the friendlier strain skinning blue dragonkin in Azshara, I learned about a different kind of person. See, I've
always approached games—the playing of games, not the schema
themselves—as an art. I play an improvisational style premised on
vision, anticipation, and instinct. Healing came more naturally than
DPS, because it has to be seat-of-the-pants. Numbers matter when
picking gear, but otherwise you're free to process the game more
as action than mechanics—art, again, more than science. I didn't
closely quantify my time. Something either *felt* worth doing or it
didn't. Leatherworking made sense because it let me craft armor;
cooking and fishing felt like elaborate jokes played on the community
by cruel developers, but anyone obsessed with truly maximizing his
character ate them up.

These people see everything differently. To them the game unfolds
in plans and boundaries, in decimals instead of integers. They look
at the swell of *WoW*'s lovingly detailed models, the flash of its spell
effects, and see the hard right angles they obscure. They find joy in
stressing those angles, trying to warp them either acute or obtuse.
They take pride in the negotiation of arcane rules, in the competition
those rules foster. Read your way through a trader's message board
and you'll find a good-natured boasting: *Just made my first 100k* or *Got
a character to the gold cap!* Some people had twenty or thirty characters
at the *Warlords of Draenor* gold cap, accounting for tens of millions
across several accounts, and *Legion* raised the cap yet again to a copper short of 10 million. It's not about having enough gold to buy

things. It's a never-ending competition, against the server but mostly against oneself, striving to inch that number ever higher. This takes a special kind of person, one driven by a very specific kind of achievement—the kind of drive that always seeks a tread to expend itself.

Gurgthock of Elitist Jerks is exactly this sort of person. His taste never ran to gold, though he made more than enough of the stuff—the man loved *WoW*'s challenges, in their various forms, and the process of cleverly disassembling them like puzzle boxes. Finesse was the key: clever tactics and perfect execution. He scorned brute force, looking down on it as a last resort for lesser intellects, and Gurgthock cared a great deal about intellect. As a brilliant individual, he was unaccustomed to suffering fools or expending energy on trivial things. In fact, "trivial" was one of his favorite words. Another was "dumb"—if Gurg didn't like something, he would probably call it dumb, and dumb was one of the worst things anything could be. If you've ever attended an elite American university, you've known folks like this: intensely elitist (to the point of running a guild named Elitist Jerks, however facetiously) but in a self-directed fashion. They demand a great deal from themselves and the people around them. They know exactly how smart they are, but they're too polite to rub it in your face and too earnest to honestly resent. That was Gurg.

Listening into Elitist Jerks' raiding channel my first night in the guild, I quickly understood why they'd been successful. Every command was clear and purposeful, each decision made for a reason. Gurgthock was at the time working as a Big Law attorney in Washington, DC. The legal profession trains many of the MMORPG world's most accomplished players, as it shunts brilliant and focused people into boring jobs with a lot of unstructured time. Cognition thoroughly wasted by his day job, Gurgthock threw his formidable intellect into *WoW* leadership. He explained things the way a good lawyer would. Even offhanded jokes made in chat would lead to thoughtful responses, delivered in a busy rapid-fire deadpan, disentangled from thorny knots into clear strands of logic. No matter what feature of *WoW* you brought up, the man knew the designers' intentions and exactly how they'd manifested or gone awry. No matter who you were, whether EJ raider or level 1 avatar created specifically to whisper the great and famous Gurgthock, he listened and he always took you seriously. This meant you sometimes had to pick what *not* to say to him, but I've always considered it a rare and admirable trait.

Those same skills would prove immeasurably valuable in the years to come, as he joined Blizzard's development team in 2008. Gurgthock the orc shaman gradually became Watcher the raid designer and then Ion Hazzikostas, game director for all of *WoW*. He never stopped leading EJ, never stopped being Gurg to us, and so it was always funny to see the same ruthless logic applied to developer blog posts or onstage for panels at BlizzCon. However you thought you felt about a particular issue, once Gurg made his pitch you always knew he was right. You'd expect to find it maddening, being outmaneuvered like that, but in practice it's remarkably pleasant, because you've just achieved clarity and learned something in the process. This is Ion's peculiar genius. It makes him an incredibly effective leader of thoughtful people, since he can win any argument without pissing them off, and an invincible foil for irrationally angry *WoW* forum posters. Spend some time around him and you can't help starting to think the way he does, attempting to see the things he sees. To this day Gurg-isms find their way into my spoken language—I'll describe things as "nontrivial" or "nonzero" and "multidetermined," careful words making a lawyer's stark yet delicate distinctions. Ion operates from a conviction that top-level MMORPG content can and should be conquered by intelligent adults with balanced lives. This conviction animates Elitist Jerks, and many of *World of Warcraft*'s latter-day adaptations can best be understood as an outgrowth of advocacy by Gurgthock and his contemporaries.

It's a generational shift of sorts, moving from Rob Pardo and Jeff Kaplan's stewardship to that of Hazzikostas, though the principals involved aren't far apart in age. The former two represented *Ever-Quest*'s legacy of hardcore raiding and infused its DNA into *WoW*, while the latter moved that same game into the mobile age by making its greatest rewards easily accessible and available to all. This is nothing if not good business, as *WoW* retains millions of active subscribers and continues to employ hundreds of talented people. Its expansions sell well, and mobile phone apps integrated into *WoW* itself allow players to interact with the game no matter where they are. Followers can be sent on missions, rewards deposited directly into players' inventory. You can banter away in Guild chat without ever logging in, so long as your *WoW* account remains active. When your guild feels like a family more than a workplace, it feels strange being without those dozens of half-strangers. Go to a family camping trip in Yosemite and you'll miss them. Saying good-bye for good can feel impossible.

WHAT WE DESERVE

No copy of my good-bye post to T K T still exists, and for that I thank the Internet. I wrote it as a message board post in one session, over forty-five minutes, crying the entire time. If an error in my browser had deleted it halfway through, I'd have lacked the emotional strength to rewrite it. It felt like moving away from my family—like going off to college for the first time, only instead of a mutual celebration it was a unilateral betrayal. Leaving a guild isn't just living somewhere else; it's an active rejection of those people with whom you've played. You're removing yourself from their world, from the daily rituals of tanking and healing and DPS that made you a family to begin with. It hurts anytime a friend leaves the game. That said, it still matters a great deal how exactly you go about it. When my college roommate Geoff decided he couldn't commit to full-time play, I was sad to lose a partner in crime but totally understanding. When T K T's main tank and my old friend Chris vanished overnight and left the guild teetering in the lurch without saying so much as a word, I was incredibly angry. It still makes me angry—not his leaving but the silence before and after, the precipitation of attacks on our family from the outside while leaving us no good answer ourselves. I couldn't do that to T K T, particularly not after shepherding them through that very same crisis.

We didn't lack for leadership, I knew. Plastico would still be around, our main tank Savena had already assumed part of the load, and the class officers were strong and vocal. The guild didn't need me to survive.* I just didn't want to cause any unnecessary hurt on my way out the door. I wanted to do right by my friends. So my farewell post—since expunged along with the rest of our ancient website—focused on those friends. I told them where I was going and why. I told them I'd picked Elitist Jerks to keep having fun in the game, because leadership was taking over my life and making me miserable, and I let them know they'd been the only things keeping me going. Only logging on every night to Meaning's sarcastic grumble and Tyrawick's Texas drawl and Plastico's honking ejaculations of nonsense held together my sanity. I apologized for my occasional outbursts, for my withering criticism, for the nights I'd taken them from their families. I let them know I loved them and I'd miss them and I'd never forget our times together. And since I couldn't forget, I begged them to forgive me leaving. I posted it and submitted the form to transfer Ghando from Detheroc to Mal'ganis. I never formally said good-bye in-game. I didn't have the stomach for it.

The responses in my inbox were astonishing. One after another, guildmates new and old (still lurking on the forums) messaged me to share their favorite memories. They were happy for me. They thought it was tremendously cool that I was joining a famous guild, even as a hired gun. If they begrudged me a thing, no one ever said it. *We love you too* was all I got back. *We want you to be happy, even if it's not with us.* In the entire human continuum there isn't a harder thing to say and actually mean. Personally I've never pulled it off. It was a uniform outpouring of affection unlike any I've ever experienced. It was far better than I could have expected, and certainly better than I deserved. But it was real. It was genuine, all of it, and if I did anything to earn this gift it wasn't leading efficient raids or putting out more healing than anyone else. It was treating people decently, being

---

* For those curious, T K T persists, still led by Plastico and Slipo and Memo, on the Illidan realm. They've transferred and rebuilt several times but never for a moment contemplated disbanding. This makes me very happy, but my time with them is over.

honest and forthright, placing values like friendship and family and loyalty over in-game rewards. It was playing the right way, living the right way, loving the right way. Plastico was something of a loon, but this he always understood better than I. When you finally quit the game, when everything falls away, all that's left is friends and memories. Time may be money and everything in *WoW* may be an intricately structured galaxy of ones and zeroes, but I owe every man and woman who ever played with me in T K T an utterly unpayable debt.

But life goes on—mine, yours, every one of my guildmates. T K T kept raiding, and having fun, and even today many of the original members play *WoW* together. Those like me, who've either left the guild or the game entirely, lurk in the website's forums. We exchange fond birthday wishes and congratulate each other as our band of wide-eyed kids marries and has kids while the older raiders' whelps (as we affectionately dubbed all their young) grow up and go to college. *WoW* left its mark on each of us, and collectively our generation has welcomed the game into our cultural pantheon. It's part of our history.

« 8 »

THE GAME THAT WON AN EMMY

A man named Barack Hussein Obama won the presidency of the United States. I know this because I watched it on television. You'll be aware of this too, via some holographic archive buried amidst the moss-grown rubble of Western civilization, but at the time the fact was really quite something to absorb. That this fresh-faced beanpole of a junior senator might mount a stage to face America as its first black president was a strange and almost radical theory until suddenly, in the campaign's last weeks with a formidable lead in the polls, it wasn't. Even so I went to cast my ballot that morning gnawingly unsure of the outcome and remained so throughout the evening. Network cameras focused on Chicago's Grant Park, where droves of Obama supporters had begun massing. One battleground state after another turned blue and the crowd swelled, pushing up against hastily installed security barriers, emitting a buzz that was thrilled but also distinctly nervous. Again, until CNN swept a jarring archipelago of colored stars across my screen and Wolf Blitzer appeared like a wizened, earnest hedgehog to formally announce the result, it didn't seem possible. But then there he was, in that gaudy studio, announcing that "Barack Obama, forty-seven years old, will become the president-elect of the United States."

At some signal in Chicago the barriers opened. Uniformed police scuttled in rows like midnight-blue beetles in their heavy jackets and they unhinged the aluminum gates and swung them aside and the crowd burst through. Hundreds of people, thousands, tens of thousands—CNN pulled its shot wider so the torrent wouldn't over-flow the frame. The wave rushed down the lawn's dark slope past the statue of Lincoln toward the portable dais erected with its back to Lake Michigan. They chanted *"O-ba-ma!"* and *"Yes! We! Can!"* while I watched from home with my girlfriend at the time, quiet on the couch, struggling to process the enormity of the image. It was an avalanche, an epoch-making event, a secular blessing on behalf of our whole society. A movement that had grown from seed and arrived but gone unrecognized finally found itself written into history. It was in many ways a coronation.

"MAKE LOVE, NOT WARCRAFT"

Barely two years earlier I'd sat on a different couch in front of a different television, watching another crowning moment. Gaming forums had buzzed for weeks and now the moment had finally arrived: *South Park* made an episode about *World of Warcraft*.

Video game references were nothing new, neither for television nor for *South Park*. At that point in its tenth season, the enormously popular animated sitcom had won an Emmy Award just the season before for an episode ("Best Friends Forever") prominently featuring Sony's PlayStation Portable (PSP) console. Yet while the PSP was an element in the plot, the episode garnered attention primarily for its allegorical depiction of the Terri Schiavo controversy over end-of-life care.

Brutally funny or unflinchingly critical when they chose to be, show creators Trey Parker and Matt Stone had grabbed hold of the entertainment industry as part of a pop culture ascent that continues unabated to this writing. *South Park* was then and remains now (for those of my generation) the definitive record of our culture. If any element of popular culture should ever find its way into an episode even in passing, it can be said to have truly mattered—at least for a few weeks—in American history. So thus, as the tomes say, it came to pass that most people with even a passing interest in *WoW* tuned in that night through their TVs and web browsers to see how it played. Following the standard Primus-backed title sequence, "Make Love, Not Warcraft" presented twenty-two minutes of catnip euphoria to MMORPG fans.

It begins with an establishing shot set to lilting woodwinds, showing us not the accustomed snow-capped mountains of the show's fictionalized Colorado but rather the unmistakable (to any *WoW* fan) backdrop of the Goldshire Inn! Stan, Kyle, Cartman, and Kenny are immersed in the game, and in the first few minutes it's clear large portions of the episode will be just like this. It's not just in-group references, like the complaint over resurrecting at the nearest graveyard. The episode is approached with the loving detail *South Park* brings to all its send-ups, made particularly acute in this case by Parker and Stone's heavy use of machinima. Machinima is a style of filming using video game footage, like a play staged inside a game. It can be used to tell serious stories furthering the game's lore, harmless comic romps rehashing popular online memes, or anything in between.

In direct collaboration with Blizzard Entertainment, *South Park* rendered much of the episode's twenty-two minutes in *WoW*'s 3-D engine (as opposed to the "2.5-D" paper-cutout animation the show typically uses), bringing entirely new strata of detail to light. The show's beloved characters are represented by their in-game avatars, reflecting not just their appearances and traits but, in classic online fashion, what those characters choose to project to the world. Cartman's speeches before battle echo the detached know-it-all tone endemic to raid leaders. Clyde, at the moment he's most needed, has stopped paying attention and left his keyboard. From the real in-game user interface to the Elwynn Forest General chat querying, "WHERE IS OLD BLANCHY?" Parker and Stone work hard to establish authenticity in presentation, despite not playing *WoW* themselves.

The plot departs from reality; after all, it's a cartoon on Comedy Central. *South Park*'s four young protagonists attempt to level their characters in *WoW*, only to be ganked over and over by an impossibly powerful player. Rather than quit the game, they commence an epically miserable grind, killing trivial enemies in a starting zone to level high enough to defeat the ganker—whose nefarious player-killing ways have begun to threaten all of *WoW*. Blizzard Entertainment makes available the Sword of a Thousand Truths,* and with this legendary weapon the boys are able to defeat their nemesis and restore order to *WoW* . . . which, in the end, only means they can get back to playing more *WoW*. It's a laugh line for mainstream audiences that also rings true for players. "You can just hang out in the sun all day tossing a ball around," Cartman sneers at the others by way of challenge, "or you can sit at your computer and do something that matters." It's a joke, but like all good jokes it inverts a commonly held belief—that real-life hobbies hold more inherent value than their online counterparts.

The same tension runs throughout the episode. When Randy advises Stan to go outside and socialize, the son exasperatedly snaps at his father, "I *am* socializing, r-tard! I'm logged on to an MMORPG with people from all over the world and getting XP with my party using TeamSpeak." Anyone who ever explained *WoW* (or frankly any video game) to his nagging parents felt this way, even if he deployed more diplomatic language. We always knew why we played! We could always articulate arguments for our preferred hobby, but our parents and teachers didn't seem to listen. For many of us, just getting consistent access to our favorite hobby was a constant struggle fraught with deception and the negotiation of strict screen-time limits. Online games represented yet a higher threshold, with broadband Internet not available in many locales prior to the early 2000s and many of our parents gravely concerned about online predators. I don't mean to dub these precautions unreasonable—if I had children I would attempt to limit their screen time and monitor their online activity—but they're doomed to fail. Children will always skirt around parental controls, particularly when it comes to technology. Try as they might, the older generations find themselves playing

---

* The Sword of a Thousand Truths was never a real item in *World of Warcraft*, though following the *South Park* episode several sly references were inserted into the game.

catch-up, hobbling along in a losing race like Stan's clueless dad trying to play alongside his son.

These ideas are not, as a matter of course, expressed on national television. To see them stated aloud in this forum of all forums was a revelation. The use of machinima, setting the episode's primary action in *WoW* while relegating the standard animation to expository scenes, inverts our expectations of sitcom structure just as it does the characters' priorities. Gamers are cynical by nature, inclined to police the borders of their culture (see, for example, the "Gamergate" campaign and its appalling suspicion of women in gaming). *South Park* attempted something that could succeed only with an earnest rendering both of video games and gaming culture, and few TV shows could have committed powerfully enough to pull it off. Watching this brilliant little tale unfold that Wednesday night, I felt truly special. Hearing the acknowledged voice of my culture speaking directly to me, and in the intensely private language of my chosen community, was the kind of "secular blessing" I mentioned early in this chapter.

Of course, the official coronation would come in the spring of the following year, when *South Park* executive producer Anne Garefino mounted a bedazzled stage in Los Angeles to accept the Emmy Award for Outstanding Animated Program. Not a coup, given *South Park*'s excellent track record in this category (2007 was its fourth win in as many years), but programs are nominated for individual episodes rather than body of work, and "Make Love, Not Warcraft"—twenty-two minutes of gleeful lunacy anchored by an authentically loving tribute to a video game played by less than 5 percent of the Television Academy voters*—was hardly critic-friendly fare. It won not because voters got every one of the jokes but because this episode made a definitive cultural statement, sanctifying video games as central to our culture. And *World of Warcraft* was no *Mario Bros.*, no *PAC-MAN*, no *DOOM*, no *Donkey Kong*. The other five games that accompanied *WoW* into the World Video Game Hall of Fame's inaugural class were accessible plug-and-play affairs built around a few

---

* Figure not remotely scientific but probably accurate.

brilliant mechanics. They were much older, with decades of history and numerous sequels. *WoW* was barely two years old, enormous and still adding more features every few months. It wasn't for everyone. Often it seemed the more you loved it the more it selfishly demanded of you. By rights it should not have driven its pilings near so deep in our culture's silty bed, and yet it spoke to so many people in such diverse circumstances that even the Hollywood establishment—for so long the epitome of sun-kissed cool, for so long hostile to gaming and fandom and anything else "nerdy" even as effects-driven fantasies accounted for many of its greatest hits—had to sit up straight and fumble for a notebook. *South Park*'s victory was a vision of (to use Cormac McCarthy's phrase) the darkening land, the world to come.

THE EXILE RETURNED

South Park was hardly alone in sowing the seeds of Azerothian fandom. *WoW* had barely been out for six months when comedian Dave Chappelle took the stage at the Punchline in San Francisco to announce, unprompted, "You know what I've been playing a lot of? *World of Warcraft!*"[*] Seeing as he'd quit his megahit *Chapelle's Show* and absconded to South Africa just the month before, scorning $55 million of Viacom's money in the process, he had a lot of free time on his hands. "I knew I had some geek brothers and sisters up in here!" he crowed at the audience's positive response. Not the hardest sell in the Bay Area, but the line wasn't uttered as a joke or as part of a larger thought. It was earnest, said off the cuff in a space between jokes, and as one of the comedian's few public missives at a time of great controversy it spread wider than it otherwise might have. It exploded on the Blizzard forums. If absolutely anything was cool in America in 2005, Dave Chappelle was cool, and he'd just declared himself for us!

They kept popping up, one at a time, these *WoW*-playing celebrities, these banner-bearers for geek culture in professions otherwise consumed by the definition and commodification of in-group status.

---

[*] The performance in question occurred the night of June 28, 2005.

Again, gaming culture is naturally wary of patronizing shills, but these confessions were so authentic, so deeply uncool to any rational calculus, that they couldn't help winning us over. Mila Kunis, already treasured by geekdom for her role as the long-suffering Meg on *Family Guy*, is the sort of sex-symbol actress a cynical sort might imagine breezily declaring her love of comic books or video games for careerist reasons. Yet in October 2008, she appeared on *Jimmy Kimmel Live!* and tensed up immediately at the mention of her gaming habits.

"Oh, you *are* gonna bring this up," she groans, shifting in her seat, gripping and then releasing the armrest, starting an explanation before arresting it, performing the classic gamer's calculation inside her head: How ignorant is my audience, and how much work will it therefore take to explain what I want to explain? "I don't know if anyone plays *Warcraft*," she says to the studio audience, long-practiced defensive instincts kicking in, assuming she's part of a cultural minority about which the majority cannot be expected to concern itself. An exchange with the host follows, revealing a great deal about their perspectives.

KIMMEL (slightly patronizing): "They do. People do. Yeah."

KUNIS: "Have you played it?"

KIMMEL: "I have not, but I've watched my son play it . . . he may have killed you a time or two! I don't know, he's good!"

KUNIS (straightening her spine, hackles raised): "I'm really good . . . like, I'm a *really* kickass mage."

Any notion of performance has now departed. Kunis isn't angry, but neither will her competitive nature allow a lazy comparison between a serious adult pursuit and the play of children. She's compelled to assert her kickass magedom even without explaining what a mage is. Kimmel, for his part, has misplayed the interview. Between his personal experience of *WoW* as a game for children and Hollywood's unstated assumptions around gaming, it does not occur to Kimmel that his guest might take this game very seriously. He cannot imagine her, Mila Kunis—global sex symbol, self-made millionaire, acclaimed and popular actor since the age of fifteen—taking *pride* in an online game. These are supposed to be trivial things, after all.

They're supposed to be places where, as Charles Barkley has said of social media, "losers go to feel important." How on earth could someone like Mila Kunis find value in such things? Kimmel gamely rolls the interview along, intrigued at her reaction.

KIMMEL: "Tell people how it works . . . you have, like, teams, right?"

KUNIS: "Well, no, you're your own person, and then you can get into a guild."

KIMMEL (amused): "Oh, a *guild*!" (laughter)

KUNIS (animated): "Well yeah, you gotta be in a guild! 'Cause you gotta do raids that require thirty or forty people, but now with the expansion pack, they're going to have raids that only require ten people . . ."

KIMMEL: "Oh, good! Whew."

KUNIS: "So it'll make things a lot easier."

She breaks into nervous laughter at the end of this statement, made suddenly self-conscious by Kimmel's (gently) sarcastic interjection, yanked from an animated explanation of a game she loves back into the reality of an ABC talk show where loving that game is no longer cool. Following the briefest of digressions into the PvP twinking scene—a discussion in which Kimmel is so lost that Kunis drops the subject completely, groaning "Oh my God"—she backtracks once again to the concept of guilds.

KUNIS: "We have a [chat] channel that's like my friends, the people that I actually know in real life . . . and then I'm in a *guild* guild, and in this guild I know nobody. They all think I'm either like a teacher, or I think I was an architect at one point, 'cause I traveled so much and I was on in different time zones and nobody understood what I did. So I was like, 'I'm an architect and I travel a lot,' and . . . they kind of just went with it."

KIMMEL: "It's because they're eight, by the way." (audience laughter) "That's why. They're nine years old. You could have said you're an astronaut and they would have said, 'Oh, awesome!'"

Though Kunis laughs along with Kimmel and the segment's tone never turns cruel, I still find it depressing to see anyone chastened for expressing what she loves. That's really what this becomes, particularly in the end: a young woman describing her favorite hobby, sharing what she likes best about it, and trying to bring more people into that experience while her interlocutor uses her earnestness as a springboard for lazy jokes. Kunis leaves herself vulnerable here. Hollywood actresses do not, as a general rule, delve into the design contrasts between MMORPG expansion packs on national television, and her host would rather wallow in preconception. He'd yelp Freudian jibes to a unicorn, but his guest, in the cosmic view, comes out on top: she gets to keep being *Mila Kunis*, Hollywood actress and (as of the *Warlords of Draenor* expansion) an NPC in *World of Warcraft*.

GEOMANCING

Oh, how things have changed! Just a few short years later, one could already perceive the altered landscape. Where the mainstream media[*] had once been content to define *WoW* as the territory of misfits and losers, they now found in its fan base a deep well of charm. The fact that normal, functional members of society played online games in a serious way was no longer treated as a troubling indictment (unhinged subversives walking among us!) of those games but rather as a positive attribute. Looking back, I see no obvious inflection point. I could pick one out of a hat, assemble an argument, and present it in glibly Gladwellian fashion as THE MOMENT THAT CHANGED OUR CULTURE, but I'd rather just explore these positive changes and the better, more open world we all get to live in! Let's stay in the talk show space, since any good *WoW* player knows to clear out all the quests in a zone.

Jimmy Fallon is not the same person as Jimmy Kimmel. I point this out because they are both dark-suited white men named Jimmy hosting late-night network talk shows, and thus can be hard to distinguish. Several years after Kimmel needled Mila Kunis about her

---

[*] This phrase is generally overused, but in this instance I take it to mean print publications, feature films, and television (both broadcast and cable).

gaming habits, *Late Night with Jimmy Fallon* demonstrated the intervening cultural shift with a short musical segment titled "We Are the
World (of Warcraft)." As a song it does little to recommend itself,
but as an unalloyed item of fan service it cannot help but succeed.
Fallon opens the segment with a quick declaration of love for the
game, and what follows is a music video in montage form, combining
footage of Fallon, *WoW*-playing celebrities Felicia Day (about whom
more later) and Chris Hardwick, Blizzard Entertainment employ-
ees, and fans around the world singing a send-up of 1985's "We Are
the World" into their PC webcams. What the presentation lacks in
polish it more than makes up for with charm—indeed, the low fidelity, poor lip-synching, and clumsy lyrics only add to the video. The
song's conclusion hides no punchline, just a globe-shaped mosaic of
hundreds of player portraits all singing along that eventually merges
into the game's classic splash screen. There's no joke. The sequence
exists purely as declarative statement: "We exist, and we celebrate
our community." That this kind of show might run this kind of piece
was inconceivable in December 2010. In June 2013, the world was
already a different place.

Just ten days following Fallon's musical number, *WoW* made
another late-night appearance, this time on Conan O'Brien's TBS
show. Among his guests was Chris Kluwe, at the time a punter
for the NFL's Oakland Raiders and a *WoW* fanatic (his Twitter
handle is @ChrisWarcraft). Kluwe appeared to discuss the gay
marriage equality debate, into which he'd repeatedly stepped with
passionate and often hilarious advocacy. After the first portion of
the interview, focusing largely on issues of equality and empathy,
O'Brien asks about his guest's gaming habits. Note how his phrasing approaches the subject differently from Kimmel and how it
reveals a different set of underlying assumptions though neither
host plays games himself:

O'Brien: "I found this really fascinating. You're quite an avid
online gamer; we talked about this a little bit before the show. You've
ranked third nationally in 'dungeon progression'—I don't even know
what that is!"

KLUWE: "I'm about to nerd everyone out here, which will be amazing. . . . So I played *World of Warcraft* for a very long time and I was in a raiding guild. And in raiding the goal of 'dungeon progression' is to defeat the bosses—it's kind of like solving a puzzle, each boss has different mechanics—and I was in a hardcore raiding guild, which means that we took it very seriously. And so at one point we were third in the United States in terms of raiding progression, which meant we stayed up very late at night and kept pounding our heads against these bosses over and over until we beat them."

O'BRIEN: "That's incredible . . . it's amazing because you're a player in the NFL, but it seems like your true dream—what you're most proud of—is that you've ranked third nationally in *dungeon progression!*"

This is the exact sandbar on which Kimmel ran aground. O'Brien approaches it from the start not as an embarrassing fact about Kluwe, not something to needle, but as something legitimately interesting. Part of that is the apparent novelty of an RPG-gaming jock, and O'Brien says as much, but when he sees the contrast between popular conception and reality his inclination is to explore rather than mock. Having elicited as fine and concise an explanation of MMORPG raiding as I've ever heard on television, O'Brien is able to cut through the dross and detail to the core issue. On some level Kimmel acknowledged Kunis's pride, but he merely snickered rather than put the pieces together and articulate, as O'Brien does, that his guest's gaming life runs parallel to his or her highly televised profession. Like most adults who love video games, Kluwe admits he works "to fund my nerdy habits." One side of his life need not inform the other. Of course there are exceptions; no human being can commit herself to two separate pursuits and hold them truly parallel, *never* intersecting. Kluwe picks up on the point:

KLUWE: "That is the only time in my life I've actually dropped the 'Hey, I'm an NFL player' card, was when I applied to the raiding guild.* I really wanted to get in, so I said, 'I'm in the NFL, let me in!'

---

* The guild in question, the Flying Hellfish of the Kil'jaeden server, were at one point the top Horde raiding guild in North America. Their kill videos were vital assets for any progression-minded Horde guild.

And they said, 'Oh my God! An NFL player is playing, so let's let him in!'"

Pushing the parallels together, forcing an intersection, is like fusing hydrogen atoms: it demands a great deal of force and it risks an explosive catastrophe. Celebrity provides the necessary energy, though it's worth noting Kluwe is unusual in allowing his online and offline personas to be linked. Elsewhere in her interview with Kimmel, Kunis mentions fleeing from a guild after speaking over Ventrilo and having her (distinctive and famous) voice recognized. "I never went back," she says, and any sensitive human being likely understands why. Anonymity privileges the least powerful person in any relationship, and while famous men may occasionally enjoy their fame online, famous women find themselves deluged with vile and toxic harassment. For women in general, revealing one's identity online is often taken by men as an invitation to engage in utterly barbaric behavior.

"Pics or GTFO"

The game's presentation of gender is one of the first things new players will see. Gender in *WoW* has always been binary, determined by a single mouse click on the New Character screen (though players can now pay fifteen dollars to change gender, facial features, and other customizable options). As has become standard in video games, male and female avatars have identical statistics and abilities. The choice is meant to be purely cosmetic, but in practice that click has profound implications for the avatar's place in the social order.

This won't come as news to any observant citizen of the Internet, but women aren't treated well online. The same structural biases permeating our society find their way onto the Internet as overt expression, as anonymity encourages performance of one's toxic attitudes and open association makes it easy to find others who share them. When angry, unhealthy people congregate, they bring out the absolute worst in one another. Barbaric behavior proliferates, decent actors withdraw from the public square, and anyone could predict the end result: many if not most online spaces are actively hostile to women. Though populated with a higher percentage of women than most online games,* *WoW* is no exception.

To create a female avatar is to mark oneself indelibly for separate treatment, even though the number of such avatars overstates the number of actual women. Researchers tracking 375 *WoW* players through a custom scenario found the male players picking opposite-gender avatars at three times the rate of women. The study's authors dug deeper for some interesting findings: while men playing female avatars tended to emote and communicate more expressively in-game, this didn't seem to be deliberate. That is to say, these men engaged in traditionally feminine behaviors not out of any impulse to deceive but because they unconsciously conformed to social expectations. This impulse is reasonably well established among social scientists. Those men also tended to prefer traditional heteronormative presentations—human over dwarf, blood elf over orc, fashion-model figures, long hair, and the like—in their chosen avatars. "I don't want to look at a dude's butt all day," goes the familiar refrain. Men who spend hundreds of hours inhabiting this avatar's skin would prefer the skin be sexually appealing. Women don't seem to share the same impulse, perhaps because video game art styles tend to be designed by men for male consumption.

Anyone who takes progression seriously in *WoW*, whether in PvE or PvP, must eventually get on voice chat. A few organized groups will allow members to listen and not speak, but most demand proof of a functioning microphone for admittance. In a pitched battle, you can't stop to type. Thus women who want to play more than casually must "out" themselves, and even a well-behaved guild can't totally protect them, because once you're a woman known as such within your realm community, everything changes. Flirtatious messages arrive in text chat, as does outright harassment, though *WoW*'s

---

* The actual percentage is a topic of debate. Nick Yee's "Daedalus Project" used opt-in survey data to arrive at a figure just south of 15 percent, while Dutch gaming analytics firm NewZoo places the number as high as 35 percent.

in-game customer service does a better job than most of responding to complaints and banning harassers. They take hate speech quite seriously, so long as it's explicit in nature—anything short of an outright slur will probably get a pass. As in real life, the vast majority of harassment is committed by people eager to exploit the rules, to stand one inch from the line jeering that it's not quite the line. Even a shade of subtlety can render something heinous unactionable.

First and most obvious to any observer of Western civilization, there's the suggestion that women are inferior gamers. Pick any activity seen as traditionally male (poker, chess, anything to do with cars) and you'll find men convinced women can't, or don't want to, compete. Whether anyone holding this belief could articulate a logically sound reason why is another question, but it's widespread in gaming. One might intuitively think it's less common in MMORPGs, with their leveling of skill disparities in favor of time invested, but that turns out only to harden the critique around a grain of truth.

Female gamers might be every bit as skilled as their male counterparts, but they tend to be older by roughly six years, and that age difference is quite significant in a population already selected for youth. Those years come with a terrible escalation in responsibilities as free time gives way to commuting, work, a spouse, children. Older gamers simply don't play as much; what Nick Yee and others call the "achievement motivation" rapidly diminishes alongside the compulsion to invest long hours in the pursuit of virtual rewards. Women also live in a patriarchal society outside of *WoW*, one that that sits in judgment of their limited leisure time and actively looks to criticize their choices. Many women report feelings of guilt and anxiety while engaging in leisure pursuits, nagged by the feeling they should be doing something "productive." Under these conditions, it's perfectly easy to understand why many women invest less time in online gaming than their male counterparts and fall prey to pernicious notions of gender disparity. To the degree that women underachieve in online games relative to men, it's the inevitable product of sexism—not a warrant for it.

Second, leaving aside all explicit value judgments, female gamers face presumptions about traditional gender roles. Women are thought—so it is written in the Codex of Misogynon—to gravitate naturally to healing and support roles, rather than tanking and DPS. Tanks in particular are always assumed to be male even if their avatars are female, due to the ideas of toughness and leadership bonded to tank roles. To the extent that women play DPS, they're thought to play ranged classes rather than melee, staying clear of harm. Blood elf hunters and night elf druids are probably the two most stereotypical character selections a woman can make.

Yet again, data-driven studies contradict the popular wisdom. Male and female players choose to heal at roughly the same rate, with the men healing slightly more.* Sadly, this argument won't change bigoted minds, both because they're bigoted and because the persistence of the women-as-healers myth is perpetuated by a phenomenon discussed earlier: that of gender-bending. Men create a lot of female avatars (33 percent of the avatars attached to male accounts were female as opposed to 9 percent male characters on female accounts) and they tend to play those avatars in ways they *believe* females behave, including a strong preference for healing. Yee explains: "Female characters had a much higher healing ratio compared with male characters. This disparity was a direct consequence of how players behave when they gender-bend. When men . . . play female characters, they spend more time healing. When women . . . play male characters, they spend less time healing. . . . They enact the expected gender roles of their characters. As players conform to gender stereotypes, what was false becomes true." The community thinks women heal more, so players with

---

* The data behind this claim, and many others in this section, can be found in Nick Yee's excellent book *The Proteus Paradox*. Parsing in-game data, Yee et al. measured "healing ratio," defined as the ratio of characters' healing to their damage, and found that across their large sample the ratio was 33 percent for men and 30 percent for women. This means that men devoted 33 percent of their combat output to healing, as opposed to 30 percent for women. Because classes are specialized, any given player's number would likely be much lower or higher (rogues near 0 percent, holy priests near 100 percent). Healing ratio attempts to isolate this particular activity from the surrounding statistical noise of class, role, and time played.

female avatars act out expected gender roles and heal more, thus reinforcing the stereotype.

Third, women gamers are said to be selfish, manipulative, and flirty in the pursuit of social or material currency. They are said to be needy and attention-seeking and just about any other negative stereotype attached to the female half of our species since the dawn of civilization. Here data is no sure guide. These are character judgments, after all, open to interpretation, contingent on context, wed to anecdote. If there's anything the online world teaches us, it's the power of perception to warp reality. Does anyone seriously believe that women perpetrate more unwanted sexual advances than men?

While I have no doubt that Blizzard, given a mechanism to erase these toxic ideas from their game, would eagerly do it, they're part of the same sexist society in which we all live. Top-down wouldn't be effective even were it practical. What *is* effective—devastatingly so—at stamping out misogyny? Why, the very same social structures that propagate it!

"IF YOU BUILD IT . . ."

Not every woman who ever logged in to *WoW* did so in the face of relentless hostility. For all the indignities of a pickup Deadmines group or Barrens General chat, women are resourceful enough to establish comfortable places for themselves. It was all about finding the right guild. Playing with friends, family, or coworkers was one way to limit one's exposure to negativity, but as discussed in chapter 4, these small guilds tend to limit one's progression. When it came to larger guilds with more ambition, more than a few guild masters were female, and many guilds nominally run by men featured female leadership. Female voices and perspectives, always valuable because they are attached to human beings, nonetheless supply a necessary counterbalance to the testosterone-addled youth endemic to online games. In my experience, the thoughtful and deliberate approach characterizing the most successful guilds bled over into their social dynamics. The more accomplished the guild, the more likely it is to be inclusive. This might seem counterintuitive to those who associate more investment in gaming with toxic misogyny, but that attitude doesn't match up with the real world. Everyone's heard of *WoW* but not many outside the community truly understand it, so it often finds itself the target of activist scrutiny, but basic misconceptions can seep into that activism and limit its impact.

Angela Washko, a visiting professor in the School of Art at Carnegie Mellon University, created a series of video performances called "Playing a Girl" in which she engaged live *WoW* players in discussions about feminism. While loitering around the Valley of Trials in Orgrimmar, Washko asks essentially anonymous players about their attitudes and opinions. Never leading the discussion but rather facilitating and perpetuating it, she records strange and fascinating and surprisingly raw chats with total strangers over gender issues. She appreciates the honesty allowed by anonymity, but I wonder if she isn't looking in the wrong places. Washko uses Orgrimmar because she figures it takes substantial effort to reach the city from starting zones, but in reality a capital city is just about the worst place in Azeroth to have an intelligent discussion. Without impugning Washko's knowledge of the game, this seems like an interesting but highly limited approach—a tactic to impress outsiders, putting a community on display without trying to know it. For a better alternative I point to another online video project, one that used an insider's perspective to engage millions of gamers around the globe: Felicia Day's legendary webseries *The Guild*.

Prior to 2007, Felicia Day was an actor best known for a recurring role in the final season of *Buffy the Vampire Slayer*. With interests ranging from classical violin to tabletop gaming, Day had passionately played *World of Warcraft* for two years (she describes it as an addiction) before quitting and finding she missed her guildmates more than any element of the game itself. Inspired by *WoW*'s diversity and camaraderie, "I decided to write something to show the world that gamers weren't just guys in their twenties who lived in their mom's basement." The resulting sitcom script went nowhere, dubbed too "niche" for television audiences, so Day recruited improv collaborators Sandeep Parikh and Jeff Lewis to help her produce it as a webseries. The first episode appeared on YouTube July 27, 2007. Six years and six seasons later, it concluded, having amassed over three hundred million cumulative views. Over its run it featured multiple Hollywood cameos, redefined the ceiling for webseries success, and turned every one of its actors into stars on the convention circuit.

The series tells the story of Codex (Day), a healing priest in a nameless *WoW*-analogue MMORPG, as she and her guildmates negotiate challenges both in and out of "the Game." A webcam-style perspective flashes between characters at their PCs, communicating over voice chat. Everyone in the Guild lives in the same area, a conceit that allows Day to bring them together in person whenever it serves the story. Social status and gender roles are the show's primary theme, as the protagonist answers her front door in the first episode to find Zaboo the warlock (Parikh) standing there with a bouquet of spray-painted roses. Having misinterpreted Codex's cavalier use of semicolons as romantic interest, Zaboo has left his mother's house to move in with her. We quickly meet the rest of the guild: uptight warrior and leader Vork, bubbly frost mage Clara, Tinkerballa the cynical and vindictive hunter, Bladezzz the vapid yet conniving rogue. The show understands the culture of 2007 with respect to games and so at first its characters seem like trite archetypes. Vork is a middle-aged bachelor living illicitly off his deceased grandfather's Social Security checks; Zaboo initially presents as a cringe-inducing stereotype of a henpecked sexually impotent South Asian man. But by the first season's end some forty minutes later (as a webseries, it is short) every member of the guild has been fleshed out in amusing and emotionally rewarding depth.

The best comedies are, at their core, about failure. Day arms her characters with a diverse arsenal of shortcomings, from Zaboo's total naïveté to Bladezzz's helplessness at the hands of his kid sister. Codex often finds herself crippled by anxiety and cannot function in any social setting. Each character has a unique relationship to the Game and makes his or her own hyperbolic compromises to play it. For all the persistent suggestion that this is unhealthy, that the characters play to fill deep wells of sadness, it's all in good fun, and by the series finale everyone (especially Codex) has grown and matured through his or her in-game exploits.

Through it all, *The Guild*'s first and last impulses are to be funny. It succeeds because of a comic premise gamers deploy all the time among themselves, transposing game values and logic onto real life. Striking out on a date becomes a failed Charisma roll; a guildmate's fire alarm clamors away on voice chat and you beg him not to leave his keyboard, insisting his character is wearing plenty of fire resistance gear. Hearing the fictional Clara groan "Ugh, husband aggro!" when asked to participate in her own family life rings like hammer on bell. *The Guild* succeeds because above all else it speaks to MMORPG gamers in their own language—their in-group references, their slang, their thorough understanding of game mechanics—with more specificity than anyone had ever before seen. I hadn't watched it myself until beginning this book, though of course I was aware of it, and even in a research mind-set I found myself laughing aloud at the cleverest in-jokes. Without spoiling anything, there exists in season 3 an absolutely sublime line about a five-piece armor set bonus. It should be impossible for a piece of popular entertainment to crack a laugh-out-loud joke about something so infinitesimally niche, but this is the world we've come to live in. This is the culture *WoW* seized on and propagated to untold millions.

The Guild changed the online entertainment ecosystem, particularly as seasons 2 through 5 found paid distribution through Microsoft's Xbox Live Marketplace. Day retained full ownership and eventually walked away from Microsoft to distribute the sixth and final season herself (along with all the other material, which can be found on YouTube, Netflix, and Hulu, among other services). From nothing but passion, free time, and—yes, let's be fair—Hollywood talent arose a permanent fixture of the gaming culture canon, built and grown and promoted and owned by a woman.

That last part is important, though Day doesn't emphasize it in interviews or even in the show itself. *The Guild* isn't an explicitly feminist show; in fact, it features a good deal of material the 2015 Internet would dub "problematic." But nearly every one of those instances is consistent with character, with setting, with the dialogue between actual gamers while comfortable in their own communities. It's real, it's accessible, and it truly loves each of its wacky characters, even the execrable antagonist Fawkes, played greasily by *Star Trek: The Next Generation*'s Wil Wheaton. It demonstrates, I think, the limitations of Angela Washko's brand of activism. Gaming culture can absolutely be toxic and misogynistic, but in the end those elements are a small (if vocal) minority generally born of ignorance. An insular culture such as this is best changed from the inside, through authentic engagement, through the building of progressive guilds and hilarious webseries, through creative construction rather than discursion and deconstruction.

Halfway to Cyberpunk

Players on every continent sampled *World of Warcraft*'s pleasures, both sacred and profane, but those in Asia had a much different experience. I note first that *WoW* has only ever been officially released in two Asian countries: South Korea and China, about which more in a moment. Everyone else on that side of the globe played the American release, buying their games on eBay, using VPNs to connect, and getting redeemable game time cards shipped around the world. Suffering from constant latency issues due to geographic distance, they congregated in their own guilds on West Coast servers to try to minimize the annoyance. *WoW* was the biggest game in the world, and this was their only way to play it. In Japan, *WoW* was never more than an afterthought—for all that nation's love of video games, they prefer their own. American-made titles have never been popular.

Korea and China represented special opportunities for Blizzard and its parent company, Vivendi Universal Games (which merged with Activision in 2008 to become Activision Blizzard). The former is a country of fifty million people, a market typically too small for

American game companies to invest much in penetrating, but Korea is a unique exception. Government initiatives have made it the most Internet-connected nation in the world, and its citizens absolutely adore video games. They love Blizzard's games in particular—1998's *StarCraft* took Korea by storm, to the degree that it is often, without a trace of irony, called the national sport. *StarCraft II* may have been the republic's most eagerly anticipated entertainment release of all time. Professional e-sports got their start in Korea, where top gamers are legitimate celebrities accosted on the streets. Blizzard properties and characters achieve Disney levels of recognition. Most American MMORPGs never appear in Korea, but *WoW* was a risk-free proposition.

WoW's Korean servers opened in January 2005, a month before the European servers would go online but with a much different business model. Blizzard's practice for their North American, Australian, and European launches, wherein customers went to a store and bought a piece of software to install on their personal machines, simply wouldn't work for Asian markets. Koreans see gaming as a public and social practice. Massive Internet connectivity and rapidly evolving hardware made the in-home PC—a staple of American gaming life, a critical component to the tired trope of portly losers in basements—an odd contrivance, one most Koreans were happy to eschew. Most gaming in Korea occurs in Internet cafés, stocked by their proprietors with row after row of flashing flatscreens, boasting extensive menus of food and drink. Gamers pay for time on the machines rather than time on their accounts, with Blizzard ultimately drawing its revenue from the proprietors rather than players themselves. Some cafés include sleeping capsules, or premium facilities with superior computer hardware. Koreans flock to these social hubs at all hours of the day and night, occasionally indulging in hair-raising binges. Every so often a truly troubled individual will perish—or worse, fatally neglect a child at home—and as those horror stories are the only press that gaming cafés receive internationally, they're what Americans think of first.

But people build real and lasting relationships at these places. They meet their spouses at cafés, congregate with school friends, establish interests and identities apart from those expressed at home. Many of my fondest adolescent memories are of all-night LAN parties with friends in someone's basement, creating the same kind of immersive private space Asian gamers have come to expect. While that same physical proximity has its drawbacks—scuffles over in-game drama, a potential element of danger introduced to women, trans people, and other out-groups (very real in homogeneous and sexually conservative societies)—it's the established way of life for gamers in much of the world.

The cyber café phenomenon extends to China, a nation much larger than Korea but not nearly so open. The government strictly regulates Chinese access to Western networks and so American developers looking to access the Chinese market must adapt their games appropriately. "Anti-obsession" mechanisms severely weaken any avatar playing more than three hours without logging out for at least five. Characters may not smoke tobacco or drink liquor. Chinese culture holds no particular mores about bones or the undead, but the government discourages explicit references to death. Undead avatars may not show exposed bones, and dead characters who resurrect find their corpse replaced not with a skeleton but with a gravestone.

With the *Wrath of the Lich King* expansion, censorship loomed as high and dark and unyielding as Icecrown Citadel itself. The new content, premised largely on undead armies, rankled Chinese officials and doomed the game to an uphill battle. Lord Marrowgar, a raid boss built entirely of bone, received such an imaginative artistic reworking that non-Chinese players expressed regret at their own model (grimly overwrought like the logo for a black metal band). The new death knight player class nearly found itself excised from the expansion entirely; in the end it remained, instead called a fade knight. Bureaucratic infighting between the General Administration of Press and Publications and the Ministry of Culture further muddied the waters. Blizzard decided to switch Chinese distributors, and the resulting server migrations took the game offline entirely for *three months*. Policy disputes between the Chinese and US governments, entirely unrelated to *WoW*, made regulatory snarls even trickier to resolve.

Wrath of the Lich King would eventually launch, eighteen months late, and players had barely enjoyed the content when, ten months later, the *Cataclysm* expansion coasted through censors to land on Chinese shores. In 2012 *Mists of Pandaria*, with its China-themed artwork and lore, faced no obstacles, and Chinese players were tackling new challenges just days after their American and European counterparts. For the first time, they felt they could compete on equal ground for world-first achievements, and Chinese raiding guilds (particularly the legendary Stars) have been fiercely competing for these honors ever since. *Warlords of Draenor* similarly saw no substantial challenges to overseas release. The People's Republic of China continues to take a strong interest in video games as a component of culture, and their officials fret openly over gaming addiction, but China has made its peace with *WoW*, and Blizzard clearly intends to keep the cyber cafés humming for as long as its millions of fans will stay.

China's affection for *WoW* loomed large as late as summer 2016, when the big-budget Hollywood film *Warcraft* appeared in theaters worldwide. Directed by promising young director Duncan Jones (*Moon, Source Code*), the movie was made through a collaboration between Blizzard Entertainment, Legendary Pictures (acquired by Wanda Group, a Chinese conglomerate, in January of that year), and venerable American studio Universal Pictures. Its plot loosely tracked the 1994 strategy game *Warcraft*, set a generation before the events of *World of Warcraft*. Players immediately recognized such series stalwarts as the tragically corrupted wizard Medivh, his youthful apprentice Khadgar, and the insidious orc warlock Gul'dan. Critics, however, held no standing affection for these characters and roundly panned the movie. It was compared, in some publications, to John Travolta's legendarily atrocious vanity project *Battlefield Earth*, widely considered among the worst movies of all time. Where fans of the series thrilled to see their favorite fantasy world brought to Hollywood life—I had to restrain myself from shouting in the theater at the appearance of tower steward Moroes, whose ghostly remains are a boss in *The Burning Crusade*—critics saw mush. More than a few reviews included "game over" jokes. I'm obviously not an objective viewer, and can understand why viewers who weren't already fans of the source material might not have liked the movie. But judged on the terms of Hollywood blockbusters in 2016, it really wasn't that bad. For all the critical savagery, *Warcraft* grossed north of $430 million in theaters, representing about a $15 million loss for its parent studios: neither a success nor a flop. Sequels have been greenlit for less.

Media commentators were surprised by how the revenue fell out. Less than $50 million came from US audiences, whereas Chinese filmgoers coughed up over $200 million. Hollywood has long relied on foreign revenues to bolster action franchises like the *Fast & Furious* movies (speeding cars translate better across cultures than dialogue), but this volume of Chinese turnout was something new. It suggested Hollywood films could make money even if they bypassed American audiences altogether, so long as they sprang from widely known franchises—and after twelve years at or near the center of online culture, few properties command more recognition than *World of Warcraft*.

A GENERATION'S WAR CRY

But there is no greater emblem of *WoW*'s world renown than Leeroy. Leeroy has endured since the dawn, as far back as anyone remembers, so long ago consecrated into legend, such a cultural totem that it seems Leeroy has always existed. I speak, as you know, of Leeroy Jenkins, the single most famous *World of Warcraft* player in history.

In May 2005 most *WoW* players were still in the process of leveling. Those at level 60 worked their way slowly and painfully through endgame content frequently beset by glitches and poorly implemented mechanics. "Broken" would be a kind word. The "whelp room" of Upper Blackrock Spire earned itself a high rank amid the game's frustrations—every single player who ever set foot in the instance wiped in that room at least once—and so when an unknown guild from the Laughing Skull server posted a wipe video on popular site Warcraft Movies (YouTube was not then the worldwide phenomenon it has become) titled "A Rough Go," everyone thought she knew what to expect. She, whoever she was, would have been wrong. What started as "A Rough Go" quickly became the most popular video on the site by a Kalimdor mile and became immortalized as "the Leeroy Jenkins video."

I don't want to describe it in much detail, both because doing so would water down the experience of watching the actual video, and because anyone reading this has almost certainly seen it. If not, take three minutes out of your life to do so. The setup is simple enough: a raid group discusses their strategy for negotiating the swarms of dragon whelps in the rookery, only to have a paladin named Leeroy Jenkins jump the gun and charge in, screaming his own name as a war cry. The entire party suffers fiery deaths. Nothing about the video's production or action is particularly noteworthy; the payoff moments charm, but they're hardly hysterical. Still, something in those three minutes captures the imagination. The video is almost certainly staged, an assertion over which Leeroy himself (in reality a lighting technician named Ben Schulz) has always been coy. "I like people to decide for themselves," he likes to say. "It's more fun that way." I don't find that question interesting; I'm fascinated by the response to the video, by its eternal life in online memehood.

With countless mirrors uploaded over the years it's impossible to tell how many views Leeroy Jenkins has accrued. Let us conservatively place the sum in the tens of millions. It is entirely possible more people have seen the video than have ever played *WoW* itself. I vividly remember a moment just weeks after the video's release when, during a pickup basketball game with college dormmates, a large and unathletic man with the ball at the top of the key suddenly bellowed *"LEEEEROOOYYY JEEEENNKINS"* and drove to the hoop like a wounded bison affixed to the prow of a locomotive. He missed. I remember laughing at the display, thinking, That's funny, Dan doesn't play *WoW*. I remember noticing I wasn't the only one laughing—almost everyone on the court was doubled over with laughter. They'd all seen the video. It was an eerie sensation, hearing an in-joke only weeks into its existence, seeing my peers collectively fall about, knowing *not one of them* played the game Dan was referencing. It may be difficult to appreciate at this late date in human affairs, but there was once a time when references to online memes based on subscriber-only video games did not generally induce laughter in human beings.

Years to come would see Schulz interviewed on NPR and numerous print outlets, make convention appearances, work as a broadcaster for *WoW* arena tournaments, and appear bellowing his famous name for Jimmy Fallon's "We Are the World (of Warcraft)," earning the montage's biggest audience cheer though few could ever have recognized his face. Blizzard at first recognized Leeroy with a special achievement awarding the avatar title "Jenkins" to anyone who slew fifty rookery whelps in fifteen seconds. The *Warlords of Draenor* expansion updated Upper Blackrock Spire to include Leeroy as an NPC players can choose to assist (again, for the title "Jenkins"). There is just something fun about Leeroy, a boundless enthusiasm indifferent to consequence, a pure silliness: traits that ultimately came to define an entire generation's tastes. Whether we're discussing LOL-cat pictures, PewDiePie videos on YouTube, or Jimmy Fallon himself playing silly games with Hollywood celebrities, this whimsical approach is the gold standard of online humor. Featuring homemade production values, a staid setup transitioning to explosive mayhem, an approach layering goofiness over apparent naturalism, and (most important!) at least one infinitely repeatable catchphrase, "A Rough Go" is an early but complete primer in viral hit-making.

It should come as no surprise, therefore, that Schulz and his comrades never made any money off their wildly popular creation. Machinima videos can't generally be copyrighted, as the art and game worlds depicted therein don't belong to the filmmakers and thus can't be traditionally monetized. Today countless video services kick advertising income back to their most popular creators, but ten years ago the idea of viral video sensations was relatively new. Schulz and company may have staged their famous video, but they were clearly not prepared for what became of it—and who, in 2005, could have been? Today anyone with viral success knows to trademark and promote their characters, ideas, and catchphrases. Models exist to follow. Not so for Schulz and his guild, PALS FOR LIFE, who found themselves late to their own party and remained in obscurity.

Proceeding in tandem with players' real lives regardless of their station or celebrity, *WoW* offered both emotional refuge and personal growth. *WoW* opened new perspective, offering an alternate timeline by which to record our lives. Because we expected that separation, it was both jarring and thrilling to see ever-increasing intersections with the familiar offline world around us. Pop culture swallowed Azeroth whole, and all parties were shocked at how easily it went down, how quickly everything changed to recognize us MMOers—we who'd long since grown comfortable being outsiders.

Of course, one cannot separate this story from the Internet at large. *WoW* grew alongside it, having the good fortune to emerge at the moment broadband was spreading like wildfire across the United States* and the creative chops to stand as the biggest and best online game in existence. *World of Warcraft* abounds with puns and referential jokes, keeping an otherwise staid high fantasy world from ever feeling heavy. Whether you're meeting a big-game-hunting dwarven analogue to Ernest Hemingway or rolling your eyes at the achievement called "Vrykul Story, Bro," playing *WoW* always feels like a tour around the Internet's sunniest climes.

Millions of people learned to use the Internet and *WoW* simultaneously; still more officially linked their online and offline personas for the very first time. As with all great achievements, whether in culture or science, what was once revolutionary has become established—a feature of the landscape, accepted, assumed, inescapable. So the Internet must seem to have always existed, though its whole

---

* Between 2003 and 2006, the portion of US households with broadband doubled from 9.5 percent to 20.1 percent, the largest three-year jump in history. The number currently stands around 30 percent. Source: Dynamic Report, International Telecommunication Union, June 2013.

lifetime is subsumed by our own, though at every step and stage we watched its development. Our speech, our deeds, and even our thoughts have grown to accommodate these features. They mark our time as surely as presidential election cycles, and so I believe there will be until the day of our species' extinction at least one soul living who remembers Leeroy Jenkins.

« 9 »

THE STORYTELLERS

APRIL 2010

♦

In the end, walking away was nothing dramatic—no failed exam, no personal crisis, no moment of truth like they contrive in the movies. You don't think in advance about how your MMORPG character's story will end, not the way football players dream of walking through confetti into the sunset like Elway. It just happens, slowly or all at once. You might see it coming in advance, attached to a specific date like a deployment to Afghanistan, or it might come up suddenly like the news you've failed advanced Chinese and won't be graduating. In my case, it happened without me really noticing. Late in *Wrath of the Lich King* I got a new job whose hours precluded raiding with Elitist Jerks, and by the time I returned to a raid-friendly schedule, the prospect didn't enthuse. *WoW* just didn't feel the same, not raiding nor arenas nor anything else. It wasn't the focused misery I'd felt in the last T K T days. I returned to the old ways and realized I simply hadn't missed them. The good old days, when Chris and I tromped through a fascinating world of mystery in search of loot and adventure, were gone. The excitement and pride of building our own guild up from nothing to top class, of learning how to play together, were never coming back. That didn't make me sad and it still doesn't. Everything comes to an end—even the best things—and we needn't cling to them. Let ends be ends. So I stopped payment on my account and uninstalled the game client, and without even a formal good-bye, I was gone.

In the months following my *WoW* account's lapse into inactive status, I'd still check up on things. Elitist Jerks remained my browser homepage—I followed their progress through the end of Icecrown Citadel—and I read up on the upcoming plans for *Cataclysm*. I'd use the fabulous but now defunct Blizzard Armory website to scan my old guildmates for the new gear they found each week. I looked at Ghando, at the accomplishments he'd earned in the in-game achievements system, the gear he still wore even in that suspended state. At the guild tag with all the prestige attached, both of which stayed precious long after it ceased mattering to anyone in my daily life. Weeks stretched into months and the checks were less frequent, like furtive glances at an old flame's Facebook page, until at last they were just a trickle. Once a year or so, I'd glance at my old account info and wonder what it would be like to play *WoW* again. Never too much, since I knew the good old times weren't ever coming back. I've never been the type to waffle on these things, and I didn't then, but it persisted as a kind of daydream. Then, one day, Ghando disappeared.

While actively playing, I'd used a Blizzard authenticator for account security—a physical object kept at my desk, which when prompted displayed a code unlocking my account. Once I stopped playing *WoW* I unlinked the authenticator and lent it to a friend for his account. Many months later when I checked my account, my alts were all in place but my treasured shaman was gone. He must have been stolen, I thought: transferred off my account while compromised by one of the many outfits constantly hacking Blizzard accounts, whose existence encouraged me to get an authenticator in the first place. This was no material blow—while at several points in the past Ghando may have been worth hundreds of dollars, his value was now confined exclusively to the sentimental. Here I could embark on a soliloquy about this loss as a kind of death, as a comment on the folly of bonding with digital avatars, but in truth it elicited no strong reaction. I was a little sad, but the episode really just confirmed the decision: I wasn't going back.

Until I did.

JANUARY 2016

It was this book that did it. You can't write effectively about a game you haven't played in years, not even about its distant history, and besides, *WoW* was the ideal medium by which to speak with those still active in the community. So at the start of 2016, well into the *Warlords of Draenor* expansion but still in advance of *Legion*, I downloaded the game client and bought *Warlords*. Before renewing my subscription I checked the account and saw the listed characters: my mage alt, my priest, and my death knight. No shaman, no Ghando. With a sigh I decided I would spend the expansion's new catch-up mechanism, a free boost to level 90, on the priest. I paid for a three-month subscription, settled into my seat, and fired up *WoW*. Following the *Warlords of Draenor* opening cinematic (spectacular in classic Blizzard fashion, as detailed and polished as a major Hollywood production), I faced the familiar login screen. The Dark Portal of Draenor stood monolithic and malevolent as it had in *The Burning Crusade*, red and orange now instead of fluorescent green, demanding only my account name and password for entry into a world of infinitely entertaining adventure. I punched it in, and the six-digit code for the authenticator I'd since retrieved. Never again would I suffer a character's permanent loss. The login server labored a moment and yielded. I was in.

And suddenly there he was. Atop my character list on the Mal'ganis realm, standing some eight feet tall, broad of shoulder with thick hunched neck, two curved horns stabbing forward like spears, was Ghando. Clad just as I'd left him, in tier 9 raiding gear with a dagger and shield, with his helmet hidden to reveal his angrily anthropomorphized bovine face. Updates to *WoW*'s character models had softened his expression, widened and detailed his eyes into thoughtful yellow-green orbs instead of the surly glare I'd picked out for him some eleven years past. Still, it was a bit like spotting a family ghost, or perhaps running into a childhood friend on the street decades later. Someone you loved dearly but made your peace with never seeing again. My Blizzard account listing, for whatever reason, had been wrong, and without an active *WoW* account I'd had no way to know. Here he was, in the flesh, and at once I felt a surprising wave of apprehension. *You can have it all back*, the game spoke to a certain nook of my brain. *All of it*. I knew this wasn't true, that there had been real love there and was no longer, that love extinguished never really returns, the way ivy scoured from a redbrick wall won't ever regrow quite the same. I knew this and still stared at the screen a long time before clicking the bright red button that started it all: ENTER WORLD.

I then applied the level 90 boost to Ghando, skipping over two expansions' worth of leveling content, so *WoW* treated me to a special experience. The boost was intended not just for lapsed players like me, whose experience with the UI and game systems allows us to jump in and quickly pick up new changes. It was also meant for new players, whose constant and surprising influx has kept *WoW* financially flush for years, and those new players can't just be dropped into the game world at level 90 and expected to fend for themselves. So Blizzard attached a scripted story sequence to characters to whom the level boost was applied, stripping them of their old gear and spells, pushing them on a madcap scramble through the Dark Portal, a massive battle sequence, and a frantic flight through the savage Tanaan Jungle. Fun but simple quests teach the game's basic mechanics, and a full complement of spells and talents gradually fill your action bars. It replicates the familiar MMORPG process of leveling in a safe and linear starting zone, only with the process greatly accelerated. Voice-acted dialogue and exciting cinematics* packed with classic characters from the early *Warcraft* strategy games make the event a fabulous introduction for new players.

On the other hand, as a veteran I found it maddening. The story, setting, and characters were great, but the game's insistence on emptying my inventory and spellbook left me feeling robbed. My old raid gear and inventory was useless at level 90, but I didn't want it

---

* Unlike the theatrical full-rendered scenes for which Blizzard is traditionally known, these scenes (first introduced in *Wrath of the Lich King*) use the in-game engine to advance major storylines in a way that feels more compelling and meaningful than traditional MMORPG story progression. More on this, and its related "phasing" technology, later in the chapter.

suddenly taken away, to be retrieved after the opening event at any mailbox. What's more, the Ghando I knew was a raid-conquering hero with a devastating arsenal of spells for any occasion, not a Lightning Bolt–spamming debutante without access to his bank, guild vault, the Auction House, or any of the countless other amenities associated with a high-level *WoW* character. Ghando, the legend brought out of retirement *for one last ride*, as the movie posters say, was being treated like a bleary-eyed noob rolled fresh out of bed. It felt a bit like the second chapter of any *Metroid* game, where having gotten a taste of the protagonist's fully kitted badassery, she loses all her weapons and must start from scratch: not exactly heartbreaking, since you know you'll get them back with time, but drudgingly disappointing all the same. The game tried to make me feel competent, like I was accomplishing important things, but instead I felt nerfed down to a weakling.

Some things I'd been able to keep. All my gold, many thousands of pieces, a modest hoard nonetheless rendered trivial by years of expansion-fueled inflation.* My mounts were still available: a solid but not exceptional collection, most notably my rank 11 mount from the days of the vanilla Honor System. I was more surprised to see the Elitist Jerks guild tag. Any large guild undergoes periodic trimming, cutting long-inactive players from the official roster to avoid clutter and confusion. Despite five full years of inactivity, I'd somehow not been purged. This came as an enormous comfort for reasons I don't myself understand, though when I looked at those Elitist Jerks currently online I recognized few of the names. Functionally anonymous, I said nothing and read little on Guild chat—though a few old friends greeted me in whispers and passed along gaudy crafted gear to help me level. Local chat was quiet too, and every other player I saw went about his questing in socially inert determination. Global Trade chat was the typical mix of spammers, trolls, and illicit ads for gold sellers with the occasional earnest request, but even that seemed muted compared to my recollection. Though I heard plenty

---

* If Senator Rand Paul is looking for a new crusade, I would suggest this.

of scripted NPC dialogue, this little corner of Mal'ganis was silent as the grave.[*]

Not that you'd necessarily want everyone talking. Video games can be wonderful things, but the Internet is a horrible place filled with horrible people, and the very same people who sustain your community can also corrode it from within. The popular gaming comic *Penny Arcade*'s "Greater Internet Fuckwad Theory" posits offensive outbursts as the medium's inevitable product. Public forum plus anonymity equals someone named Plainbagel hurling wild abuse at complete strangers because he wants to be dispelled faster in a five-man instance. This sounds reasonable but falls short because it lets game designers off the hook. Plainbagel is probably a functional if not high-functioning human being, not a sociopathic monster nor a child lacking self-control. His behavior is not innate but learned: because he has seen other people behave in this way without censure or consequence, he perceives social gain for mimicking the behavior.

In theory it's easily remedied: allow players to report each other's bad behavior, actively punish people who misbehave via bans from the game, and notify the reporter that some action was taken. But in practice, even attentive game developers can only do so much. Automated reporting systems are obvious targets for fraud and exploitation, so the system demands human eyes reviewing chat logs. Consider a single *WoW* server and all its myriad interactions between tens of thousands of players, twenty-four hours a day. Multiply that by the several hundred realms spread across the globe; it's more ground than a single software company can cover, unless they're willing to invest huge sums of money hiring thousands of workers with the sole aim of policing in-game behavior. Blizzard hired hundreds back when *World*

---

[*] I should note, for context, the highly unusual demographics of Mal'ganis: per http:// realmpop.com, its players are 95 percent Horde and 5 percent Alliance. Considering the global *WoW* population is almost balanced (52 percent Alliance, 48 percent Horde), a high-population server sporting this kind of imbalance is almost impossible to imagine, and yet a handful of servers have worked their way to this kind of homogeneity, either favoring the Alliance or the Horde. The phenomenon hasn't been studied in detail, but it occurs gradually over the course of many years. As a server acquires a reputation as Alliance-tilted or Horde-tilted, players on the underside of the population imbalance migrate and reroll elsewhere.

of Warcraft was new, and it used to offer fairly robust reporting mechanisms where players could lay out their complaints in detail. These days, in the game's twilight years, the infrastructure has been streamlined and reporting occurs via pull-down menu: cheating, language, spamming, inappropriate name. No option for sexual harassment, for racism or homophobia unless perhaps it's expressed with especially foul language or by a character named Hitler. The Ignore feature can block individual characters but provides no meaningful safeguard against sustained harassment. Blizzard cares, in an abstract and academic sense, how people behave in Azeroth. They're just not going to do much about it. Establishing healthy, fun social environments is up to the players, and we've gotten pretty good at sorting ourselves by humanity.

The developers, to their credit, have removed some of the natural friction points between players. Relative to the total population, only a handful of players are truly awful, and they're easily blocked in the game. Most bad behavior occurs because a player is angry or frustrated at something that's happened in the game. Ease those points of frustration, keep them happy, and they're much more likely to treat each other well. For instance, loot distribution in most dungeons is now automatic—no arguments, no dice rolls, no theft. *Legion*'s "multi-tap" system is a particularly good example of smart social game design. If several competing players have each damaged a monster in the game world, every one of them gets his own loot without having to share. Now players don't argue over monster taps; in fact, they go out of their way to help strangers beset by foes, because they'll get loot and quest credit too. I've even helped Alliance players out on my PvP server because certain tough monsters were better tackled as a pair. We couldn't heal each other or speak, and we had to be careful not to accidentally damage one another, but we shared a fun experience thanks to good game design and clever implementation. Blizzard's emphasis on consistent "quality of life" improvements in the game make the lousy moments easier to stomach. If some asshole decides to boot you from a dungeon run just before the final boss, the Looking for Group feature will find you a new party in minutes. No harm done, right?

But if you played for years on end, you'll start to notice a downside to the automated matchmaking, to the instantaneous queues for any dungeon or battleground you might choose to play. MMORPGs are about persistence, slow accumulation over time. They're about permanence. Convenient on-demand rewards undermine that very ideal, making a weakness of a strength. I'd argue that *WoW*'s years-long trend toward convenience, toward merging realm servers into giant pools of players easily matched for on-demand activities in instances, has weakened the social bonds that made it great. In the old days, guilds and relationships were everything. Treat someone badly and she'd tell her guild about it, which sullied your reputation with dozens of people. That antipathy might reach further than you; every time you grouped with anyone else or opened your mouth in chat, you carried your guild's reputation on your back. Guilds would routinely refuse to deal with each other due to past instances of petty assholery. None of this is true today, because modern *WoW* has functionally obliterated its own intraserver social structures. That's the unfortunate compromise for MMORPG developers: the only proven and economical way to address harassment is to make other players so ignorable, so disposable, that it undermines the game's reason for being.

I emerged from the Tanaan Jungle entry event to a snowy windswept slope and the rudimentary beginnings of a fortress tucked into a bowl-shaped depression in the earth. A few point-and-click quests officially established my garrison, a new feature in *Warlords of Draenor* and more or less in keeping with the latter-day video game trend of persistent base building. Timed construction processes and carefully doled-out rewards encourage players to come back every day, if only for a few minutes to set their NPC minions on the next six-hour task. Tie-in mobile apps let players develop their garrisons while on the toilet at work or slouching in line to get coffee. I understand these things, why developers use them and why they elicit quantifiable responses in players, but personally I've never had the patience. Simulators and strategy games like *Civilization* will consume me for hours at a time, but in action-focused games like *WoW* they feel like tedious tack-ons. Put simply, if I have dynamic real-time control of an avatar, any time spent in menus detracts from the experience. Garrison construction felt like a chore, albeit a relatively cool one.

The game also gave me a set of quests to fill in early progression, but these felt more like errands than exploration. Quest-guide mods had always been popular, but now they were integrated directly into the default UI. You never had to wonder where quest objectives were—just run to the highlighted spot on your map! Even though I saw other players running the exact same quests, I felt no connection to these people. Each of us pursued his own garrison, his own private story, all layered atop each other but yet invisible to the others. If you've ever read China Miéville's strange crime procedural *The City & the City*, it was something like that.

It was also of a piece with the cinematics, the scripted events, the writing and pacing of the quests, the division of characters into one of several hard talent specializations, with just a handful of choices on a linear talent tree. The vanilla talent trees were awful, of course— gnarled and overgrown with terrible talents you often had to pick simply to access a necessary one higher on the tree. Hybrids abounded, with Mortal Striking tanks and arcane / frost mages. Hunters specced for melee instead of their typical ranged attacks. A thousand builds to pick from, nearly all of them less than optimal. Raiders and high-end PvPers gravitated toward a handful of optimized builds, and in those contexts it felt you had no choice, that anything less than the settled science let down your teammates.

So I understand Blizzard's choice to pare away the choices. I understand why the modern *WoW* offers less intimidating if less meaningful options, why dungeon-finding is a simple menu rather than a harrowing journey to the gates of said dungeon, why one may find oneself in a battleground with total strangers as the sole representative of one's realm server, why so much of *Warlords of Draenor* centers around the construction of a stockade fort in a wilderness hollow. It's all fabulously designed by smart people. Today's systems are unequivocally better than yesterday's. But that same obvious, data-fed care also renders them sterile.

It neuters the old axiom of the game as a harsh and unforgiving master never to be pleased; substituted is the more market-friendly concept of game as service, player as customer. The game now seeks the player's approval, not the other way around. An in-game Adventure Guide lists the bosses to every dungeon along with short biographies, which seems innocent enough until you look closer and realize it also lists those bosses' abilities and how best to counter them! Players used to learn these themselves, either through explanations in Party chat or trial and error. The first time you saw any given boss monster, you often had no idea what to expect. Imagining the bosses' backgrounds and roles in whatever nefarious doings was part of the fun! Wipes were the price, of course, and there's the rub: players don't want to wipe learning encounters in organic fashion. Certainly not during the leveling process! They want to get into dungeons and clear them expeditiously, knocking out daily quests and accumulating loot. Lest you think I'm forcing the corporatist angle, a large tab in the Adventure Guide is named "Suggested Content." Not even a pretention to adventure. Everything is a commodity. Everything is content.

Some nods to mystery remain. Though the mini-map points me anywhere I want to go and stocks every zone with ample flight paths for easy transit, I find myself spending a lot of time just riding around on my Black War Raptor, admiring Draenor's savage beauty and the interesting places populating it. Orcs and ogres huddled in a fortress built in the rib cage of a colossal beast's fossilized skeleton. Windswept plains abound with packs of hulking, snow-dusted clefthoof, and around an exposed magma fissure I encounter seething, hissing fire elementals (which, curiously, aren't resistant to fire damage). Zooming along on an errand I nearly miss a narrow passageway between two crags, an ice cave at the back of which sits a blocky iron treasure box. A rare monster squats in an icicled hollow and, when killed for the heck of it, drops a fine piece of leveling gear. Hunters pursue the clefthoof, and NPC soldiers from various factions tussle in the open spaces between towns. Small scripted events abound, offering optional entertainment for small rewards, usually for my garrison. This is new—or, rather, it was not the case ten years ago, when monsters loitered aimlessly about their designated areas and many quests were roughly painted on a naked landscape. It dawns on me that the mini-map and its helpful arrows are like the big screen at a stadium concert: an easy, seductive distraction from the real action. You'll get much more from pulling your eyes down to the performers, but doing so takes a conscious effort.

The game itself, the essential mechanics of movement and combat and casting, is still pretty fun. I'd leveled many characters of different classes through various expansions, but never before had I felt so strong. Modern *WoW* gives players of any class an arsenal of skills both formidable and diverse.* Where at first I found the system narrow and constraining, I soon begin to appreciate the subtleties—how changing a single talent reordered my whole damage rotation just by emphasizing one buff over another. Questing offers a diverse palette of challenges, often with fun mechanics cribbed from other games.† The quest writing and dialogue are dramatic but never lose sight of the light, referential humor for which Blizzard is known.

Returning to *WoW* took me right back to the old ways and familiar rhythms. Hours fell away, and every time I stopped to take the dogs out, the game exerted a telekinetic force. What quests were next on the docket, and when would be the best time for dungeon runs? What was going on with my garrison? While busy with real life I'd still make time to log in, if only for a few minutes to assign my "follower" NPCs fresh missions—the mechanics of which, flipping through assignments to match their particular skills with the mission parameters, elicit an elementary pleasure not unlike pushing wooden blocks through appropriately shaped holes. I pad through my darkened house, toothbrush pinned between back molars, and fire up *WoW* to send out garrison missions before bed. Bathed in

---

* That's even more the case in the latest expansion; *Legion* pared away several expansions' worth of dross and rebuilt each class around four or five core abilities.

† *Legion* would also further revamp the approach to leveling by allowing the game world to scale dynamically with characters for the very first time—players can tackle any zone in the new continent (the Broken Isles) in whatever order they choose, and even old zones offer tough enemies to players at the level cap.

pale blue light, I lay out my followers into valuable ten-hour errands that proceed while I sleep. Every hour of the day made productive.

All of which is to say, *WoW*'s PvE experience has never been better designed. For all the nostalgia contained in these pages, only with the rosiest of tinted glasses could anyone argue for the vanilla regime, or *The Burning Crusade*. More than a few fans would vote for *Wrath of the Lich King*, so thoroughly rooted in Azeroth's lore. I'd agree that's where *WoW*'s modern age began. But the systems were never so clean, the rewards so sculpted to challenge and necessity. Like its predecessors, *Wrath* was packed with petty indignities: incredibly long and geographically complex corpse runs, redundant leveling zones, badly imbalanced crafting professions. Players flying cross-continent had to steer clear of the Wintergrasp PvP zone, lest they find themselves abruptly dismounted a mile up in the air. *Cataclysm* demolished and overwrote a game world players had grown to love, and *Mists of Pandaria* felt like a niche product for those already invested in Blizzard's adorable / insufferable pandaren race.* *Warlords of Draenor* returned the game to its roots in the tale of a savage orcish horde pouring through a Dark Portal, told through classic characters animated and voiced like never before, and *Legion* throws back to *The Burning Crusade* with a demonic invasion of Azeroth and the return of a legendary franchise favorite, the demon hunter Illidan Stormrage. At some point in the endless construction of new content, in the narrative's forward march, Blizzard seems to have remembered what everyone loved about their games to begin with and made a conscious effort to get back there.

MMORPGs, more so than other online games, warp conventional senses of time. I don't mean the sessions that devour three or four or six hours at a clip, though those happen—I mean the way their narratives sit static. I can delve into a necromancer's lair and slay him for a

---

* A race of anthropomorphized panda bears, the pandaren first appeared as novelty characters in *Warcraft III: The Frozen Throne*. The race builds and dresses according to a simplistic and stylized East Asian aesthetic that (to this writer) seems totally out of place in Azeroth. They also display an alarming sexual dimorphism, wherein the males are enormous and tubby while the females are cute little runts. The males also have accents, whereas the females do not. I'll let the reader draw her own conclusions about this.

major quest, but if I walk back into that cave fifteen minutes later all his acolytes have respawned and the man himself once again stands cackling over a violet-smoking cauldron. Nothing can ever really change, because the next player in line (or one player, with many alts) needs to finish the same quest. It's a bit like a theme park, animatronics reset for every fresh run. It's hard to legitimately advance a story and impossible to develop characters. Since *Wrath of the Lich King*, the game has gotten better at presenting epic moments, through the aforementioned in-game cinematics and new "phasing" technology that allows select portions of the non-instanced game world to appear differently to different players. (It's phasing that allows each player to build his own garrison on the same windswept slope.) But these innovations don't really help the characters. We accept stories as arcs, as sequences of events summing up to a progression, but characters are different. Characters we see as static; they're people frozen in amber at the ends of their respective stories. We see them and think only of the conclusion, not the journey. Darth Vader is Luke Skywalker's father and savior, not a mass murderer, because we've watched his arc to the end. MMORPG characters, even such momentous figures as Jaina Proudmoore or the former warchief Thrall, have no proper end, and as such can only be appreciated as specters of the *Warcraft* characters we already knew. Nothing in an MMORPG has a true future, only an entertaining present and a past sustained through players' nostalgia. Saving the world inaugurates no Pax Azerotha; in fact, you're going to save it all over again next week for another goddamned hunter weapon.

WoW's decade-plus perch at the top of the heap has built a churning population of players like me, whose subscriptions may occasionally lapse, even for years, but who eventually return to the fold. Old friends beckon alongside new content, but what I personally find most appealing is the familiarity even years later with totally overhauled talents, spells, and systems. Like riding a bike, it never really goes away. Instinctive shift-clicks to loot all items from my kills; turning Ghando's body sideways when fleeing from monsters so I'm not hit in the back and dazed; constantly spamming the jump button while running because, well, they gave me a jump button, didn't they? Habits honed over years and laid to rest resurrect themselves the moment I log back in. My pinky finger hovers ever over the Shift and Control keys, ring on the A, long on W and index on D, though in an instant any of them may leap up to the number keys to cast a spell. The body remembers, sometimes better than you do. Even your motor neurons recognize these rituals.

So it should come as no surprise that *WoW* players adore the past, constantly celebrating the old and defunct. They keep old gear (I still have my Earthfury Boots from Molten Core, the first epic item I ever received), they use that old gear to transmogrify their current equipment to *look* like old gear, they traipse through old leveling zones, and they delve back into old dungeons. Years after the legendary-quality sword Thunderfury faded into obsolescence, players still ran Molten Core every week for a remote chance at acquiring it. For many players *WoW* is a pleasant bath of old memories, of adventures with friends both present and departed. As a guildmate whispered to me in the hours after Ghando's return, *They always come back.*

Blizzard recognized this with their Timewalking events. Five-man dungeons have long been the game's most popular attractions (aside from compulsory leveling zones), but once characters progressed past a given dungeon, nostalgia used to be the only reason to return. *Warlords of Draenor* changed this, in June 2015, by introducing Timewalking. For a weekend at a time, players may visit dungeons from a prior expansion under special conditions: all players entering those instances find their gear and abilities automatically scaled down, so monsters once again offer a challenge.

WoW leverages its own nostalgic appeal to keep you coming back, to reinforce the feeling of home. If that seems like an obvious and cynical ploy from developers chasing their bottom line, consider that it's only possible because the game endured so long and won so many devoted fans. The loot dropped by Timewalking bosses is "timewarped," meaning that gear from level 70 or 80 or 90 gets automatically boosted up to level 100 power the moment you leave the Timewalking instance. Players also acquire tokens redeemable for more high-end items. The dungeons themselves are a delight, particularly given *WoW*'s new and improved combat. I found myself taken immediately back to the early days in Shattered Halls, in Gundrak, in the Pit of Saron.

I cleared these dungeons with total strangers, but it became apparent we were really sharing the space with the ghosts of our memories. Deaths were more funny than annoying, since most derived from peculiar boss abilities long since forgotten. *Oh yeah, the old Lightning Nova. LOL!* After a wipe on a pack of trash monsters, our tank started marking targets and calling out assignments. *Holy shit*, noted our paladin. *We're going old school now.*

I can't Hex undead, I typed into my Party chat window. *Remember when we had to actually pay attention?*

I know, it's BS.

Now we just AoE everything, chirped our warlock.

He was absolutely right: In days past, every engagement in a dungeon used to require exquisite pulling, crowd control, and focused fire. A single loose monster would probably kill the healer and wipe the group. Now tanks used their improved survivability and ample threat generation to corral all the monsters of a group into a pile to be melted by intense area-of-effect damage. Easier and more fun, but less demanding, which is as good a two-phrase description of modern *WoW* as I've ever heard. Players enjoy this but also lament it. There is no surer way to start a long and boisterous conversation with a *WoW* player than the formulation "Hey, remember X?" where X is a frustrating hardship from years past.[*] Challenges, however trivial, breed camaraderie. Game director Ion Hazzikostas—my guildmaster Gurgthock—acknowledged the value of danger in explaining why *Warlords of Draenor* and the future *Legion* expansion wouldn't allow mounted flight at launch: "World of Warcraft is full of memorable moments that are only possible when players explore the world by ground. . . . The world feels larger, more dangerous. There's more room for exploration, for secrets." What's the essence of any story?

---

[*] Parents: this is an excellent way to connect with your *WoW*-obsessed offspring. It may, in fact, be the only way.

A character who wants something, runs into obstacles, and overcomes them. That's *WoW*: an endless series of entertaining challenges, a new chapter of your avatar's story every day of the week, because unlike NPC characters your own can be contemplated in situ. You're the sole master. A populated online world must present itself as a public attraction, and that's why its best storytelling will always come from the players themselves.

LORE AND LEGENDS

Though a small chunk of chapter 6 lays out the important distinctions between PvE and PvP environments, veteran *WoW*ers will have noticed I have barely touched upon another major category of realm server. Role-playing (RP) servers existed from the very first day, offering a different spin on the experience for those players most interested in storytelling through Azeroth's lore. Put simply, to RP is to play as though the game world were real and your avatar an actual person inhabiting that world. Speech adapts first; the more extreme RPers might speak in flowery fantasy language, peppering their chat with "thou" and "thee," but the vast majority are more subtle. They avoid the constant acronyms and typical Internet shorthand associated with MMORPG chat, taking more care with their communication. RPers make greater use of the /say and /yell commands, speaking out loud in character and dexterously cycling through custom emotes to express themselves. Different rules apply to whispers, Guild chat, and other features too video gamey to pass as anything else. These are taken as out of character (OOC) by default, for personal communication and practical planning. While adventuring or running dungeons, players keep their chat serious and in character. These guidelines vary from server to server and guild to guild, maintained and policed by the community itself. Players on role-playing servers aren't forced to role-play. Indeed, many choose not to—for them, being on an RP server is happenstance. Blizzard makes no attempt to enforce role-playing etiquette, though RP servers are subject to more stringent naming guidelines (you can't name yourself Luvtospuuj on an RP server), and players who spam others with OOC messages or otherwise aggressively disrupt the environment are punished. Put simply: role-play as much or as little as you like, but don't harass others out of their own immersion.

The appeal should be obvious to anyone with a bit of imagination. Since tabletop role-playing games and live-action role-playing have both been popular for decades, computer RPGs were the next obvious step. All the fun and storytelling possibility without the tedious rolling of dice and scanning of tables! *WoW*'s RP servers offered on-demand fun with a never-ending supply of partners.

I dabbled myself in the early days, leveling a feeble paladin on an RP-PvP server. Since the avatar was chrome-domed and sported an imposing mustache, I played him more or less like Samuel L. Jackson in his unfortunate latter-day remake of *Shaft*. Thankfully I kept no chat transcripts from that time, but rest assured it was cringeworthy on more than one level. Still, nobody in any of my Deadmines runs complained about it, and most even seemed to enjoy the change of pace. Some took the character seriously, more or less, while others shifted their own personas to match. I was, on more than one occasion, berated for my antics by a gruff if well-intentioned "police chief" character. Though the escapade started as a joke, I quickly saw the doors it opened. Regardless of the character I chose to play, merely playing one inspired others to do the same. It was a bit like dancing at a wedding reception: one person can break the ice. Even if I never saw these people again and we never hashed out any rules between us, RPing gave us another dimension in which to play. It created lasting memories (I still snicker over those moments a decade later) although nobody ever received a material reward for RPing. But they did it all the same, in the simple spirit of pure fun.

Of course, some delved deeper than others. RPers certainly raid, run battlegrounds, and compete in arenas, but you'll rarely see dedicated RPers atop the ranking. It's a question of personality, of one's instinctive approach to the game. RPers aren't inferior players, but legitimate success requires you conceptualize *WoW* as a *game* and all its designs as competitive rules to be manipulated. It demands acronyms and careful adherence to the latest meta-game and humping pillars rather than tooth-rattling battles for honor and glory. Playing *WoW* in this way rarely feels heroic. Grinding rarely builds fond memories. RPers set means above ends because, as argued previously, obstacles and struggle are the essence of any good story.

Often this means subjecting themselves to special challenges. This might be as simple as a strict "Red equals dead" rule: your character so despises her enemies, she'll attack anyone from the opposing faction on sight. This inevitably gets her into trouble, more so than strategically "carebearing," as most players do while attending their business, but it's part of the character and so any distractions acquire that extra dimension of fun.

As with anything *WoW*, a few players took this idea to strange and extreme lengths. A Hunter named Gweryc Halfhand achieved notoriety for his insistence on fighting only with melee weapons instead of ranged—a choice forced, as the story went, by the unfortunate mangling of his right hand. Swinging various heavy weapons alongside his trusty wolf Cafall, Gweryc struggled his way to level 70 without any assistance from others. He published a blog detailing the finer points of his exploits, forcefully arguing for the value of unconventional approaches in a game: "My monthly subscription rents me a playground, not a bunch of pixellated penis enlargers, not a spot as somebody's slave in a raid guild. It's about fun, and I get a major kick out of pushing the envelope." He decided the character's mulish personality was best suited for a dwarf and thus forsook other races with better innate bonuses for hunters. Through his writing the process seems a nightmare, but he delights in its peculiar challenges.

Brave souls undertook even harder tasks, like pacifist leveling: no kills of humanoid opponents, or even no violence whatsoever. Noor the Pacifist was a rogue, inspired by Gweryc's blog, who refused to engage in combat of any kind or receive experience from those who did. He snuck his way through the retrieval quests sifted from WoWhead. He scoured what few experience points he could from exploring new areas and scraped a few more from daily battleground quests. Reaching the level cap was practically impossible, but that was never why Noor (a "fifty-year-old male computer programmer," by his description) played. It was technically possible, given a long enough journey, and the journey was the point. Other notable characters included Rotgut the Naked Troll—nudity was actually quite a popular theme, with more than a few players using no visible clothing. Jewelry and weapons alone were enough for the skilled and patient to fight their way through most leveling content.

Among those intentionally fettering themselves, twinks form their own category. The term "twink" in gaming has several meanings but generally refers to under-leveled alternate characters or accounts; an experienced player limits herself to a smaller rule set for practice or amusement. Twink characters usually benefit from a powerful and well-funded main character funneling them resources like the proverbial rich old uncle. In *WoW* twinks have always been organized around PvP, specifically battlegrounds. Battlegrounds become available at level 10 and players are matched by graduating brackets (10–19, 20–29, and so on), so each level number ending in "9" has its own twink community. Swarms of players forever frozen at level 19 clash in Warsong Gulch, rushing into battle on foot since they can't yet ride mounts.* They wield the absolute best gear available for their level, crafted and enchanted to maximize combat output. Normal characters don't have nice gear while leveling because they'll just replace it soon, the way children aggressively outgrow their shoes, so twinks barely notice them in the course of battling among themselves. Because the community is small and they play battlegrounds almost exclusively with each other, rivalries grow intense. Twinks have some of the fiercest flame wars on the Internet.

In a certain sense twink players prize process over outcome, but their ultimate objective remains winning. They're just hunting a

---

* In the early days, aspiring twinks had to be very careful and diligent with their gearing process. Every dungeon run for better gear tacked on more XP and threatened to push them into level 20, ruining the character entirely. At the behest of the twink community Blizzard implemented special "experience eliminator" NPCs in the PvP areas of Orgrimmar and Stormwind City, with whom players may speak to turn off character XP gain entirely. The world was thus made forever safe for twink-kind.

leaner (perhaps purer) species of competition. Role-play, to return to the thread, has a trickier relationship with competition. The people RPing may be competitive and their characters possessed of an unholy determination to succeed, but the act of role-playing is inherently collaborative. Like improv acting, it asks all participants to work together, to take risks and give of themselves in pursuit of a shared experience. Everyone labors a bit harder, but they have more fun in the process.

This is the very reason RPing returned to fashion. What flourished with vanilla *WoW*'s infinite possibility and faded as *The Burning Crusade* and *Wrath of the Lich King* placed an ever greater emphasis on achievement has made a comeback. *Mists of Pandaria*'s extra-fanciful settings and pandaren populace (always a cult favorite) inspired a new generation of RPers, and *Warlords of Draenor*'s dense lore only expanded the burgeoning community. *Legion* followed in the same footsteps, adding extensive and well-written "artifact quests" attached to each specialization for every class. They never really went away, of course; Blizzard always maintained a separate message board for RPing and fan fiction, "*WoW* Roleplay" has its own popular sub-Reddit, and mods like MyRolePlay give players a blank canvas to flesh out their characters in full, florid detail.* Quickly peruse the forums and you'll find remarkable testimonials of longtime players who've recently turned to RP. They love how the game feels like home, but for those not focused on beating Mythic-level raid dungeons, the daily grind of *Warlords of Draenor*'s follower missions and work orders left them feeling cooped up in their garrisons. Even *Legion*, at its endgame, comes down to endless dungeon runs under progressively more masochistic conditions. Class halls, cool as they are (warriors literally leap up through a golden beam to Valhalla), aren't effective social spaces. Nobody ever assembled a dungeon party or made a new friend in a class hall. RP colors in the map's edges, makes the world seem larger and older and more dangerous, lets play-

---

* Using these mods, players write up lengthy passages describing their characters' appearance, past, and attitude so other players with the same mod can inspect and read them. Saved templates allow quick switching to match any mood, costume, or setting.

ers forget how incredibly powerful and well-designed their characters' abilities are. It turns out being master of the universe is kind of a chore. Little people in a big world have the freedom to be frivolous.

That's why most RPing activities aren't dungeon runs or ranked battlegrounds or questing expeditions at all; they're social events. A glance at Blizzard's official RP forum shows recruiting posts for guilds and notices of upcoming events, some open to the public and others by sign-up. Players explore such ideas as "Daycare of Warcraft," a space where players pretend to be infant versions of their characters. Think *Muppet Babies*, with baby night elves and worgen pups instead of Baby Kermit and Babby Fozzie. It includes "adult" roles—caretakers and nannies for the youth. No players, the post specifies, may take any action inflicting serious harm upon any of the babies. Others organize *Night of the Living Dead* events where a powerful warlock raises swarms of "zombie" undead players dressed in rags for grim and shambling marches on the mist-shrouded Alliance town of Darkshire. "Shadow Sermons" hosted weekly in Silverpine Forest induct fresh corpses into the Horde's undead subfaction, the Forsaken. Some events are quite literally tea parties: sin'dorei (anyone #woke and up on her lore knows "blood elves" is a slur) conjure food and drink from the arcane and perhaps a warlock gets incensed enough to summon an infernal, but the tablecloths are barely singed and everyone socializes and has a gay old time.

Storytellers are always socializing their pastime. A great story is best shared, so RPers seek out and provoke each other to play. They solicit and dole out advice on each other's stories—correcting lore where it might drift astray or agreeing, *Yes, that's a brilliantly fresh take on the Illidari*. One player states he'd like to play a pandaren ninja and another replies that while *WoW* has no ninjas as such, a close approximation might be a Shado-Pan from this clan and that spot on the Wandering Isle. The feedback isn't really the point, of course, any more than advice columns are about solving folks' thorny issues. It's about the act of sharing, and partaking of what's shared. It's about sustaining a proud community. RPing is *loud* if nothing else, between the insistence that players communicate in /say or /yell instead of private chat and the constant seeking of social reinforcement. New RPers marvel at the community's boisterous warmth, especially compared to the sterile silence of leveling zones or the white noise of spammers and gold sellers in Trade chat. If you feel as though *WoW* has become indistinguishable from the rest of the Internet, spend an evening role-playing on one of the established RP servers (Wyrmrest Accord has become something of a hub). It's an old way of doing things, harking back to the ancient days of text-based online games played over Telnet. Without graphics, players had to dream up their own identities; all you could ever know about your fellows was the description text they wrote for themselves.

Of course these practices lead to their own conflicts. As a communal activity, RPing relies on certain common assumptions—accords easily made among friends or in Guild chat but poorly communicated to the world at large. Game critic John Brindle once wondered about ownership on *WoW*'s RP realms: "In the age of Twitter timelines and filter bubbles, we've become used to inhabiting tailored slices of reality. But in 2004, hanging out together in one big shared space . . . was still the dream of the Internet. *WoW* had no player housing, no private space, and while it has since added some of each, they are limited in the big hub cities where most people want to RP. The result is a scarcity of useable space, even in the midst of geographical abundance."

So on RP servers, self-appointed Stormwind guards found their halls packed with scheming thieves, and members of the Church of the Holy Light grumbled endlessly about cultists gathering for dark rituals in the nave. Everyone felt entitled to his own interpretation of the game world, his own backstory, while also implicitly relying on the larger community for immersion. As Brindle notes, "It was actually criminal roleplayers who had the biggest stake in maintaining these presences; crime is no fun without someone who is trying to catch you. So most people basically agreed that a Guard should exist, even if there was sometimes dispute about who should run it or how it should work." Occupying customary spaces with the expected behaviors and hewing to the game's visual presentation are the best guidelines to widely accepted RPing. Very few people are going to read the in-depth guide to your guild's lore that you bump to the top of the realm forums every few days. Without the ability to really own any given space, RPers must start from a solid premise and work to convince others of its legitimacy. Needless to say, this is a difficult task. Few players are up to it, and so it's no wonder Blizzard has continued their progress toward a game as private and personalized as the rest of the Internet.

BOUNDED IN A NUTSHELL

As I worked Ghando up to level 100, from the questing zones and back to the Tanaan Jungle,* I found myself missing that kind of connection. There was a gulf of sorts—between the cozy bustle of a full quest log and the long, empty hours of waiting for work orders, between rapid progression and the trickle of scarce garrison resources necessary to access the best content. Without that sense of forward momentum I was left with two depressing shades of quiet: the soft quiet of waiting and the harder one, loneliness. General chat was empty, and anyone I saw was a silent automaton on an errand. Even stealing someone's monster kill or mining node no longer elicited an angry response. It was a waste of time; they merely moved along to the next resource. In dungeons, the Adventure Guide explained each player's role in any given fight, so there was no real need to communicate. I'm chatty by nature in games, and yet I found myself proceeding in exactly the same silence.

So alone I played. Ghando roved across the wilds of Draenor following tiny icons pasted on his map, collecting garrison resources twelve or fourteen at a time when thousands were needed, finding the odd apexis shard when again thousands were needed. The comically mismatched numbers seemed to mock me, though with focused grinding they added up quick. If you're willing to spend a whole day

---

* Tanaan, first glimpsed on the run in the expansion's introductory event, returns as a full-fledged zone—and a richly cultivated gear farm—for max-level players.

working at something, *WoW* is happy to reward you for it. The game guarantees you Y reward for X effort, and this is probably the single biggest reason it's more appealing than the rest of life. It's also why modern *WoW*, in contrast with its own past, feels more like a game these days than a place. Between the game's crisply designed systems and the cornucopia of add-ons to assist me, the work was enjoyable enough but clearly work. For some people that's perfect. Elitist Jerks' raiding core appeared online for perhaps an hour each week to clear old content—I never saw them otherwise—and they seemed content with that arrangement. If they logged on apart from that it was to run specific errands, after which they logged out.

If players aren't pushing the envelope, what exactly are they doing? Checking off daily quests, pushing for ever-higher arena ratings, accumulating wealth and upgraded gear through the ample and easily accessed endgame events. It wasn't that *WoW* lacked for things to do. I just struggled to escape the unsatisfied feeling that had led me away from the game years before. It's fun—and how can anyone really complain when a video game is fundamentally fun?—but these days it's too nested in comfort to ignite anyone's passion. The developers provide their customers with an excellent product, yet we find ourselves looking back most fondly to years-old pain and suffering. I understood acutely why so many choose the social embrace of role-playing. I was halfway there already, imagining the tales of my garrison and its followers' exploits, because those were all I saw happening. Hours of exploration, of treasure-seeking, and all for a few more points in a giant pile of integers that would eventually let me upgrade a garrison building in order to build *another* garrison building and thereby access Tanaan Jungle. It feels like progression, activates the associated neural circuitry, but delivers only in the minutest sense. By the same token, more than a few players spend all their in-game time (and heaps of their real-life dollars) collecting cosmetic pets, which in *Mists of Pandaria* were granted the ability to battle each other *Pokemon* style. Even the most obscure features of a character may represent hundreds of hours of mentally engaged play. One dungeon run saw the matchmaking system pair me with a guildmate, and neither of us even noticed each other until most of the way through, because we paid no attention to anything outside ourselves. The end result feels like treading water in a busy, warm bathtub. We're all in complete control of our destinies and we know exactly when the next reward comes. Again, I cannot stress enough how well designed the World of Warcraft is. Its designers have labored to be everything to everyone, and they're damn close to pulling off this impossible task—but it is, after all, impossible.

WoW has always been a cyclical experience, tuned not to seasons or the calendar year but Blizzard's regular expansions. It's not quite clockwork, but players have always been able to expect new expansions about every two years. My experience playing *Warlords of Draenor* came at the low ebb of what the community consensus has dubbed a front-loaded expansion. They feel there just wasn't enough to do, particularly as the two-year cycle approached its end. *Legion's* release at the very end of August 2016 abruptly kicked the game back into high gear.

Whether you're a new or returning player, a new expansion is the best time to throw yourself back into *WoW*. Your garbage gear won't matter for the first month at least, which gives you an opportunity to catch back up to the hardcore players if you want. Expansions are great fun—charging through the leveling zones, exploring new areas and living fresh stories and getting new gear and immersing yourself in this vibrant virtual world alongside your guildmates. Even if they're total strangers you can run dungeons together and commiserate over a handful of obnoxiously bugged quests in Val'sharah. Crafting professions feel relevant as you build yourself useful items; gatherers make piles of money hocking their wares in a desperate seller's market.

As of this writing, late in the year 2016, it's too early to render any big conclusions over *Legion*, but playing it reminded me of the best in *WoW* for all the same reasons *Warlords of Draenor* represented the worst. Seldom does a game last long enough to see the industry change around it and react—over the years *WoW's* clever designers have swiped mechanics from other popular games, from *Pokemon's* monster collecting and battling to platforming and rail-shooting and the infamous "pikmin" dungeon in the *Legion* zone of Suramar. Even rarer is a game that gets to learn from itself, to exist so long with so much security that the designers can react against their own prior choices. *Legion* represents a conscious reaction against its predecessor; Hazzikostas himself stated in a Twitch Q&A the week after *Legion's* release that the developers wanted to "step back from the *Warlords* garrison model." Dynamic zones keep every region of the Broken Isles engaging and tough, especially since frequent "world quests" with meaningful rewards draw players out of their capital cities. Player-versus-player combat is reborn, as world quests draw the Alliance and Horde into close contact in the open world and some explicitly reward killing the opposite faction. In battlegrounds and arenas, the game steps in to normalize players' gear—newbies and fresh rerolls no longer get their faces stomped as the price of admission, and hardened veterans can earn a long succession of valuable class-specific perks for their valor. Stripped-down spellbooks for every class keep the action comprehensible; you can pick up the basics in just a few hours. Guild rosters bulge with names old and new, every one of whom has a demon hunter alt. Green chatter fills your screen at all hours of the day and night as the hours flash by. This is how MMORPGs are meant to be played, in wobbly nascent states exploding with promise. Many people take a week off work just to immerse themselves in the juvenile madness. Just to have a prime seat at the show, a great perch at a party that's not meant to outlast the night.

We circle around to find once again that the best parts of online gaming exist in our choices, in expressing ourselves better than words alone permit. Work for years in someone's cubicle or live as housemates and you might still barely know her; play with her for an hour on voice chat and you've learned more than any details of biography could reveal. I don't need to know where you went to high school. Show me how you tank, how you burst, how you peel. If we're going to live in a permanently connected world that so vividly transmits pain and anger and madness, let the things we do for each other be just as real. Let our friendships endure.

« 10 »

WHAT IT MEANT TO US

E ven gone and departed, I thought about *WoW* all the time. Even before this book and the research that came with it and the inevitable renewal of my subscription, I missed the game's order, its schedule, the weekly rhythm of clearing and progression. I missed having a crew of friends waiting for me every weeknight and arena partners to pass the rest of the time. At the same time, I knew those pangs represented nostalgia more than any contemporary need. The *WoW* I had loved so much had changed, was gone and couldn't return. Only a relative handful of crusty old raiders would even want it to. So while from time to time I found myself missing the bygone days, I was more conscious of the various ways *WoW* had altered my brain. From everything I can tell, these changes are permanent.

It happened most often while driving—something about the displacement of driving a vehicle, surrounded on all sides by the kind of rushing chaos only gaggles of complete strangers can animate. Everyone operates according to her own peculiar logic. We're all trying to get somewhere, but not all to the same place and certainly not by the same route. And yet we all coexist in the same space, affecting each other if only by our presence, forced to negotiate the various challenges of our proximity. My fellow drivers feel like "randos" picked up in the Looking for Group menu. I'm handling my own vehicle, but like piloting a *WoW* avatar, the skill cap of highway driving sits low. Keep going straight, maintain speed, change lanes as appropriate, and check blinds spots as you do. Driving demands perhaps 15 percent of a smart, aware person's mental bandwidth. Most people devote their remaining brainpower to the appreciation of music, or grumbling assents along with talk radio hosts caught in a permanent stasis of rage, or thumbing through their Twitter feeds. I don't; instead I watch the other drivers. My inner raid leader can't help but monitor them as though they might need healing or a quick dispel. Seeing the sudden flare of brake lights I track the propagating red, down the lanes and across them. I see every reaction and I judge by its quickness the soul behind that wheel. The fastest you'd want in your crew. The slowest would stand mired in hazards—bubbling lava or a seething violet miasma of shadow—with their health ticking down and down and down, moving at long last but only quick enough to drop dead a step from the periphery. They represent a massive psychic underclass visible only to those with the refined and misanthropic perspective of an MMORPG veteran.

The phrasing is tongue-in-cheek, not the sentiment. MMOs don't have the highest individual skill cap, but they teach their players a kind of broad-spectrum awareness most other games don't. The diversity of classes and their various specializations and the talents attached to those specifications could fill their own informative but crushingly dull book. Playing at a high level demands a complete and intuitive grasp of all that information: what every class does and how they do it. In chapter 6 former *WoW* arena (and current *Hearthstone*) star Rumay "Hafu" Wang described her long and granular learning process, dueling every class until she understood them inside and out. Hardcore *WoW* players know more about the game than many people know about their own jobs. They have to recall, process, and apply that information in a huge variety of conditions and under brutal time constraints. Retaining and quickly calling upon this knowledge to inform decisions becomes, more than anything else, the mark of a quality player. Ideally everyone would be able to handle this, but it's a lot to ask. A good guild like T K T can expect perhaps three quarters of its players to meet this standard. Even great guilds like Elitist Jerks have weak links here and there, usually among the DPS for whom raw numerical performance can make up for the odd death. It's hard to attain this level of awareness, harder still to maintain it. *WoW* teaches players to pay constant attention to their surroundings, to be mindful of their actions, to monitor every branch of the decision tree regardless of circumstance. Any organism on earth can react to stimulus; true intelligence anticipates. To an experienced eye the difference is plain as day.

Which makes it difficult, at times, to exercise patience. I see someone else approaching a circumstance, know exactly what he should do and why, and I know he won't do it. I see the mistake someone's about to make (for example, switching lanes neither checking his blind spot nor applying a turn signal) and I know how to avoid it, but she goes ahead and does it anyway and I just want to scream. More than a few fellow *WoW*-heads can relate. How on earth, wonders the gamer, am I paying more attention to your business than *you* are? I could remote-control you using half my attention and still make better choices! Of course, nobody says this out loud. Doing so would paint us as irretrievable assholes—tryhards of the worst kind, uptight type-A personalities more suited for cutthroat law firms than decent society. We must settle for expressing it in the pages of books, themselves monuments to ego.

You didn't have to count yourself hardcore to be changed forever by the game. You never forget your first MMO, to mangle an old phrase, and for much of the Internet-native generation, *WoW* was their first. It layered the game world persistently over their own in a way most had never experienced. I certainly hadn't, despite a lifetime of playing RPGs and other immersive video games. If some players are motivated by winning, I'm motivated by learning, and *WoW* offered a wonderfully bottomless well of knowledge to plumb. As I learned Azeroth's every intricacy I felt a degree of mastery over the real world too. Events in my life made more sense. Dynamics in the large multiteam office where I worked aligned with a realm server's jostling population, its yammering factions. When I got home, a four-mile run became a daily quest to be ground out no matter the misery attached. The fiction I wrote in a darkened room under an overbright desk lamp was my raid—abrading frustration with a sweet payoff cooked somehow into the process. Which isn't to say I glimpsed the secret topography of our universe or some marketable shortcut to success. I did find that what I saw made more sense.

One event proceeded more logically to another the way the highway turned to a flickering game board.

School and work fall out much the same way. Long-term goals that might otherwise overwhelm can be broken down to small, achievable tasks. If you consistently knock out these tasks, their benefits—slight but not trivial, concrete but not quite tangible—add up like gear upgrades over the course of a long arena season. Life is less predictable in its rewards, but the principle remains the same: focus intently on whatever's in front of you today, and things will probably work out in the end. If you ever ground a faction reputation to Exalted, you probably have the discipline to better your station in life. Just about everyone I know from *WoW* enjoys a successful and personally rewarding career despite their diverse backgrounds and circumstances. Kids from the violent Texas border town of Juarez grew up to be engineers. Utterly confused teenagers worked their way through college and law school and the Georgia bar exam. They learned the valuable lesson that organizations are what their members make of them, that hard work won't necessarily take you to the top of the world but it will get you incrementally closer, and that wherever you find yourself might still make you pretty damn happy.

Ask them what they got from the game and they note the satisfying connection between investment and reward. Playing the game, even when it most resembled work, still felt good. As one says, "Even the grindy, miserable parts of it never dissuaded me from continuing. I was a chronic procrastinator (and a recovering one still) but in *Warcraft* I never felt the need to put things off, because I enjoyed what I was doing. Even the grinds were worth it because of the payoff . . . I think that the MMO nature of the game—the social interactions and ability to compare oneself [to others]—only adds to that." The same player demonstrates the value of a persistent game world when he notes that fully instanced RPGs like Blizzard's own *Diablo* never held the same appeal. Each day in *WoW* was populated by the same people, the same cast of characters to share in your successes and failures. "The people," says another player when asked what kept him playing. "Definitely the people." Group play binds people together. It affixes strong emotional stakes to any challenge. Play badly and you've done worse than lose—you've let down your teammates. Even if they don't blame you, you'll blame yourself. Fidelity to friends, real or virtual, is the biggest single motivator in *WoW*. More matches were won and bosses downed for mutual love than ones and zeroes arranged into a piece of epic loot.

Friends learned these precious lessons together, and perfect strangers bonded in the learning. T K T and Elitist Jerks were two of the coolest organizations I've ever been associated with, containing brilliant and kind people I will always consider my friends no matter how many years or circumstances come between us. Perhaps it sounds silly to someone outside gaming culture, but it's absolutely true. Every day I chat with *WoW* friends as we go through our workdays; we're part of each other's lives. The first day I joined Elitist Jerks, I was hanging out on their IRC* channel and received a message from a stranger: *Hello, I hear you will have the privilege of healing me* ☺. It was EJ's main tank, Paches, reaching out to a player he knew had freshly transferred with no social network. I needed a friend and he appeared. We partnered in arenas, whispered constantly during raids, and though we've never met in person and haven't played *WoW* together for the better part of a decade, I talk with him more often than anyone but my wife. We see the world similarly; we think the same things are funny; we love video games. From what else on earth are friendships built?

If guildmates held our fiercest affections at the time, passing years have made flame wars and other petty conflicts feel much the same. For all the sparring I did on Blizzard's message boards (the ups and downs of which are whimsically recounted by an anonymous scribe on Detheroc's WoW Wiki page), a decade later I feel genuine affection for all my antagonists. In researching this book I got back into contact with the turncoats who left T K T in such an awful lurch years ago, and while I verified the basics of my recollection, never a cross word passed between us. It's so far from mattering now; the good times we had together are all that remain. We learned the value of

---

* Internet Relay Chat is an ancient mode of communication whereby text messages were scrawled on clay tablets and launched pneumatically through the InterTubes.

persistence, focus, and work, but because we learned them together, we couldn't help but become acutely aware of how our powers interfaced. Talented as we might have been, we were absolutely great as a team. Not even the fiercest ego could see Ragnaros burst into cinders and his great hammer plummet to the ground and think of himself. There's only the guild, the comrades who've nursed each other through a hundred wipes of heartbreak now screaming themselves hoarse on voice chat. "Fuck the beef," as Dr. Dre once said of a departed friend. Adults let any good outshine all the bad.

There's a lesson in that too, about friends and colleagues and how to treat them. A few leaders might have powered their guilds through sheer iron-fisted force of personality, but they were exceptions. Great guilds functioned because their leaders persuaded, cajoled, bribed, and pleaded to pull them through tough times. If folks weren't having fun on a nightly basis, they wouldn't play with you. You needed to value your guildmates as people, even online, even when they committed aggravating errors.

We learned so much about ourselves through these virtual challenges, and the game gave those better selves expression. It gave us a venue to be loud and stupid and sometimes cruel, to try new things and make mistakes. I'd argue that *WoW*'s insistence on consequence-free death led to more personal growth than significant portions of the typical high school curriculum.* Arriving when it did, at a highly formative period for my age cohort, the game couldn't help but splice its way into our DNA. Of course it meant the world to us. Of course it still feels like home, when we think back to it or renew our subscriptions for three slow months of the summer.

PALS FOR LIFE

The infamous Leeroy Jenkins video gained viral traction not because it was terribly funny on its own terms or because it referenced something specific from *WoW* but because it spoke to a deeper kind of

---

* Full disclosure: I received a D in softball class and a B- in something called Introduction to Art.

shared experience. It cleverly rendered the goofy mayhem that can ensue when good friends engage in spirited play. One thing goes wrong and someone can't help but tug at the thread, or perhaps they started the unraveling to begin with. Chaos is the essence of fun—it ensures unpredictability, diversity, possibility. Break a rule and you've made the world anew. Leeroy's guild was called PALS FOR LIFE, and since the video's release, one can find identically named imitators on every server. That is the ideal of a guild, after all: friends bonded for the duration, not for one game or one expansion or one tier of content. No matter how time passes, anyone who ever played in T K T is my brother or my sister, and I really mean that. I'm thrilled to see them wed and it kills me when their exes won't let them see their kids. They're my friends, and we'll always have our times together. The best guilds become exclusive social clubs where the only members are the only people you'd ever want there. But you don't need to have fought shoulder to shoulder with someone for *WoW* to bring you together. Anyone who ever held an active account unwittingly inducted herself into a vast and disparate family.

When I started a new job in April 2008 at a large game developer, my neighboring work station was occupied by a young man named Dante. Dante loved *WoW* with every fiber of his being. "Hey man, you play *WoW*?" was the first non-work-related sentence he spoke to me. He played a rogue in a small guild working its way through Karazhan, and we'd chew up slow hours with idle conversation about each and every one of its bosses. In a matter of weeks we'd bonded over the game without any particular effort, though we hailed from totally different backgrounds and had little superficially in common. As tends to happen, things got more personal. I told him about my anxieties over moving in with a girlfriend. He described the spectacular drama engulfing his mother and sister, whose screaming fights kept him up all night. He laid out the predawn bus transfers necessary to get him to his carpool's meeting spot in the distant East Bay. This was why, he confided, he often struggled to stay awake during the afternoons. It was a problem; our boss hated him for it, suspected him of being high, though I never smelled or saw anything of the sort. It was just a bad circumstance. When he couldn't sleep any more, Dante would pull his laptop out from under the rickety hide-a-bed and farm gold in deserted zones before embarking for the bus. He'd tell me about his latest ganking exploits ("Alliance is some *punks*, nigga. Can't never fight solo.") and the loot he hoped to get that week. Prince Malchezaar dropped a fabulous dagger he coveted more than anything in the world, but it just refused to drop for him. The man was born with no surfeit of luck. In chaotic circumstances *WoW* became a refuge, a part of his life he could control while his family life spiraled out of control. It was something he felt good at. It offered comfort, friendship, and the feeling of reward even when nothing else in his life was going right. I don't know if he ever got his dagger, aptly named Malchazeen. They fired him not long after.

I bring up *WoW* quite a bit with people I meet today, for reasons of professional interest if nothing else. Everyone under the age of forty seems to know someone who played, and if they themselves once held an account I'm guaranteed a warm and friendly conversation. Attend Blizzard's annual BlizzCon convention some autumn in Anaheim (indistinguishable, it turns out, from any other season in Anaheim) and you'll be astonished at the good cheer and affection radiating between the thousands of attendees. They might be there to meet guildmates or cluster around cocktail tables emblazoned with the names of realm servers, but everyone shares the same barely restrained glee at being in this celebratory space. In this space no one will snark at the things you love and everyone will always know what you're talking about. Most gamers hold their gaming lives close to the vest. Professional and family settings attach a time-wasting stigma to MMORPG play, so they don't get to talk about games nearly so much as they'd like. This is one of the reasons I came to love sports late in life: they represented a kind of game I could discuss in just about any setting without anyone thinking me strange.

This is an underserved need. *WoW*'s unified, persistent game world provides the kind of universal reference point people can draw on in casual conversation. If I meet someone who plays or played *WoW*, I can learn a great deal about them simply through their experience with the game. It lets them tell me who they are in a way that's as personal and private as makes them comfortable. *WoW* is a great way to make friends and meet people, even if you don't meet them in the game. A woman I know from the early vanilla days explains, "I can still sit at a bar and look down it and just know who I could impress by saying I raided at the level I did." Your mileage may vary, of course, but anyone who played the game knows the special thrill of meeting a kindred spirit. The staggering millions who've passed through Azeroth make them easy to find. In an increasingly fractured cultural landscape, where tastes in entertainment are badly fractured, the World of Warcraft represents one of precious few touchstones.

FOLLOWING THE FLOOD

If the players were shocked by *WoW*'s mammoth success erupting seismically beneath their feet, the gaming industry stood no chance. Millions of copies flew off the shelves—literal copies off literal shelves, since digital distribution was still in its infancy.* The game shipped in a hefty cardboard box adorned with a double front flap that opened like the pages of a book into four gorgeously decorated panels promoting the game. Inside was a sheaf with four CDs containing the game's basic files, since DVD players weren't yet common enough to ship in that medium. A glossy-paged product catalog advertised Blizzard's entire catalog to date, including the upcoming *StarCraft: Ghost*—a game the studio famously axed before it ever saw the light of day.

Perhaps the biggest anachronism to the modern consumer is the game manual. In 2016 games rarely include physical manuals even if purchased in hard copy. *WoW* shipped with a manual two hundred pages long. It's littered with beautiful art and contains some of the

---

* Interesting coincidence: *Half-Life 2*, which introduced Valve's now ubiquitous Steam network to the general public, came out just seven days before *World of Warcraft* in November 2004. Blizzard eventually embraced digital distribution, but only through their own proprietary network, Battle.net.

best technical writing I've ever seen, covering every element of the game in meticulous detail (at least as it existed in 2004) without ever resorting to jargon or becoming condescending to the reader. Relentlessly informative but never didactic, it encourages new players and assures them they need never be overwhelmed. The glossary lays out such common community terms as "mob," "aggro," and "kiting" so simply and concisely it makes me feel resentful as a writer. The first week I owned *WoW* I found myself marooned in an airport for six hours and I passed the time by reading the entire thing cover to cover. It made the unsatisfiable need to play the game almost physically painful. These kinds of manuals have gone the way of the dodo. Not enough players read them, the conventional wisdom goes, to justify the expense of writing, editing, printing, and shipping such things. A game's official documentation, such as it exists, will generally be thrown up on a website and updated perhaps once a year. Better yet, the community will likely do the work themselves and populate a well-maintained public wiki on their own time and someone else's web-hosting dollar. That's how things work in 2016, with sophisticated gaming resources at everyone's fingertips. Gamers watch YouTube walkthroughs on their phones while playing on their PCs, and *WoW* has since moved its guides online with the expectation of almost exclusively digital sales.

WoW's creators always understood that its goal was to be the MMORPG for people who'd never played an MMORPG. That fabulously hefty manual promised an adventure of endless depth and promise, with adventures made dangerous but never punishing. Death was an inconvenience, so no mistake could ever cost you more than a few gold coins. Bright and colorful continents packed with fun quests limited the tedium of grinding for levels, keeping casual players interested and moving from zone to zone in a logical progression. Even the time they weren't playing yielded some value, piling up "rest" that was rewarded as double experience from killing monsters. Diverse classes rooted in classic Warcraft lore tempted crossover gamers, the UI was easy to understand (if profoundly limited without add-ons), and it wasn't too mechanically complex to play. I never played an MMO before *WoW* and I haven't played many since, though of course I take a professional interest. Only a highly accessible title from a proven developer like Blizzard could have convinced me to give it a shot. Millions of others felt exactly the same, which is one of the reasons why *WoW* achieved such penetration across the culture. It's why I've heard from so many players while researching this book, "Literally everyone was playing *WoW*." Now, that statement isn't literally true, but enough people say it that I couldn't help but notice. Their friends were playing, so they played, and the playing was that much better for it. A social network's value increases with its population, since each may connect to all the others, and so *WoW*'s networking effects made it the MMO of choice throughout the Western world (and much of the world beyond).

Competitors appeared. It was inevitable—*WoW*'s massive commercial success guaranteed more money flowing into Blizzard's coffers every month than most studios make in a year. The annual figures are a topic for debate, but they're in the hundreds of millions and *WoW* has cumulatively generated $12 to $13 billion since the game's late 2004 launch. Successful MMOs were for many years the best and most reliable sources of continuing revenue a game company could have. So if Blizzard could have ten million concurrent users, its competitors reasoned, there was room in the market. In the two years following *WoW*'s launch, just about every major publisher undertook its own competing game—sometimes more than one. They sunk massive resources into development. Games are always pricey to make, since they require so many specialized skills attached to highly educated white-collar professionals, but MMORPGs might be the very hardest to get right. To be "massively multiplayer" they must convey tremendous volumes of data between their servers and thousands (or millions) of clients. The engineering work alone lies beyond the means of all but the biggest and richest studios. Then there's the work of designing hundreds of features across all areas of the game in order to give users a full and functional experience. Combat mechanics, crafting, character progression, user interface, and social systems represent just the tip of the proverbial luxury liner–foundering iceberg. You must also consider character and world design, along with all the art and animation and sound and music. All this and you still haven't given players anything to actually *play*. Quest, dungeon, and raid design represent epochal undertakings on their own. MMORPGs are the world's biggest and most complicated pieces of retail software. Simply getting one to a functional public beta test demands hundreds of workers' labor over half a decade, at a minimum cost in the tens of millions. Phenomenal talent and hard work are necessary but insufficient. Reaching *WoW*'s lofty pinnacle is almost impossible and probably miraculous, even considering Blizzard's considerable advantages.

So the competitors' failure might have been inevitable. "Failure" is a relative term, of course. Many MMOs have made money and kept hardworking developers employed for years, powered by modest but dedicated fan bases. Hell, there are still a lot of people playing the original *EverQuest*. But more than a few had been called *WoW*-killers, had implicitly or explicitly courted the label, and none came close. They had their own flaws in design or endgame content or server stability or marketing, but more important the gaming industry's moneyed leaders had misread the market. Most games sell like books, in that people consume them serially and move from one title to the next. They'll buy more games than they have time to play just as they buy more books than they'll actually read. The point is to have it, to express your taste, to support creators, and so on—you obviously buy books and know what I'm talking about. Traditional MMORPGs are different because of the subscription attached. Rare is the player willing to maintain paid subscriptions on several MMOs at once. Hang the expense; it's simply bad business. MMOs reward cumulative time investment, and there are only so many hours in a day. Invest yourself in one and you can conquer the world. Invest in several and you'll be a noob in all of them.

So while some *WoW* players devoted to the form might dabble in *Age of Conan* or *Star Wars: The Old Republic* or *Black Desert Online*, they'll eventually pick one or the other, and *WoW* simply offers more reliable yield for your entertainment dollar. No matter how long you've been away, you can come back to *WoW* knowing it will be accessible and enjoyable. You can join a well-populated server with a bustling economy and plenty of guilds seeking recruits. You know you're paying for a known commodity. What's more, even the exciting unknown quantities of the latest expansion feel more or less like *WoW*. As the first MMORPG for an entire generation, it defined their expectations and set the bar quite high. Challengers were expected to offer the same copious features, and they responded by becoming more like *WoW*. A tutorial for every system. Instanced player-versus-player combat on demand. A bright yellow exclamation point hovering over every fresh quest giver. Guild chat defaulting to green, whispers to purple. Each game made some novel changes to the formulae, but never enough to wrest away a critical mass of players. Because network effects are so important to an MMO's success, *WoW*'s position on top gave it the consistent player base to stay there.

Of course, none of it would have mattered without new players. Most MMOs start out with a base of excited players that gradually withers over years of play—they get burned out or bored and move to other games. And often prospective new players are turned off by the years of established content. They don't know it the way old players do, and they feel they can never catch up. Blizzard attempted to kill both birds with one proverbial stone: their release schedule. *WoW*'s success assured them ample resources to develop new content, so they never stopped cranking it out, and players could rely on several major "free" content patches to keep them occupied between expansions. As for the expansions themselves, they went far beyond content. Blizzard used these forty-dollar retail products as opportunities to totally overhaul major game systems. This let the developers get creative, knowing anything they got wrong could be replaced wholesale in two years' time. Even if some changes proved unpopular, this approach to the expansions kept the game from getting stale for old players. Each expansion also rendered old gear obsolete, so newcomers were never too far behind and could catch up to the competitive endgame in just a few weeks' time. Most MMOs find a formula and stick to it because their small-yet-dedicated community craves stability. *WoW* went in the opposite direction, and it's the single biggest key to its singular success.

One by one the competitors faded into obscurity or died outright, their servers taken offline or converted into free-to-play. The companies that had been so eager to hurl gobs of cash at any credible MMORPG project turned in the opposite direction. MMOs have been tried to death, the wisdom now goes. The only big one is *WoW*, and you'd be a fool to try to compete.

The end result is odd to contemplate: *WoW* manages to stand as both exemplar of its genre and the last of its kind. Studios don't make these kinds of games anymore, nothing so ambitious and certainly nothing with a fifteen-dollar monthly fee atop full retail price. Even if someone tried, the video game market has changed so dramatically it's hard to imagine such explosive success replicated. Gamers are more fragmented now, balkanized by the Internet into smaller factions. Just as television no longer revolves around the programming on a handful of broadcast networks, game developers seek smaller audiences they can rely on over time to buy sequels and downloadable content. We'll never again see a game grow monolithic the way *WoW* did. Nothing will match its primacy in popular culture—though *Minecraft*'s popularity with children informs a generation of parents alongside. *WoW* stamped an entire generation with its ambition, with its attention to detail and devotion to games as accessible mass entertainment. Complaints about "epics for casuals" sound like the first wave of MMO players pining for the days of XP loss on death. The *WoW* generation insists that risk-taking be encouraged rather than punished and work be rewarded on a fair, consistent basis. Nobody ever wanted to wait six months for a purple piece of loot to drop, or to grind for hours making back the losses from every wipe. In keeping with its origins at the dawn of the modern Internet, *WoW* established a streamlined on-demand culture that can't be rolled back.

TOO MUCH BIRTHDAY

Because it was by and for and of the Internet, *WoW* suffered many of its peculiar pathologies. First and foremost among these: anything fun can (and will be) taken too far. *WoW* became such a cultural phenomenon that after a while we couldn't play it without being identified with it—without family, friends, and classmates gently jabbing our choice of hobby, insinuating a social invitation was declined "so you could fight the ogres," thoughtfully forwarding *Wall Street Journal* articles on gaming addiction. Some people played too much, sacrificing grades or girlfriends or jobs, but that's true of any time-consuming activity. *WoW*'s bottomless nature means no end to the potential time investment, and so it held a natural appeal for any soul inclined to intemperance.

I don't use the word "addiction" with regard to video games. It trivializes the suffering of real addicts, whose bodies and minds are often destroyed by their disease in ways video games can't manage. It is possible, if one looks hard enough, to find isolated horror stories, like the parents who neglect their children for marathon gaming sessions. I would suggest these incidents stem from broader mental illness and reflect very little on video games. Still, it's indisputable that many people struggled to balance *WoW* with the rest of their lives.

It's more fun than your life; that's really the problem. Human existence teems with responsibilities of one kind or another, and as a result each of us spends hours of the day doing things we'd rather not. We might enjoy our schooling or our jobs—we might feel very fortunate to be in those spots—but for almost everyone, life is a series of chores broken up by the occasional good meal. We amuse ourselves with TV shows or video games, but in most cases these entertainments include natural stopping points. The credits roll, the lights come up, and we're treated to a teaser for the sequel. Even the deepest, darkest binge-watching holes (*Gilmore Girls*, for example—that Rory could never find the right boy!) end once you're out of episodes. *WoW* never does. It's there at two in the afternoon, at three in the morning, rain or shine and independent of federal

holidays. It's there on your best and worst days, filled with friends
who'll commiserate or celebrate as the situation demands. In T K T
one of our officers, a beautiful Mexican mom named Laura and one
of the kindest people I've ever known, religiously maintained a reg-
ister of guildies' birthdays. We'd log on to find the Guild Message
shouting out our special days, with gift-wrapped mystery presents
in our mailboxes. If things in your life weren't going the way you
hoped, *WoW* offered a reliable source of warmth and joy in your
darkest hours. Nothing ever really went wrong in Azeroth—deaths
and wipes just meant you were having fun. If sleep wasn't coming,
you could play all night. Years came when you just needed someone
else to celebrate your birthday.

But like any coping mechanism, it may become its own unhealthy
need. It felt as though any time you invested in *WoW* was rewarded in
one fashion or another, so more than a few players played more than
a bit too much. In chapter 4 I discussed the strife that engulfed T K T
in the aftermath of our main tank's resignation—my good friend
Chris, who'd made some poor academic choices and compounded
them by playing *WoW* all day and night. It wasn't pathological. It
didn't persist past his decision to quit. It just offered more fun and
better rewards minute to minute and hour to hour than just about
anything else he could do. So it consumed his free time, all of it,
before encroaching on social time and class time. A mutual friend's
wife recalls making a trip to visit Chris two states away only to find
him unwilling to leave his dorm room.

Other players tell eerily parallel stories of leaving and returning,
entering Azeroth with an unexpected bolus of free time only to quit
months later when old habits returned. It simply feels good to play,
and the more you play the better it feels. "I was a chronic procrastinator and am a recovering one still," one of these serial players explains,
"but in *Warcraft* I never felt the need to put things off, because I
enjoyed what I was doing. Even the grinds were worth it because of
the payoff . . . some combination of none of it feeling like work, the
predictable input to output, and the desire to be the best at things led
WoW to consume me in ways that nothing else really has."

A former player with whom I'd crossed paths in T K T always struggled with balance. I knew him as a kind of adorable flake, the sort of player who'd grind for potion materials all night and then sleep through scheduled raiding time. Gabriel "Mew" Gonzalez Ponce tells his story more vividly: "I made a ton of friends that eventually became real-life friends. However, just like many others I let the game take over a lot of my time and effort. I failed two subjects, lost one girlfriend, and was fired from two jobs due to my excessive play time. By December 2009 I was unemployed, failing at my senior year in college, no girlfriend, and broke . . . but I had the biggest achievement score on the server, with the most Exalted in-game reputations and pushing for world-first raid kills. I guess that was the breaking point: if I failed at school I had to go back to Mexico, and that's no fun. I sold my computer and *WoW* account, got myself a girlfriend (now married to her), focused in school, and so on." I asked Mew how he felt about his youthful indiscretions, and given his earlier phrasing I was surprised at the answer. "Do not get me wrong, I do appreciate my time in *WoW* and by no means regret playing it for the time I did. I *firmly* believe and can't emphasize how much I do believe that playing this game helped me at my job. I think it made me smart, I think it made me more analytical. I didn't know shit about Excel but I taught myself in order to do theorycraft.* It made me more resourceful and taught me I could be good at something as long as I focused on it. It taught me how to deal with jerks, how to deal with criticism, how to follow and lead and how to strive to be the best."

At my wedding I asked Chris (who was a banker before becoming a successful professional poker player) whether he missed those days. "Of course!" he said immediately. "All the time. It was great." Our mutual friend's wife, also present, took this opportunity to remind everyone of Chris's old excesses. He flashed his tooth-baring grin back at me: "See, these noobs don't understand," he pronounced, "what it takes to be pro." Even those souls most ostensibly damaged

---

* "Theorycraft" is a bit of tongue-in-cheek jargon describing the process of optimizing your character. *WoW*'s combat is fundamentally just algebra, so players can use Excel spreadsheets or even just the back of an envelope to plan out their talents, gear, and in-game tactics.

by the game's all-consuming qualities miss the good times for what they were. None of us would have missed it for the world. We'd get it back now, if we could. For any ups and downs *WoW* is part of our lives, our youths, and the self-directed formation of our selves. We might not volunteer this to prospective employers, but it'll always be part of who we are.

A Great and Scattered Tribe

Life rarely plays out as scripted. I never planned to play any MMORPG. I bought *WoW* only due to my friends' cajoling, and yet it was their desertion that spurred me to embrace it. Five years later I quit to pursue a career in writing, and then it was the writing that washed me back upon Azeroth's white, sandy shore. I led one of the world's top Spanish-language raiding guilds without, aside from a few vulgarisms, speaking a lick of Spanish. What was stigmatized ten years ago as an isolating, alienating pursuit now sparks warm and friendly conversations whenever I mention *WoW* to anyone under the age of forty. It's an institution, a fixture of the cultural landscape, an unacknowledged public utility along the lines of Google Search. *WoW* annually makes happy millions of people who play in addition to millions more who take comfort knowing they could resub at any time, that their avatars are waiting just past the horizon.

If a few brought grief upon themselves through intemperance, I suspect (and they seem to agree) that it brought them great joy as well. *WoW* isn't a drug or a singularity impelling impressionable college kids down its throat. It's a group of people brought together by the serendipitous circumstance of play, a group of people who might never exchange a word but are still necessary to a game they all love. Even if I despise someone in-game, that passion provides a kind of psychic framework powering and animating the fictional world of Azeroth. One can't write a good story without conflict, without characters, and *WoW* has always been fabulously engineered to provide them. Recently at a party I met a father who never played *WoW* but whose nine-year-old daughter was obsessed. "All she wants to do," he told me, "is watch these streamers play. I won't let her play, but she can watch and she just loves it. The colors and the characters, it's just a really cool world for her." A cousin in the sixth grade told me he'd rather watch streamed games than play them himself. A whole new generation is growing up with *WoW*-as-institution, a game released before their birth, a game they might not have ever played but that they can sense (in the canny but inchoate nature of children's understanding) informs everything around them. They're attracted to it because of the people who play and their obvious passion.

It was always about the people. Anything that was ever truly good came from them: the bickering in Barrens General chat, the futile urgency of Tarren Mill and Southshore battles, the late-night gankfests in the Searing Gorge and the high-noon duels outside Ironforge, the comically long traipse to acquire the key to Onyxia's Lair, the mad kiting of raid bosses with the raid half-wiped until that 1 percent ticked zero and everyone just *screaming* like you'd won the damn Super Bowl. *WoW* makes us friends. It can even make us family. It's part of who I am, and who we all are now, and it was only ever really supposed to be a fun video game. Nobody could have predicted it—predicted success, perhaps, or years of healthy profit, but never this. We took a piece of retail software and made it into a civilization. It's a hell of a story. It runs as long as we need.

ÎNDEX